THE BACK HOME SERIES

I0518871

SERIES TITLES

WILDLIFER

Wisconsin Origin to Climate Change

NEIL F. PAYNE

CORNERSTONE PRESS
UNIVERSITY OF WISCONSIN-STEVENS POINT

Cornerstone Press, Stevens Point, Wisconsin 54481
Copyright © 2024 Neil F. Payne
www.uwsp.edu/cornerstone

Printed in the United States of America by
Point Print and Design Studio, Stevens Point, Wisconsin

Library of Congress Control Number: 2024948267
ISBN: 978-1-960329-15-8

All rights reserved.

Cover and title page photo: Neil Payne checking wooden live traps for rabbits, Hog Island, Virginia, 1962.

This is a work of nonfiction. All of the events in this book are true to the best of the author's memory. Some names and identifying features have been changed to protect the identity of certain parties. The author in no way represents any company, corporation, or brand, mentioned herein. The views expressed in this book are solely those of the author.

Cornerstone Press titles are produced in courses and internships offered by the Department of English at the University of Wisconsin–Stevens Point.

DIRECTOR & PUBLISHER
Dr. Ross K. Tangedal

EXECUTIVE EDITORS
Jeff Snowbarger, Freesia McKee

EDITORIAL DIRECTOR
Ellie Atkinson

SENIOR EDITORS
Brett Hill, Grace Dahl

PRESS STAFF
Chloe Cieszynski, Grace Dahl, Kirsten Faulkner, Maddy Mauthe, Sophie McPherson, Lauren Rudesill, Katie Schimke, Ava Willett

To my brother Glenn Payne in TX

my sister Virginia (Ginny) Harris in VA

my lifelong best friend Sam Lev in WA

my kids Adam (born CA), Mark (born NL), Erin (born WA) in WI

my step-kids Patty, Shari, Gail in IL

my relocated wife Jan in WI

*And in memory of my parents, Forrest and Ruth Payne,
and my grandparents, Charles and Gertrude Payne, in WI*

ALSO BY NEIL F. PAYNE:

The Newfoundland Mystique

Wildlife Delights and Dilemmas: Newfoundland and Labrador

Wildlife, Conservation, and Human Welfare: A United States and Canadian Perspective (with Richard D. Taber)

More Wildlife on Your Land: A Guide for Private Landowners

Techniques for Wildlife Habitat Management of Uplands (with Fred C. Bryant)

Techniques for Wildlife Habitat Management of Wetlands

Environmental Impacts of Harvesting Wood for Energy (with James E. Johnson, Philip E Pope, and Glenn D. Mroz)

Wildlife and Fisheries Habitat Improvement Handbook (with Fred Copes)

Top: white-tailed deer; *Middle*: badger; *Bottom*: prairie chicken
Courtesy of Al Cornell

CONTENTS

*How much biodiversity will humans damage or destroy before they,
like other animals, feel the consequences profoundly?*

A healthy ecosystem is the foundation of a healthy society.

END OF AN ERA:
REMARKS BY ESTELLA LEOPOLD

Estella B. Leopold, Aldo Leopold's last surviving child, died in 2024. Aldo Leopold's last surviving graduate student, Richard D. Taber, my former colleague and book co-author, died in 2016. The last direct connections to Aldo Leopold, both are recognized with extreme accomplishment and honor in the wildlife profession. Both are featured in this narrative. Estella and I attended the University of Wisconsin in Madison ten years apart and worked at the University of Washington in Seattle, but we missed each other by several years. Never having met her personally, I nonetheless was audacious and pretentious enough to ask her, at age 94, to write the foreword to what would become this book. She agreed at first, but then reconsidered, at her age. To my delight, she graciously praised the contents and wished me well in this email of 1 November 2020. To my delight and honor, we became email pen pals.

REMARKS BY ESTELLA LEOPOLD

Dear Neil Payne! I have now read your book manuscript with great interest and pleasure! I am indeed flattered by your request, and want to tell you how much I have enjoyed reading your new manuscript!!

I am happy to accept your challenge, but need to know the time line you need to follow for it. There is so much in your story that I have real interest in, and much that tells me about the challenges in your interesting life! I feel like I already know you in many ways and want to compliment you on this achievement! Marvelous writing—and exciting coverage over many years! I send warm thanks and much appreciation for what you have done here!

I knew Dick Taber when he was a graduate student with Starker Leopold in Calif. He did some interesting work on nutrients & deer browse, etc. after fire!

With sincere appreciation, Estella Leopold

* * *

ESTELLA LEOPOLD (1927–2024) was a University of Washington professor emerita of botany, forest resources, and quaternary research. She served on the board of the Aldo Leopold Foundation as lifetime director and lived in Seattle, Washington, until her death.

FOREWORD

As a hunter, angler, conservationist, and public servant, I was honored to accept Governor Tony Evers' appointment to serve as Secretary of the Wisconsin Department of Natural Resources (DNR). As I begin a new chapter, Dr. Neil F. Payne is writing his last. In his 85th year, Dad is publishing his final book, an achievement years in the making and the icing on the cake of a unique life.

The book provides an extensive overview of the wildlife profession's beginning in Wisconsin. I was honored and humbled to write this foreword, and it was heartwarming and gratifying to learn more about the man who had such a profound influence on my life, and countless students and colleagues.

This informative book provides unique insights into the origin of wildlife management, the father of wildlife management Aldo Leopold, his family, his students with some of their personal and significant contributions to the profession, and others. The book also provides an overview of the vast importance of wildlife habitat, wildlife ecology, wildlife management, Wisconsin land and water, environmental education, and the DNR. I enjoyed learning more about Wisconsin, its key and influential national leaders, and the numerous organizations that champion the critical importance of biodiversity.

Each chapter presents a distinctive focus, overview, and approach. Some are written in a candid and direct writing style you would expect from a proud Wisconsinite, sharing the many "firsts" in the origin of the wildlife profession. Other chapters are written more in an academic style you might expect from an avid researcher and teacher. Throughout the book, you will enjoy some personal stories, humor, and the strong opinions of a seasoned professor of wildlife ecology.

Neil F. Payne has lived an exceptional life. He honorably served his country as a marine in Vietnam, raised a loving family, and has made and continues to make a substantial contribution to the singularly important profession of wildlife management. This book will undoubtedly help the reader better understand why the wildlife profession, biodiversity and ecosystem management, environmental education, leadership, and relationships are key to guiding society for generations to come.

—ADAM N. PAYNE
Former Secretary
Wisconsin Department of Natrual Resources
2023

PREFACE

Rabbit, you started it all, I said to myself as I watched a cottontail rabbit pause outside my window in the sunroom on the shore of the Wisconsin River in Plover, Wisconsin, at 7:15 a.m. 21 June 2016. There sat that remarkable creature, with its profound effect on the biodiversity of the complicated ecosystem because it was the right size to support most reptilian, avian, and mammalian predators around: hawks, owls, bobcats, foxes, coyotes, weasels, snakes, etc. To replace their numbers and feed the carnivorous community, rabbits breed like crazy. For protection, they jump, run fast, have long ears and bulging eyes—and an extensive diet. Cover is their main limiting factor.

When I was a grad student at Virginia Tech, I had to build 120 wooden box traps for my rabbit research project. My dad wanted me to drive into New York City to get my younger brother Glenn who had been stationed in Germany and was being released from his time in the U.S. Army. But I had traps to build. Dad said he would help, and arrived in Blacksburg with my mom and sister. After the traps were built, I drove to New York City for a family reunion, then to Sheboygan Falls, Wisconsin with my brother in tow, then back to Blacksburg, Virginia via train. Handier than I by far, Dad was delighted to build those traps. Without Dad taking the lead, I'd still be at it.

I can sex a mean rabbit. Using wooden box traps without bait during fall 1962 and 1963, I pulled rabbits 857 times from my live traps. (Nervously and embarrassingly, with the refuge supervisor watching, I mishandled my first rabbit, which escaped!) That total involved 516 rabbits—479 cottontails and 37 marsh rabbits.[195x] Some rabbits became trap addicts, re-entering the traps, while others became trap shy. I also caught other animals,[202x] e.g., 62 opossums, which the refuge supervisor wanted removed from the refuge because they were serious predators of waterfowl nests. I loaned the traps with opossums to a refuge worker, who took them to an acquaintance who ate them. I didn't know what a marsh rabbit was, only that it was grayer and struggled more when handled, which I noted. Finally, I figured it out; my first technical publication was about its range extension.[195x] At Dr. Henry Mosby's request, I prepared a study skin for the wildlife collection at Virginia Tech.

With my bare hand, I reached into the trap, grasped the rabbit by the hind legs, and pulled it out. While standing, I placed the head upside down between my legs, pried the legs apart, and sexed it, looking for the vagina because the penis and clitoris are about the same size (juveniles more difficult), then sat on the trap to place a numbered ear tag in each ear before releasing the rabbit: 253 males, 263 females.

I went from live-trapping little cottontail rabbits[202x] to live-trapping big black bears next,[195z] my first in Newfoundland in 1968. (A graduate student of mine with whom I became particularly close was Ned Norton, who worked on black bears[189y] for me in 1981, and Wildlife Biologist Bruce Kohn with the WDNR.[205x] After that, Ned became the WDNR wildlife manager for the unique state Sandhill Wildlife Area. In time he was unable to speak; he talked to me by typing on his computer which had a speech generating device, no tone inflection, before he died in 1993 of Lou Gehrig's Disease, ALS, at age 43.)

I got to thinking that I'd come a long way since I grew up in Sheboygan Falls, Wisconsin, too nervous to conduct a proper meeting as president of our high school freshman class, and pulled my first rabbit from a live trap in 1962 in Virginia. But to get there, as a college senior at the University of Wisconsin I was offered a fellowship by Dr. Burd McGinnes at Virginia Tech and was being considered for a teaching assistantship by Dr. Reuben Trippensee[258] at the University of Massachusetts. I phoned Dr. Robert McCabe, chair of the UW Wildlife Department, for advice. McCabe advised me to tell Trippensee to "fish or cut bait." I wasn't so blunt, but Trippensee informed me I wasn't as qualified as someone else. In the wildlife course I took at Virginia Tech, Dr. Henry Mosby used Trippensee's two-volume set of wildlife textbooks.[251, 252]

In 1957, I graduated from high school in a class of 66, having grown up in a blue-collar neighborhood in Sheboygan Falls, home of Bemis where my parents were factory workers making toilet seats to adorn toilets made by the nearby Kohler Co.; my dad had worked there too as an unskilled laborer. He grew up on his parents' small dairy farm and had no high school degree. My mom grew up in the village of Cascade and graduated from high school, her father a tavern owner during Prohibition. My folks had absolutely no familiarity with college. I worked as a window-washer for my summer college job in nearby Sheboygan, hanging out with a bolt belt (if window screens were hinged at the top) or a stirrup belt (if screens were hinged on the side) from windows of tall buildings. With my parents' support (40% theirs, 60% mine), I earned a bachelor's degree in Zoology at the University of Wisconsin-Madison (1957–61), where I was captain of the fencing team (Big Ten Champs, 1959) and met Jan in January 1961, only to marry her exactly 25 years later. As an MS graduate student on fellowship at Virginia Tech (1961–64) in Blacksburg, Virginia, maybe the greenest graduate student in history, I conducted my research project on the Virginia Commission of Game and Inland Fisheries' 3,908-acre Hog Island Wildlife Management Area in the James River in southeastern Virginia, across from Jamestown, those early settlers releasing their hogs there in 1608 (none now). There I learned firsthand about managing salt marsh with flapgates in culverts to regulate tidal flow in marshes for waterfowl.

There I lived alone on my meager monthly stipend in a house trailer, no phone or TV, referring to myself as a "Professional Hermit." My mom gave me an old 90-page cookbook from 1934, with her notes that I still have. Later, she wrote that our household dog had died. I always admired collies, so I drove to Richmond and bought a collie pup; I registered her "Reine de l'Isle" (Island Queen), calling her "Reina." She became my constant companion everywhere I moved except Vietnam. She even graces the cover of this book.

In the fall of 1962 and 1963, I set out along a trapline of about 4 miles the 120 unbaited wooden live traps 200 feet apart, in rabbit leads on 12 linear plots at least 500 feet apart, and calculated the population estimates. I checked them daily by vehicle along gravel road and field edge, or on foot when it rained and fields were muddy. The handiest place to get groceries was at a little convenience store/gas station eight miles away with two entrances labeled "Colored Only" and "Whites Only"—a cultural, and shocking, eye-opener for a guy from Sheboygan Falls. I hadn't really grasped that I was stepping into one of the most complex, important, and essential professions in the world—maintenance of the biodiversity of ecosystems required by all life. I would live and/or work on the shores of four great rivers—the James River and the Potomac River in the East, the Columbia River in the West, the Wisconsin River in the Central—and along the Atlantic Ocean.

Living in a house on Hog Island refuge was Clyde Abernathy, refuge supervisor. Stocky, savvy, and assertive, with little education, he intimidated me at first. We became good friends.

Hog Island had been an Indian hunting area; I found numerous stone arrowheads and even a stone knife along the shore when the tide was out. I also found pieces of green glass bottles and clay pipes there from early colonists at Jamestown across the James River from Hog Island. One day while on the beach, I saw a human skull protruding from a tidewater-eroded bank of soil. I dug it out before it eroded out and washed away, and placed it in a cardboard box in my house trailer where I left it. I found out that Hog Island had also been a burial ground for slaves, and that in all likelihood I had discovered the skeleton of one.

During my lonely existence at ages 23 and 24 in a house trailer on the refuge, I was learning sound field discipline in checking my traps daily, rain or shine. One time, I sang "Waltzing Matilda" at the top of my lungs for morale while slogging alone through muddy fields during a rainstorm, my boots heavy with mud. As I was returning from checking my trapline on 22 November 1963, Clyde Abernathy met me to say, "The president was shot." Confused, I asked, "What president?" He replied, "President Kennedy."

I saved my trapping and tagging records of those rabbits I handled during my research on them over half a century earlier.

In 2015, I removed them from the back closet and was all set to throw out that stack of old data cards I carried in my backpack every day (a duplicate set in my house trailer then) while checking my live traps on Hog Island some 55 years ago. But I just couldn't. I still have all those rabbit data cards. Just think how excited some descendant will be to display that old stack[194] of 516 data cards elegantly in some conspicuous place of charm in the living room.

My first indecision was contemplating quitting college in my freshman year at the University of Wisconsin in Madison, away from home for the first time, intimidated by the culture shock between high school (300 students) and college (23,000 students). My second indecision also occurred while at the University of Wisconsin where I had taken an aptitude test to see if biology or linguistics were for me, having done well in introductory German, French, Russian, and Spanish. Although with lower grades, biology was more interesting. My third indecision was at the end of my MS degree at age 25; uncertain of wildlife as my chosen profession, I made a lonely decision to buy some time and in 1964 I went to Richmont to join the Marine Corps. The recruiting officer asked, "What's with the beard?" I responded jokingly, "I suppose there are more of us with beards in the Marine Corps." He replied un-jokingly, "No, there are less of you." I shaved, joined the Marine Corps, and became a combat engineer for three years (and a possible 20-year career), starting with Officer Candidate School on the shore of the Potomac River in Quantico, VA (where the FBI also trains). Married to Eileen Tagge in Wisconsin in 1964, I was in Vietnam when the Red Cross informed me 12 February 1967, that my son Adam had been born two days earlier in California. That same day, 12 February, I heard my friend 1st Lt. Donald "Bucky" Egan get killed in Vietnam—a day of mixed emotions (see Appendix 7).

I must have been expensive to the taxpayer, for in those three years the Marine Corps moved me from my home of record in Wisconsin to Virginia, North Carolina, Puerto Rico, California, Philippines, Okinawa, Vietnam (Vietnam War[194x, 196x]), back to California, then finally back to Wisconsin. Until my sophomore year in college on the varsity fencing team, the only time I had been outside Wisconsin was by bus on the high school senior class trip from little Sheboygan Falls to Chicago, 144 miles away.

During my first ten years after high school (1957–67), I earned a BA degree, an MS degree, and the rank of Captain in the Marine Corps, and lived in four states, one U.S. territory, and five countries, including in a war zone and the Canadian province of Newfoundland and Labrador. I began my wildlife career at age 28. In May 1967, I was an officer in Vietnam; three months later I was a wildlife biologist in Newfoundland, having traveled 12,313 miles to get there.

As to the other animal besides the cottontail rabbit (MS degree[194]) so important in my career development, as the first fur biologist with the Newfoundland and Labrador Wildlife Division (1967–71), I determined that the fur value and trappers' interest in beaver (PhD degree[195]) warranted my initial attention. I coordinated the largest single-season aerial census of beaver in history (220 hours, 9,902 mi²),[196] dividing Newfoundland into 12 beaver management areas with legislative support[195zzz] and 310 beaver traplines; examining 668 beaver reproductive tracts for placental scars, corpora lutea, and embryos; counting cementum annuli to age teeth from 5,346 beaver jawbones (oldest 20 years). I also coordinated snaring lynx around caribou calving grounds, initiated research live-trapping and tagging black bears,[195x] sea-going river otter, the endangered Newfoundland marten,[195zz] and the introduced red squirrel.[207x] I designed the iconic caribou arm patch for the Newfoundland and Labrador Wildlife Division (p. 241).

In my four years as a wildlife biologist with the Newfoundland and Labrador Wildlife Division, I was sent on conferences to Toronto, Ontario; Ottawa, Ontario; Edmonton, Alberta; Calgary, Alberta; and Whitehorse, Yukon Territory. After two more moves, to Utah (PhD on beaver, Utah State University) and to Washington state (University of Washington, where I considered pursuing environmental law), I returned by coincidence, at age 36, to my home state of Wisconsin, to the delight of my parents.

After four years with the Newfoundland and Labrador Wildlife Division (1967–1971) and over two years with Aldo Leopold's former graduate student Richard Taber[235] at the University of Washington's College of Forest Resources (1973–1975) in Seattle, most of my career (1975–1998) was as a professor of wildlife ecology at the University of Wisconsin–Stevens Point (UWSP) in the College of Natural Resources, with wildlife disease specialist and college dean Dan Trainer[44, 250] (see Appendix 2).

My entire wildlife career and most of my life, with its initial uncertainty and indecision, are now history. I held four types of wildlife jobs: wildlife biologist, wildlife professor, wildlife researcher, and wildlife writer. I spent most of my career teaching thousands of college students about wildlife, taking students to study natural resources in Iceland, Poland, Germany, and Costa Rica, doing some research, and writing articles and books, notably two big ones on wildlife habitat.[197, 203] As a faculty member at UWSP, I personally presented BS/BA degree diplomas to my son Mark, my daughter Erin, and my grandson Forrest (Adam's son). I retired in 1998, although I wrote four more books since then, including one with Richard Taber,[235] and one about the wildlife of Newfoundland and Labrador.[200] I figured if I could write a book about the wildlife program in that province after having worked there for four years (and now live there part-time), I ought to write a book about the wildlife program in Wisconsin, where my connection was so much longer and stronger.

So now, I have written my eighth and final wildlife book, this time about Wisconsin, where my roots are, where I was

born, where I grew up, where I spent most of my professional life in an interesting, satisfying, sometimes frustrating, and low-paying wildlife career, and where I spent most of my retirement. After living in eight states and one province, I retired where I began, in Wisconsin, 59 years after I began and 36 years after live-trapping my first cottontail rabbit.[199]

During 2023, I enjoyed the thought of my son Adam as the Secretary of the Wisconsin Department of Natural Resources—the department with which I have interacted most of my career!

Time has its way.[199] So much of it has passed for me that the past now seems surrealistic, as with most folks my age. What occurred to me where and when it did seems like another time, another world, another me. It was.

Yes, Rabbit, you started it all. Well, actually, my grandfather Charles Payne did, when I was a kid. His farm animals fascinated me. I was going to be a farmer just like my grandpa. I never lost my interest in animals, but I never became a farmer. Among other animals, I worked closely with rabbits (MS[194]) and beaver (PhD[195]). I became a wildlifer.

—NEIL F. PAYNE
Plover, Wisconsin
November 2023

Neil Payne tagging rabbits, Hog Island, Virginia, 1962

PROLOGUE

This is where it happened—where it all began for the world. Wisconsin. In 1933. Six years before I was born here. Less than 100 years ago. A new profession. There had been foresters for decades—formally trained, university-educated men in the forest management profession. But there had not been formally trained, university-educated wildlifers. (That name was not used until decades later; my computer still doesn't recognize "wildlifer," but it recognizes "forester.") The profession of wildlife management began in Wisconsin.

The process of transforming an idea into a book is long, complicated, and tedious. I struggled with the title and a sub-title. I vacillated at times in feeling pretentious and presumptuous about taking on this comprehensive project, especially alone. Although I strived for 100% accuracy, I suspect I failed somewhere. Despite the many references and tedium with finding them, a concern of all writers is that they missed something important out there. I share that concern. Perhaps I did not include enough of the voluminous literature that the talented wildlifers of the Wisconsin Department of Natural Resources and the University of Wisconsin produced over the years, especially for Chapter 5. As I review the data collected, I worry that I screwed up somewhere. I'm hoping any omissions are not noticed.

This book complements *The Gamekeepers*;[67] it is mainly a historical account of the wildlife profession—its origin and development in my home state of Wisconsin before it expanded nationwide and worldwide. It is also a reference book. Where I could, I injected myself here and there into the narrative to try to connect myself to it. It is no memoir *per se*; I wrote an unpublished memoir, hardbound, for my descendants some time ago.[199]

The wildlife profession began, and developed its first wildlifers, in a state with unique contrasts: glaciated and unglaciated landscapes with lakes and rivers that affected wildlife habitat, and large-scale human-caused economic habitat alteration typical of North America and the world. The world's life-sustaining natural environment is now imperiled by a combination of problems including human population growth, economic growth, pollution, waste management, global warming, nuclear arms, and environmental ignorance. Because of the wildlife profession's vast comprehensive knowledge and understanding of the complex biodiversity of the ecosystem, wildlifers are among the few folks who can help remedy the situation.

Several Wisconsinites have made wildlife or wildlife-related contributions nationally. Four major wildlife leaders, national and even worldwide, have Wisconsin roots: Aldo Leopold, Jay N. "Ding" Darling, John Muir, and Gaylord Nelson.

The fascinating geology, plant, and animal communities in Wisconsin influence the abundance and variety of wildlife here and are mainly responsible for the fourth-ranked industry in Wisconsin—tourism. People from other states and Canada visit Wisconsin to view wildlife, sight-see the geologic formations and landscape, boat, snowmobile, and cross-country ski, and hunt and fish; the many cottage resorts along Wisconsin's many lakes are a testament to tourism for fishing and hunting. (Unlike other states and provinces, Wisconsin has retained its unique, traditional, popular Friday night fish fry, with a beer or a Wisconsin brandy old-fashioned. A holdover from when Catholics were not permitted to eat meat on Friday, the "Friday Night Fish Fry" remains attractive in Wisconsin's bar and grill scene, as well as its many unique "supper clubs." The menus include Wisconsin walleye, perch, and bluegill.)

Human interaction notwithstanding, wildlife throughout the world is completely influenced by its landscape and climate. In

Wisconsin, the landscape is particularly variable and fascinating. The state is bordered by the Mississippi River and the two largest Great Lakes: Lake Superior and Lake Michigan. The mighty Wisconsin River flows through the state. Producing land with thousands of lakes, streams, and wetlands and riparian area, forest, prairie, and agriculture, the Wisconsin Glacier covered part of the state with rolling hills and boulders, and left part of the state—the Driftless Area—unglaciated and flat.

The Niagara Escarpment extends from Niagara Falls into Wisconsin. Wisconsin has a transition area of variable width called a tension zone, running through the state and dividing it into northern and southern species of plants and animals. Wisconsin is unique in its two continental watershed systems. All this interesting landscape diversity produces a diversity of natural communities—with associated plants and wildlife diverse and abundant.

As in all states, wildlife in Wisconsin has seen major disturbances throughout the state from major habitat alteration for financial profit. Wildlife is somewhat unique in the United States by being a public resource that occurs on mostly private land. To manage its profitable but less economically measurable wildlife resource, a state or provincial wildlife agency exists in all 50 states of the United States and ten provinces of Canada. In Wisconsin, the Fish, Wildlife and Parks Division of the Wisconsin Department of Natural Resources has developed into a major force for wildlife management.

Wisconsin had the first formal wildlife instruction in the world, at the University of Wisconsin-Madison, educating students to become wildlifers of the future. The University of Wisconsin-Stevens Point had the first department of conservation education in the world, developing into the world's largest natural resource program with the world's largest undergraduate wildlife major.

Wisconsin—the origin of the wildlife profession—has made a tremendous contribution to wildlife management and the natural environmental culture of the world.

* * *

The years 2020, 2021, and 2022 are of particular and unusual historical note due to the Covid pandemic, a pandemic not experienced since the Spanish flu pandemic (1918–20) 100 years ago that began at the end of World War I (1914–1918). Although not addressed in this book, the Covid pandemic occurred during development of it, and atypically affected the wildlife programs—university and agency—in Wisconsin and elsewhere.

GREAT POSSESSIONS

If Charles Dickens hadn't written a book called *Great Expectations*,[46] the name of Aldo Leopold's book would have been *Great Possessions*.[174] That was Leopold's preference. The publisher said no, too similar, although in 1944, Leopold had begun considering changing the title to something with "almanac" in it. His preferred title *Great Possessions* having been reluctantly discarded, Wisconsin's Aldo Leopold used the unseemly name *A Sand County Almanac*.[140] (What's a sand county and who's gonna read an almanac about it?) Initially unpopular, it eventually caught on. Published posthumously in 1949 by his son Luna and then again in 1966, Leopold's futuristic book, begun in 1941, became a classic. Strange as the undescriptive, unexciting name might seem, *A Sand County Almanac* has been published in 15 languages and is a best-selling, ageless collection of 60 philosophical essays considered the most important contribution to environmental thought since Henry David Thoreau wrote *Walden*[249] a century earlier. The environmental movement has now developed into one of the strongest and most influential social, political, and economic forces of our time, with more than 400 non-profit environmental groups.

But the name "Great Possessions" was not to be forgotten. To commemorate the 100th anniversary of Leopold's birth, in 1987 the Wisconsin Chapter of The Wildlife Society commissioned artist Jonathan Wilde to paint a picture of The Shack and surrounding landscape, with Leopold standing shovel in hand watching 22 Canada geese in flight. Matted and framed 24 inches by 33 inches, it is titled "Great Possessions." In my house in Newfoundland and Labrador hangs print 128 of 450 produced. The lower left corner of the frame has attached to it a pin I received from the Aldo Leopold Centennial Symposium in 1987, held at the University of Wisconsin–Madison. It simply says "424," the house number where Aldo Leopold had his office and taught—and began the wildlife profession.

ALDO LEOPOLD CENTENNIAL SYMPOSIUM

The Aldo Leopold Centennial Symposium, a celebration of Aldo Leopold's life honoring the 100th anniversary of his birth, coordinated by University of Wisconsin–Madison wildlife professor Dr. Robert A. McCabe, was held at the university, 23–24 April 1987. I attended with Dr. Richard D. Taber and his wife Pat from Missoula, Montana. All of Leopold's living former graduate students, including Taber, were asked to participate: 19 did, two did not, and five others had died. I knew eight of them (see Appendix 7). The symposium proceedings were published by the University of Wisconsin–Madison Department of Wildlife Ecology as the book, *Aldo Leopold: Mentor by His Graduate Students*.[169] The book is "likely to be the last written on Aldo Leopold by persons who knew and worked closely with him" (p. i).[169] The book lists all 26 of Leopold's students, with information about these accomplished wildlifers.

At the proceedings, I heard Leopold's 93-year-old brother Frederic Leopold (1895–1989) speak. (After returning from Europe and World War I, he enrolled at Wisconsin, and, in 1919, joined the social fraternity and literary society of Alpha Delta Phi, the same one I joined four decades later, as did Aldo Leopold's grandson, Dr. Bruce Carl Leopold, psychiatrist, at Amherst College [and Franklin Roosevelt and Theodore Roosevelt]. Aldo Leopold's father wanted him to join a fraternity, but he never did). Active in wildlife conservation, Frederic has a collection of papers located at Iowa State University. Famed limnologist Dr. Arthur D. Hasler (my university advisor for three years) chaired a session. He had known most of the Leopold students. Two of Leopold's children also chaired sessions—Luna Leopold and Nina Leopold Bradley—as did his son-in-law Charles Bradley.

One of the speakers, Dick Taber, had been my former boss at the University of Washington in Seattle, and some years later invited me to be his junior author of a book[235] he had been working on for years. Dick, his wife Pat, and I had lunch together the first day of the symposium, joined by my son Adam, a student at the University of Wisconsin–Madison (and eventually Secretary of the Wisconsin Department of Natural Resources).

That afternoon, a photographer took a remarkable photo of 17 of Leopold's graduate students attending the symposium. Pat and I stood together just left-front of the former graduate students, off the picture, watching it being produced for the book, *Aldo Leopold the Professor*.[167] If I had had the presence of mind to stand with Pat in the far-left corner where those other two guys are, she and I would have gotten into that historical photo!

* * *

In 1957, nine years after Leopold died, I enrolled at the University of Wisconsin–Madison and, in 1960, entered that same 424 University Farm Place, demolished four years later, where Leopold's department had been housed and where Leopold had taught his graduate and undergraduate students. It was then occupied by Leopold's faculty successors and former graduate students Dr. Joe Hickey, Dr. Bob McCabe, and Dr. Bob Ellarson. There I took Wildlife 118–Wildlife Ecology, from Hickey, the same course Leopold had taught beginning in 1939. (I got a B). I also took a limnology course and a fish ecology course from famed fish limnologist Dr. Arthur Hasler (my advisor), one of the centennial symposium session chairs. I also took plant ecology from famed plant ecologist Dr. John Curtis, who, in 1937, Leopold had recommended for a position at the university, and who, in 1959, produced the iconic, highly respected 657-page book *The Vegetation of Wisconsin: An Ordination of Plant Communities*,[39] so helpful to Wisconsin wildlifers.

In 1961, I graduated from the University of Wisconsin–Madison with a bachelor of arts in zoology, including the wildlife ecology course—unaware that I had just been exposed to the most historic and iconic formal wildlife education program in the business.

1.

BEGINNERS

THE AWARD

One Wisconsin wildlife legacy presented in North America every year is a reminder of how far the wildlife profession has come, how broad it is, and what it stands for. The day Aldo Leopold died, 21 April 1948, Durward Allen of the U.S. Fish and Wildlife Service told Bob McCabe of the University of Wisconsin in Madison that he had been thinking about establishing an annual award for its most distinguished living wildlifer, who made an outstanding contribution to wildlife science.[167] It would be the most prestigious award in the wildlife profession. The most prestigious organization in the wildlife profession, The Wildlife Society, formed a committee to discuss a design.

The 2.5-inch bronze medal has the extinct passenger pigeon depicted on one side as a symbol of a lesson in wildlife conservation, poignantly presented in Leopold's article "On a Monument to the Pigeon" in *A Sand County Almanac*.[142] The other side bears a sculpted profile of Leopold, from a photograph of him that Bob McCabe took at The Shack in 1946.[167]

The Wildlife Society's Memorial Committee makes the annual selection of a person to receive the medal. The president of The Wildlife Society presents the medal, inscribed with the recipient's name and the year.

Diverse wildlife professionals have received the medal: researchers, teachers, writers, administrators, politicians. In 1965, Aldo Leopold's son, A. Starker Leopold, received the medal. Four of Leopold's former graduate students received the medal: Joseph J. Hickey in 1972, H. Albert Hochbaum in 1980, Robert A. McCabe in 1986, and Richard D. Taber in 2008. Ernest F. Swift, former director of the Wisconsin Conservation Department, received the medal in 1959, and in 1989 so did Laurence R. Jahn, who worked for the Wisconsin Conservation Department and the Wildlife Management Institute.

The first medal went to J. N. "Ding" Darling in 1950. The next year, 1951, was the only time the medal was presented to more than one person: Carl D. Shoemaker received it that year; so did Mrs. Aldo Leopold—Estella—in honor of her late husband: the Aldo Leopold Memorial Award, The Wildlife Society's highest honor.

HIS FIRST STUDENT

"Schmidt's death is the first fatality in that young profession known as wildlife management."

—Aldo Leopold, 1936[137]

After working as a field naturalist for the Chicago Field Museum, Franklin J. W. Schmidt entered the University of Wisconsin in Madison in 1927.[167] Upon graduation, he worked on a prairie chicken project for the Wisconsin Conservation Department. He published seven papers on mammals, reptiles and amphibians, and prairie grouse, viz., sharp-tailed grouse and prairie chickens. He co-authored a paper on painted turtles, establishing the modern view of that genus as a single species with many subspecies. In 1934, he became Aldo Leopold's first graduate student and would be the first person in history with university training in wildlife, using his work on prairie chickens toward a PhD dissertation and a monograph. He planned to start a consulting service to assist midwestern states in managing prairie grouse. Before he could make his contribution to the new profession of wildlife, Franklin J. W. Schmidt, 34, and his mother died in a fire on 7

August 1935, at his farm house in Stanley, Wisconsin. His five-year prairie chicken data died with him, including seven papers in preparation.[137]

HIS LAST STUDENT

On 8 November 2008, in Miami Beach, Florida, 60 years after Aldo Leopold died, his last surviving graduate student, Dr. Richard D. Taber, at age 88, became the 60th annual recipient of the Aldo Leopold Memorial Award. I was with him, as was his son Doug and my wife Jan.

A Wisconsin farm was home to Dick Taber's grandfather until, as a boy, he left with his parents for the California goldfields during the Gold Rush of 1849–1855, California having been recently acquired in 1848 from Mexico after the Mexican-American War (1846–1848).[232] So Dick grew up in San Francisco, where, at age 14, he obtained a copy of Aldo Leopold's book *Game Management*,[133] and began to think his outdoor interests might lead him in that direction.

In 1942, he graduated from the University of California–Berkeley with a BS in zoology. He served as a commissioned officer (Captain) in the U.S. Marine Corps during World War II. While serving in the Marines (1942–1946), he published his first paper, which was about the birds of Adak Island, Alaska, where he was stationed.[230] Then he joined Leopold in 1946 at the University of Wisconsin to begin work on his MS degree, which he obtained in 1949. For the degree, his research project, which he conducted in a marsh near Baraboo, was entitled "Observations on the Breeding Behavior of the Ring-necked Pheasant (*Phasianus torquatus*)." In 1949, a year after his advisor Aldo Leopold died, Taber published a research paper on pheasants.[231]

Taber's Wisconsin connection goes further. He obtained his PhD in 1951 at the University of California–Berkeley from Aldo Leopold's son, A. Starker Leopold, who grew up in Wisconsin. Taber was the only graduate student of Aldo Leopold to receive graduate degrees from both father and son: MS from Aldo Leopold and PhD from Starker Leopold. In California, Taber studied black-tailed deer, publishing his results with fellow graduate student Raymond Dasmann.[233]

In September 1953, Taber was startled when Starker Leopold proposed that they co-author a second edition of Starker's father's famous *Game Management* (1933),[133] "the bible of the field,"[232] wrote Taber (p. 99). Insufficient time prevented it.

An eloquent writer, he published 125 writings, including chapters in the first four editions of The Wildlife Society's prestigious *Wildlife Techniques Manual* (1960,[182] 1963,[183] 1969,[66] 1980[216]). Dick would be my boss at the University of Washington in Seattle (1973–75) and my co-author for reports on uncommon wildlife of the Mount Rainier National Park area[206] and the wildlife in riparian habitat of the Columbia River,[207] then a book.[235]

Taber was professor emeritus of forest zoology at the University of Washington. His main areas of professional interest were the ecology and conservation of mammals, and human welfare relative to wildlife conservation. As Leopold's former graduate student, he extended Leopold's legacy by working with many governmental and nongovernmental conservation organizations in North America, South America, Europe, and Asia. He was elected to the American Institute of Biological Sciences and the American Association for the Advancement of Science, among other professional awards.

After a career as a wildlife professor at the University of Montana (1955–1968) in Missoula and the University of Washington (1968–1985) in Seattle, where he had many MS and PhD graduate students, Taber resumed his Wisconsin connection by inviting me at the University of Wisconsin–Stevens Point to co-author a book he had been working on part-time for some 25 years: *Wildlife, Conservation, and Human Welfare*,[235] published when Dick was 82. He wrote the Foreword to two of my books when he was 74[203] and 90.[200]

Taber's wit, sense of humor, and inclination to socialize are revealed in the book he published (in Wisconsin) at age 79 with his wife Pat in 1999: *Parties without Pain: Your Guide to Healthy Humor*.[236] Around 2012, he self-published a hardbound copy of a memoir he called *Lucky Dick*.[232]

One of the things Dick and I had in common was the Marine Corps. Before our wildlife careers, Dick had been a captain during World War II; I had been a captain in the Vietnam War. For 20 years, until 2015, Dick and I had been old-fashioned pen pals, exchanging personal letters written in longhand; Dick didn't do computers.

All of them are gone now. Dick Taber was a first generation wildlifer in this new wildlife profession. He and his generation of wildlifers laid a solid foundation for the young wildlife profession, for its advancement by all wildlifers who follow. Dick was my boss, colleague, mentor, co-author, pen pal, and friend. I am proud of my link to this renowned wildlifer partly because of his accomplishments, partly because I liked him and his clever ways, partly because of our association and friendship, and partly because through Dick Taber, like other wildlifers who have known him, I can personally and vicariously stretch back through our professional wildlife history to the very beginning of it, to Aldo Leopold, Dick's major professor.

Born 22 November 1920, Richard D. Taber died in Missoula, Montana, on 24 January 2016, at age 95.[162,202] Among the items in the Richard D. Taber Scholarship display in the University of Montana Wildlife Conference Room of the Forestry Building is a shadow box with the Taber and Payne book[235] in it. Taber's death ends the last personal wildlife connection to Wisconsin's Aldo Leopold, the Father of Wildlife Management. With the death of Taber, the beginning of the wildlife profession is no longer as close and personal. My friend Dick Taber was the last survivor of Aldo Leopold's famed graduate students, the last of the first generation of students formally educated in the new profession of wildlife management. The death of Richard D. Taber represents the end of an era.

HIS MERE FIFTEEN YEARS: 1933-1948

Of all locations in the world, the state of Wisconsin was profoundly fortunate when Aldo Leopold settled in. How could a man who started a new profession and worked in it *a mere fifteen years* have so much enduring worldwide influence in it? Fifteen years: 1933–1948! Meine[174] provided a detailed historical account of Leopold's life. Other publications about Leopold and his life followed.[58, 153, 175, 177, 179]

He went hunting with his father and enjoyed both gun and bow. He was seldom without a dog. From 1890 to 1948, he had owned at least nine dogs (four named Flick): three spaniels, two setters, an Irish terrier, a collie, and two German short-haired pointers named Gus and Flick.[21]

He was christened Rand Aldo Leopold, the first name or initial never used. Aldo (1887–1948), Marie (1888–1983), Carl (1892–1958), and Frederic (1895–1989) were born to first cousins Carl Leopold (1858–1914) and Clara Starker (1859–1948) and reared in Burlington, Iowa. Aldo was a wildlife visionary. When he was born, no forestry profession existed in America. No wildlife profession existed in the world. A few European-trained foresters existed in North America. The first forestry school opened at Cornell University in 1898. In 1900, Yale University opened a graduate school in forestry. The first university training in wildlife would have to wait until 1933 and Aldo Leopold.

Working for the U.S. Forest Service in Arizona and New Mexico since 1909, he began publishing, and in 1915, wrote the "Game and Fish Handbook"[126] followed by various other wildlife articles.[127, 128] After his transfer in 1924 to the U.S. Forest Products Laboratory in Madison, he continued writing wildlife articles.[129, 130, 131, 132]

On 16 July 1932, Leopold sent the final draft of a manuscript to Scribner's, and applied himself to his consulting business.[131] *Game Management*[133] was published in May 1933. (In it, Leopold still spelled the word "wildlife" as two words.) It was Leopold's crowning work in game management, and utilitarian in game production some 30 years after Gifford Pinchot, first Chief Forester, applied utilitarian techniques in forest production. But *Game Management* was more than utilitarian; it also espoused an environmental ethic. The principles discussed applied to nongame as well as game species of wildlife. The 481-page book of 18 chapters (Chapter XVIII entitled "Game as a Profession") had a profound effect among game conservationists throughout the

United States and Canada—except here was a wildlife textbook for which no wildlife course existed, nor a formally trained wildlife profession! In *Game Management*, Leopold mentioned the reign in Asia of Kublai Khan (1260–1294) as producing the first, and only, documented program of game management.[256]

Here's where his mere 15 years began, starting and developing the wildlife profession—at age 46. On 26 June 1933, Harry Russell, former dean in Madison of the University of Wisconsin's College of Agriculture and then first director of the Wisconsin Alumni Research Foundation—the university affiliate for research funding—informed Leopold he had a job with the university within the Department of Agricultural Economics. (In 1962, Russell would have a future wildlife building on campus named after him—Russell Labs—with the Aldo Leopold Wing added in 1989.) At a budget of $8,000/year, including salary and expenses, Aldo Leopold became the first Professor of Game Management in the world, earning him the sobriquet, "The Father of Wildlife Management." Leopold began training students at the University of Wisconsin to become wildlifers, providing the first formal wildlife education to students pursuing that new profession.

His students and others referred to him as "The Professor." (He couldn't be called "Dr. Leopold," for he had no PhD.) In 1939 (the year I was born), Leopold authorized the first academic department in the world dedicated to the emerging field of wildlife management. He accordingly named his department the "Department of Wildlife Management," within the University of Wisconsin's College of Agriculture. For nine years, until his death in 1948, Leopold was chair of this department—chair of a wildlife department—and a professor of wildlife who had no degree in wildlife because no such degree existed until he developed it!

That same year, 1939, Leopold first taught Wildlife Ecology 118. (Born that year, I took that course 21 years later). By that time, he was established enough to participate on the Committee on Professional Standards for The Wildlife Society.[144]

Leopold was a prolific writer. During his 61 years, he produced 352 publications, including three books. At least a third of those were published in peer-reviewed journals. Of these, about 30 were research papers. From 1916 until he was appointed to the first wildlife faculty position in the world in 1933, he produced 119 publications (7.0/year). After that he produced 233 publications (13.7/year). Areas covered personally by these publications included New Mexico, Arizona, Utah, Oregon, Wisconsin, Ohio, Indiana, Michigan, Illinois, Minnesota, Iowa, Missouri, Manitoba, Mexico, Germany, and Czechoslovakia.

Leopold had an MS degree in forestry, but no PhD. Because no university wildlife program existed until Leopold's appointment with the University of Wisconsin, his formal training in a university consisted of his forestry program, which probably included a course in biology. Thus, his background in wildlife consisted mainly of curiosity and OJT, i.e., on-the-job training.

In addition to his teaching and writing, Leopold accepted many other wildlife responsibilities, with accompanying contributions.[110, 152, 173] During the early 1930s, Leopold became involved with establishing the University of Wisconsin Arboretum and Wild Life Refuge, which was officially dedicated 17 June 1934. That same year, Leopold, Ding Darling, and Thomas Beck were the three people appointed to President Franklin Roosevelt's Committee on Wild Life Restoration.[11] Leopold was appointed chair of the National Research Council's Committee on Wild Life, 1934–1936. During that time, research activities were increased, along with advisory support for creating a national system of cooperative wildlife research units, contemplated by Ding Darling. Also in 1934, Ding Darling resigned as head of the U.S. Bureau of Biological Survey (renamed U.S. Fish and Wildlife Service in 1940), and the position was offered to Leopold, who declined it to remain in Wisconsin. The position was given to Ira Gabrielson, who held it from 1935 to 1946, when he became president of the Wildlife Management Institute until 1970. As an incentive to remain at the university, Leopold had been offered his own department.

In 1935, Leopold was among the 6 founders who organized The Wilderness Society. That same year, Leopold was one of six foresters invited to study forestry methods for 3.5 months in central Europe, specifically in Germany and Czechoslovakia. He also studied game management there.

After the Wisconsin state legislature passed a law in 1935 requiring schools to teach conservation, teachers needed ideas, and some regularly wrote to Leopold, who always responded with references.

At the first North American Wildlife Conference in 1936, Aldo Leopold and Herb Stoddard served as counselors to the first president, Ralph T. King, of the "Society of Wildlife Specialists," which became "The Wildlife Society" the next year, 1937. Leopold also was chair of the Society of American Foresters' Committee on Forest Game Policy. In 1936, Leopold also served as director of the Audubon Society.

In 1936, Leopold began a friendship with Gordon MacQuarrie (1900–1956) when he became the outdoor editor of the *Milwaukee Journal*. MacQuarrie is the first professional full-time outdoor writer in America[38] and a member of the Wisconsin Conservation Hall of Fame.

In 1937, Leopold co-authored the report "The University and Conservation of Wisconsin Wildlife"[143] when he chaired an intra-university committee that included Chancey Juday (pioneer of North American limnology), Norman Fassett (published botanist), and Leon Cole (geneticist and ornithologist). Also in 1937, as chair of the Technical Committee of the American Wildlife Institute, Leopold was instrumental in establishing a waterfowl research station, which would become the famed Delta Waterfowl Research Station on the marshlands of southern Lake Manitoba near Winnipeg. Leopold's graduate student, Albert Hochbaum, who became renowned as a wildlife artist and author, was the first director of Delta, 1938–1970.

Throughout the 1930s, Leopold's main contribution to the Wisconsin Conservation Department (WCD) was consulting. In 1933, the WCD was reorganized and given legislative authority to set seasons and bag limits on big game—a historical landmark in state game and fish administration. In December 1933, Leopold was appointed to the WCD's new game and fisheries committee. He became friends with Ernie Swift, a warden then, who became WCD's director from 1947 to 1954 (and recipient of the Aldo Leopold Award in 1959). Leopold had a profound effect on Swift, reflected in Swift's career.

In 1943, the governor nominated Leopold to the Conservation Commission (now the Natural Resources Board), which Leopold helped establish in 1927. He was confirmed overwhelmingly by the state senate, the only natural resource type on the board and the first wildlifer, serving until his death in 1948. During this time, he became embroiled in "The Deer Wars," so-called because of the contentious issue about reducing the deer herd by shooting does in order to preserve the carrying capacity of the deer habitat that starving deer were damaging in winter.[67] The release of the Walt Disney movie *Bambi*, in 1942, did not help, with its interesting and endearing story but inaccurate biology, although it helped stimulate interest in wildlife.[105]

In "Game as a Profession," the last chapter of *Game Management*[133], Leopold described the training needed in wildlife management, listing courses in the sciences and arts, but none specifically in wildlife science. As a member of The Wildlife Society's Committee on Professional Standards, he published "Academic and Professional Training in Wildlife Work"[138] that the committee had developed in 1939. It included a master's degree. He wrote, "the basic skill of the wildlife manager is to diagnose the landscape, to discern and predict trends in its biotic community, and to modify them where necessary in the interest of conservation."[138] In 1939–1940, Leopold was President of The Wildlife Society, as well as active on committees and boards of more than a dozen university, local, and national organizations.

His involvement in current wildlife affairs could leave him unfamiliar with some mundane affairs. Once when his son Starker tuned into a football game on the radio, his dad asked who these Packers were.

Leopold focused on his select few graduate students, of which he had 26 from 1934 to his death in 1948: nine PhD and 17 MS students. Three of his MS students also got their PhDs from him. Thus, he administered 12 PhD degrees; three others did not finish. The first of Aldo Leopold's graduate students to obtain a degree in wildlife—the first in the world—graduated in 1939. Leopold's three graduate students to graduate before that, in 1937, would have had degrees in zoology, for the wildlife department did not begin until 1939, when the university approved it for Leopold.

Of Leopold's 26 graduate students with degrees,[167] seven of them worked for the WCD: Jim Hale, Donald R. Thompson, Cyril Kabat, Fred Hamerstrom, Fran Hamerstrom, with Irv Buss and Lyle Sowls temporarily. *Game Management*[133] was used to produce university-trained wildlifers throughout the country, as more universities began developing wildlife programs.

In 1947, with his professional standing at its apex, Leopold was elected an honorary vice-president of the American Forestry Association and became President of the Ecological Society of America—testimony to his high regard in the scientific community and the major conservation organizations. Also in 1947, Leopold served on the advisory council of a new conservation organization called the Conservation Foundation. Due to ill health in 1947, he had to cancel an anticipated consulting trip to Isle Royale National Park. Later in 1947, he was re-elected Vice President of the Wilderness Society.

Aldo Leopold was not alone in writing early wildlife books (Appendix 1). In 1947, Leopold was planning to update *Game Management*[133], which he considered out of date since he had published it in 1933, and write a book of ecological case studies which he had been considering since the early 1940s. He never did.

Here's where Leopold's mere 15 years end. In February 1948, U.S. Secretary of the Interior Julius Krug appointed Leopold to serve with about 40 American advisors on a United Nations conference sponsored by its Economic and Social Council, to be held in the U.S. in 1949 or 1950. It was called the International Scientific Conference on the Conservation and Utilization of Resources. Leopold accepted this final appointment—but could not make it. He died in April 1948.

In a mere 15 years, Leopold began and developed a new profession and was instrumental in revolutionizing the world regarding wildlife management, biodiversity, and ecosystems.

Leopold's view of wildlife management was both utilitarian and preservation-focused. He advocated "wise use" and wilderness. His students reported him to be kind and gentle, but a persuasive and eloquent fighter for what he believed in, which made him a remarkable personality because gentle people often are not fighters.[58]

In 2004, Wisconsin passed a law designating the first weekend in March as Aldo Leopold Weekend. In 2014, a new residence hall opened for 172 students at the University of Wisconsin-Madison. The building's focus is on conservation and sustainability, with solar panels, electricity monitors, and a greenhouse on top. It was named the Aldo Leopold Residence Hall.

Aldo Leopold, from Wisconsin, began in Iowa and returned to Iowa for burial in Burlington. Estella, his wife from New Mexico, is beside him.

What Aldo Leopold accomplished in his 61 years of life—especially his last 15 years—was formidable. It is safe to say that Aldo Leopold was the only wildlifer whose fame and name every other wildlifer recognized by the time Leopold died in 1948. It holds true today. Aldo Leopold is recognized worldwide as one of the most influential people of all times in wildlife conservation and stewardship of land.

HIS SHACK AND HIS BOOK

by Neil F. Payne and Richard D. Taber

If you travel in Wisconsin along I-90/94 or I-39, you will have to cross the Wisconsin River somewhere near Portage. Paralleling the river is a road called Levee Road. Along that road is The Shack. A shack, you say? No. *The Shack.* Much of world-renowned conservationist Aldo Leopold's futuristic and classic book, *A Sand County Almanac,*[140] was inspired by what he experienced near the chicken shack on 80 acres of worn-out farmland he bought in 1935 in the Wisconsin River floodplain of Sauk County near Baraboo, and eventually five parcels totaling 250 acres.

In 1947, when the junior author of this article was a graduate student of Aldo Leopold at the University of Wisconsin, "The Professor" would open each of his spring lectures in the now-historic course Wildlife Ecology by asking, "Who has a phenological observation to share?" *Phenology* is the study of seasonal events in nature. It would not do to say "The birds are back" when you really meant that you had seen the first robin or heard the first winnowing flight of the snipe that spring. For the thinking investigator, a close focus on the seasonal phenology of the same species in the same location in a long series of years might reveal different species' responses to variable environmental factors including climate change.

During Leopold's formative years, the earlier emphasis on taxonomy and, for game birds and mammals, food habits, had provided a base of knowledge concerning the individual animal or plant. As he worked through the concepts in his famous book *Game Management*[155], Leopold dealt with species' populations. His thinking continued to advance toward a more comprehensive vision of "habitats" of interacting species' populations. By 1937, he was "digging deeper," as he would say, into the topic of the seasonal patterns of species and the annual variations in those seasonal patterns, that is, the responses of community members and individual species to the variations in environmental factors.

Leopold had been gaining fame as a conservationist,[58,174] but the posthumous publication of *A Sand County Almanac* brought everlasting fame for him and The Shack that helped inspire the book. It was on these grounds that he died of a heart attack at age 61 while fighting a neighbor's grass fire in 1948. The following year, his son Luna took his father's manuscript to publication with Oxford University Press in New York, from whom Aldo Leopold had learned, just weeks before he died, that his manuscript had been accepted for publication. Then, Luna arranged to have some of his father's other previously unpublished essays published, in a book titled *Round River*.[141] It took a while for *A Sand County Almanac* to catch on; it is published in 15 languages now. In

1966, Luna Leopold combined all of *A Sand County Almanac* with eight essays from *Round River* into the best-selling book it continues to be today—*A Sand County Almanac: With Other Essays on Conservation from Round River.*[142] Charles W. Schwartz illustrated it with 28 birds, 20 mammals, and one fish.

Leopold began his book with, "There are some who can live without wild things, and some who cannot. These essays are the delights and dilemmas of one who cannot."[142] No one has examined just what these "wild things" are in so famous a book, the essays encompassing every month of the year in diverse locations in North America: seven states in the United States, two states in Mexico, and one province in Canada, with other examples throughout the U.S. and the world.

These "wild things" that Leopold mentioned in *A Sand County Almanac* occur in 140 greater and lesser habitats mentioned in the narrative. These wild things are used throughout the book, often repeatedly, to illustrate Leopold's ecological observations, ideas, and philosophy. These wild things are mentioned by common name for 376 species or genera of animals and plants: 34 game mammals, 14 nongame mammals, nine domestic mammals, 26 game birds, 82 nongame birds (three alien), three herps, 11 fish (one alien), 16 invertebrates (one alien), 14 coniferous trees (two alien), 30 deciduous trees (five alien), 36 shrubs (two alien), 73 wild forbs (eight alien), ten domestic forbs (flowers and vegetables), 12 wild grasses (four alien), three domestic grasses (grains), three grass-like plants, plus six plant and animal diseases. Of these, two mammals (mammoth and mastodon), two birds (great auk and passenger pigeon), one order of reptiles (dinosaurs), and most of a class of invertebrates (crinoids) are extinct.

Most of these plants, animals, and habitats are sprinkled generously through the first two parts of *A Sand County Almanac*, viz., in "Part I: A Sand County Almanac" and in "Part II: The Quality of the Landscape." Fewer occur per page in the last two parts of the book, viz., in "Part III: A Taste for Country" and in "Part IV: The Upshot," which tend to be more philosophical. Of the phenological observations of plants and animals by Leopold and Jones in 1947,[145] 118 were mentioned in *A Sand County Almanac*:

eight mammals, 35 birds, one invertebrate, 15 trees, 15 shrubs, 39 forbs, four grasses, one grass-like plant. Most (68%) of these 118 animals and plants mentioned in both sources occur in Part I and Part II which deal more with phenology, although some of the observations are repeated in Part III and Part IV.

In 1947, Leopold and Jones[145] published a ten-year phenological study (1935–45) for Sauk and Dane counties that included both animals and plants. Indeed, Leopold began *A Sand County Almanac* with a phenological account of January through December. Leopold probably used some of the information from his and Jones's study[145] to help tell the story in the book.[142] Since then, phenological studies in Wisconsin have been conducted during 1976–1989[25] and during 1994–2004.[271] Such studies are useful in determining and comparing ecological change wrought by climate change.

Leopold's *A Sand County Almanac*[140] took time in developing, of course.[31] For example, a portion of the essay quoted most often, "The Land Ethic," was originally published as "The Conservation Ethic."[134] Meine[172] described the chronology of *A Sand County Almanac*: "Aldo Leopold's *A Sand County Almanac* has brought a generation to a groundswell change in environmental consciousness – and conscience" (p. viii).[31,175] The principal themes, often reflected in Leopold's earlier writings, are conservation ecology, natural aesthetics, and environmental ethics,[59] which apply to both private and public lands worldwide, although the book was written about North America, with examples especially from Wisconsin. This famous book was instrumental in bringing posthumous fame to Aldo Leopold and The Shack and its grounds, and the development of the Aldo Leopold Foundation, with its headquarters near The Shack. Aldo Leopold's daughter Estella expanded on The Shack and *A Sand County Almanac* with additional stories.[147]

In 1935, not long after Leopold's appointment as the nation's first professor of wildlife management at the University of Wisconsin, where the profession of wildlife management thus began, he bought a retreat for his family along the Wisconsin River near Baraboo—old worn-out farmland with an old chicken coop that he cleaned up and converted into confined living quarters, eventually calling it "The Shack."[147] It was a retreat into a rural area from the hustle and bustle of Madison where they lived, yet within easy driving distance (less than an hour away). The Shack and its grounds are operated by the Aldo Leopold Foundation. Founded in 1982 by Aldo Leopold's children, the Foundation is deeply committed to restoration ecology, land stewardship, and ecological study. Leopold's Shack has become its icon that inspires a reverence for all who visit it. Tours can be taken of The Shack, the Foundation buildings, and the grounds. In 1978, the area was placed on the National Register of Historic Places and in 2009, designated a National Historic Landmark, with its own "green" building headquarters, the Aldo Leopold Legacy Center, built nearby in 2007.

In 1969, the senior author received his hard-bound copy of *A Sand County Almanac*[142] and inscribed it then, "Perhaps my most valuable book." It continues to be read by the environmentally concerned public and used at various universities throughout North America as supplemental reading for classes in wildlife, forestry, other natural resources, and environmental ethics. Although written over the course of 40 years preceding Leopold's death in 1948, the book reveals an early perspicacity about such present-day concerns as biodiversity, fragmentation, area-sensitive species, core reserves, human population limits, and climate change, some of which are just being addressed these many years later. With regard to altering the land mechanism, Leopold's classic saying applies: "To keep every cog and wheel is the first precaution of intelligent tinkering" (p. 177).[142] As the world finally begins to recognize the severity and urgency of, and react politically and economically to, its severe environmental wounds, Leopold is recognized as one of the most influential people of the 20th century. Aldo Leopold should have been listed with Rachel Carson[32] and others among the "Scientists and Thinkers of the 20th Century" described in the cover story of the 29 March 1999 issue of *TIME* magazine.[51]

HIS KIDS

Aldo and Estella Leopold had five children. Aldo's professional influence on all five is remarkable. Like their father, all five, incredibly, became professionally engaged in some phase of natural resources. This strongly hints of their admiration for their father and for the natural resource work that he did. All five became accomplished at it. Like John Muir,[186] who lived in Wisconsin just 14 of his early years, the five Leopold kids, professional conservationists all, lived in Wisconsin 12 years (Starker and Luna), 17 years (Carl), 21 years (Estella), and 87 years (Nina). All were born in New Mexico except the last one, Estella, born in Madison. Three of the Leopold children have been appointed to the prestigious National Academy of Sciences: Starker, Luna, and Estella—the only family so honored.

STARKER LEOPOLD

When easy-going Starker (1913–1983) discovered girls and alcohol his freshman year at the University of Wisconsin, his grades plummeted. When his girlfriend totaled Leopold's new family car, Starker's father first expressed genuine concern about the girl, then jerked Starker out of school and placed him at the state game farm to work for awhile.

In 1934, Starker graduated from Wisconsin with a BS in soils and agronomy. After two years of study in the School of Forestry at Yale University, he transferred to the University of California in Berkeley, and in 1944 received his PhD in zoology. Of the Leopold children, Starker followed most closely in his father's footsteps. Starker's PhD in zoology was more suitable to the pursuit of a university career in wildlife than his father's MS in forestry, although Starker had no coursework in wildlife ecology either, unless he took his father's course in it while an undergraduate at the University of Wisconsin.

Starker never traded on his father's famous name. Because Starker was in the wildlife profession like his celebrated father, the ghost of his father's reputation never quite left him, but he made his peace with it. Ultimately, Starker would become a recognized wildlife authority[146] at the University of California-Berkeley, where he was professor of zoology and forestry. He declined the offer to succeed his deceased father at the University of Wisconsin in 1948 (even though it would mean being in Madison with his mother). Starker went on to award one of his father's

MS students (Dick Taber) a PhD in 1951, write five books and more than a hundred scientific articles on wildlife, be an active member of numerous conservation committees and organizations including as president of The Wildlife Society, and receive the Aldo Leopold Memorial Award in 1965, among other awards and honors. He retired in 1978. He had two children: Frederick and Sarah Klock. Starker was 69 when he died.

LUNA LEOPOLD

When his father died in 1948, Luna took his father's masterpiece manuscript, *A Sand County Almanac*,[140] to publication in 1949 (see *Great Possessions*, in Prologue).

Luna (1915–2006) received his BS in civil engineering from the University of Wisconsin in 1936, his MS in physics-meteorology from the University of California in Los Angeles in 1944, and his PhD in geology from Harvard University in 1950. He worked for the U.S. Geological Survey from 1950 to 1972 when he joined the faculty at the University of California–Berkeley as a professor in the Department of Geology and Geophysics and Department of Landscape Architecture, retiring in 1986 an accomplished hydrogeologist. Like his brother Starker, also on the UC–Berkeley faculty, Luna was a productive writer and wrote some 200 scientific articles and six books, was an active member of numerous conservation committees and organizations, and received awards and honors. His hobbies included playing guitar, singing, composing guitar and piano music, dancing, painting, writing poetry, acting on stage, hunting, and fishing. Luna had two children: Bruce and Madelyn. Luna was 90 when he died.

NINA LEOPOLD BRADLEY

Nina (1917–2011) received her BS in geography in 1939 from the University of Wisconsin. Like all the Leopold kids, she spent many a happy weekend at The Shack—an old chicken coop renovated for family use near the shore of the Wisconsin River near Baraboo. The Leopold Shack and environs ultimately became the Leopold Memorial Reserve. She and her husband Charles facilitated research at the Leopold Memorial Reserve, initiating the

Leopold Fellows program that enabled many graduate students to conduct research for their MS and PhD degrees. In 2007, the Aldo Leopold Legacy Center opened for Leopold scholars and ongoing education programs. It is the headquarters of the Aldo Leopold Foundation, a National Historic Landmark, and Nina served on its board until her death. More than anyone else, Nina spoke at meetings and banquets about the Leopold legacy. The work and contributions of Aldo Leopold, through his daughter Nina, became more widely recognized and appreciated worldwide. In 1988, Nina received an honorary Doctor of Environmental Science from the University of Wisconsin–Madison. She was inducted into the Wisconsin Conservation Hall of Fame. Nina had two children: Nina Loeffel and Trish Stevenson. Nina was 93 when she died.

A. CARL LEOPOLD

I found this story by Curt Meine (p. 455–456)[174] compelling, I suppose partly because, like Aldo Leopold's son Carl, a first lieutenant in the Marine Corps in a war zone at age 25 during World War II (1939–1945), I was a first lieutenant in the Marine Corps in a war zone at age 27 during the Vietnam War (1965–1973). I had an MS in wildlife but did not go bird watching in Vietnam due to landmines and snipers. Unlike Carl, I could inform my parents and wife about my location.

I Know Where Carl Is!

"Of more personal concern, Aldo and Estella had not heard from Carl for several weeks. The family knew only that he was somewhere with the Marines in the south Pacific. Carl wrote home regularly, but his letters did not relate the full story of his war experiences. He was now a first lieutenant, and his company had taken part in the grievous island campaigns of 1943. In order to keep Estella calm, Carl kept the letters cheery. Then, early in 1944, military secrecy tightened and no mail at all was allowed through. Finally, in February, after a month of mystery, one letter made it to Madison. Carl was forbidden, for security reasons, to give his location, but he did describe the local bird life. Wildlife ecology did have its quite practical applications: with this

scant information, Aldo was able to pinpoint Carl's location. He had a grand smile on his face as he excitedly told Estella, "I know where Carl is! I know where Carl is!"

Carl was in the Marshall Islands probably on the island of Kwajalein or Eniwetok; later in 1944 he was on the island of Guam.

Carl (1919–2009) received his BS in botany in 1941 from the University of Wisconsin. He enlisted in the U.S. Marines during World War II, after which he received MS and PhD degrees in plant physiology from Harvard University, joining the faculty at Purdue University in 1949 as a professor of physiology in horticultural crops, earning a reputation as an outstanding scientist. In 1975, he became Graduate Dean and Assistant Vice President for Research at the University of Nebraska. In 1977, he moved to the Boyce Thompson Institute for Plant Research on Cornell University's campus in Ithaca, New York, retiring in 1990. He published some 200 scientific articles and five books. He was active in environmental issues until his death and received many honors and awards. Carl had three children: Lucia Wolf, John, and Susan Freeman. Carl was 89 when he died.

ESTELLA LEOPOLD

A paleobotanist and conservationist, Estella (1927-2024) was born in Madison and spent 21 years in Wisconsin. She received a BS in botany from the University of Wisconsin in 1948, an MS in botany from the University of California–Berkeley in 1950, and a PhD in botany from Yale University in 1955. She has conducted groundbreaking research on fossilized pollen. She specialized in a form of paleobotany known as palynology, i.e., the study of pollen. From 1955 to 1976, she worked for the U.S. Geological Survey. She collected and compared fossils from the Rocky Mountains and other places in the U.S. and the world. When the rich fossil beds of some 1700 species of fossils, from flies to sequoias, in Florissant Valley near Denver were threatened with development, she guided a conservation effort that led to the area being protected in 1969 as a national monument—Florissant Fossil Beds National Monument. She also helped establish Mount St. Helens National Volcanic Monument in 1982. She helped stop construction of dams in the Grand Canyon and helped prevent shipment of nuclear material through Puget Sound. For 30 years she was a professor of botany in the Department of Biology at the University of Washington in Seattle. Estella was active in environmental concerns and served on the boards of various environmental organizations. She published more than 100 scientific articles and three books, and received many honors and awards. She was president of the Aldo Leopold Foundation in Baraboo, Wisconsin. Estella was 97 when she died.

HIS WIFE

She wasn't a famous Wisconsin wildlifer. She wasn't famous or a wildlifer. But for 36 years she was the wife of the world's most famous wildlifer and the mother of their five children, all of whom were world famous in natural resources. This is more a human-interest part about the Leopold family. Estella Bergere Leopold (1890–1975) was born in Santa Fe, New Mexico and as a little girl probably did not dream about moving to Wisconsin and raising her family in the winters of Madison or cleaning out and living in an old chicken coop, calling it "The Shack." Estella was a schoolteacher. She met Aldo, of course never realizing any more than he did that he would become the most famous wildlifer in history. They married in 1912, had four children in New Mexico where he was working for the U.S. Forest Service, and when he was transferred they moved to Madison in 1924, where their fifth child was born. A cultured woman of many talents, Estella descended through her mother from a Spanish land grant family. Her father was a concert pianist. She taught her kids to love Spanish classical and folk music. In such a family, she developed into a skilled outdoors-person, winning the Wisconsin women's archery championship five years running. Northland College in Ashland, Wisconsin, bestowed on her an honorary doctorate degree in 1973. In honor of her late husband, in 1951 she received the Aldo Leopold Memorial Award, The Wildlife Society's, and the world's, highest wildlife honor. She played a huge supportive role in the development of her family. Their extreme accomplishments can be considered a tribute to her as well as to Aldo. Aldo's dedication in *A Sand County Almanac*[142] reads, "*To my ESTELLA.*" She died at age 84.

HIS PROTÉGÉ: BOB MCCABE

"McCabe was a feisty product of the ethnic neighborhoods of south Milwaukee" (p. 401).[174] On a football athletic scholarship in 1935, Robert A. McCabe (1914–1995) attended Carroll College in Waukesha, received his BS in biology, then switched his interest to wildlife. Beginning in 1939, Aldo Leopold served as the major professor (advisor) for Bob's MS in 1943 on Hungarian partridge and PhD in 1949 on ring-necked pheasants.

During Leopold's last six years, McCabe was his assistant, working closely with him on research, academic affairs, and professional concern—the daily involvement producing extraordinary rapport.[167] McCabe "…worked with him, talked with him, [was] counseled by him and [was] professionally trained by him during his most productive years" (p. ix)[167] (see University of Wisconsin–Madison, in Appendix 2). McCabe knew personally all but three of Leopold's 26 graduate students who completed all requirements, and all five of Leopold's secretaries. An observant McCabe wrote, "The seemingly unimportant nuances during [Leopold's] university years provide a measure of the man who more than any other gave meaning to the environmental movement" (p. ix).[167]

In 1952, McCabe became Leopold's successor as Chair of the Department of Wildlife Management, directing that prestigious program for 27 years. Renowned for interacting personally and humorously with his students, he brought to thousands of them knowledge of new techniques for studying the complexities of wildlife ecology. Also during that time, McCabe's advice was sought at state, national, and international levels as he served on various committees, including as president of The Wildlife Society.

McCabe[167] wrote a personal account (p. x) of his "remembrances and recollections" of Leopold, stating, "This compendium includes places, events and people who were, as I saw them, part of the ménage that was the Leopold era at the University of

Wisconsin, when the profession of wildlife management was evolving as a major thrust in resource conservation."

In his well-written, informative, personal, touching book, *Aldo Leopold the Professor*,[167] McCabe referred to Leopold as A.L. and included more than 100 photos of the Leopold era, some taken by Leopold. The book is a legacy.

In honor of Aldo Leopold's 100th anniversary of his birth, Bob McCabe coordinated and assembled (and I attended) the Aldo Leopold Centennial Symposium, held at the University of Wisconsin-Madison, 23–24 April 1987. The personal accounts about Leopold from 19 of his graduate students and 1 secretary are a legacy[169] (see Aldo Leopold Centennial Symposium, in Prologue).

Bob McCabe and Leopold's son Starker became close friends. The highest award in the wildlife profession, the Aldo Leopold Memorial Award, was awarded in 1965 to the University of California–Berkeley's A. Starker Leopold and in 1986 to the University of Wisconsin–Madison's Robert A. McCabe. McCabe[167] wrote (p. 159), "Mrs. L. inscribed my copy of *A Sand County Almanac* with the words, 'A son by affection to Aldo.' I certainly like to think so, as he was 'by affection' a father to me."

Bob retired in 1979 and was inducted into the Wisconsin Conservation Hall of Fame. He died at age 81.

EARTH DAY, WORLDWIDE: GAYLORD NELSON

Earth Day. 22 April. The world's largest environmental movement. U.S. Senator Gaylord Nelson (1916–2005) of Wisconsin, a more contemporary conservationist but no trained wildlifer, was disturbed that an issue as important as our environment was not addressed in politics or by the media. So, 22 April 1970, he created the first Earth Day, where an estimated 20 million people nationwide attended festivities.[35] Over the next ten years, known as the environmental decade, Congress passed 28 major laws protecting water, air, wetlands, and endangered species. In that decade, more environmental legislation was produced than in U.S. history.

Nelson viewed stability of the nation's population as an important aspect of environmentalism. He wrote that the economy is a
wholly owned subsidiary of the environment, not the other way
around[188]—a truism generally unrecognized by society, with its
capitalistic lust toward unrelenting economic growth.

Gaylord Nelson was an Army combat veteran (in the vicious
Okinawa campaign of WWII), Wisconsin state senator (1948–
58), Wisconsin governor (1959–63), and U.S. senator (1963–81).
Nelson (LLB WI '42) authored the Wilderness Act, the National
Trails System Act, the National Wild and Scenic Rivers Act, and
the National Environmental Education Act of 1990. Due to his
efforts to have Apostle Islands National Lakeshore created in
Wisconsin, 80% of the park is designated the Gaylord Nelson
Wilderness. Governor Nelson State Park, on the western shore
of Lake Mendota near Madison, bears his name. So does the
Gaylord Nelson Institute for Environmental Studies (Nelson
Institute) at the University of Wisconsin–Madison.

Each year on that day, 22 April, Earth Day is celebrated
worldwide with various events demonstrating support for environmental protection. Earth Day now includes events in more
than 193 countries, all started by a person from Wisconsin. Gaylord Nelson[188] was 89 when he died.

OTHER EARLY NATIONALLY RECOGNIZED WISCON-SIN-CONNECTED WILDLIFE LEADERS

The 1930s were a banner decade in the origin of wildlife man-
agement. Early wildlife leaders, who had influence on society
before Leopold's time, were outdoorsmen/naturalists,[166] artists,
or writers. Early wildlife leaders who were contemporaries of
Leopold included J. N. "Ding" Darling, Herb Stoddard, Walter
Taylor, John Phillips, E. A. Goldman, W. L. McAtee, Stanley
Young, Wallace Grange, Charles Elton, David Lack, Olaus Murie,
Paul Errington, Ira Gabrielson, Gardiner Bump, and Reuben
Trippensee. Most were wildlife researchers, but like Leopold,
Paul Errington and Reuben Trippensee became involved with
teaching students to become wildlife managers. Darling became
an organizer and activist in the wildlife profession.

Aldo and Ding; two singular names. Contemporaries. Two different personalities, both with Wisconsin and Iowa connections. They got things going and they got things done. One lived in Wisconsin but was educated elsewhere; the other was educated in Wisconsin but lived elsewhere. Both had lived in Iowa at one time. One was an educator who trained future wildlifers; the other was a cartoonist and dynamic organizer of wildlifers. Aldo Leopold and Ding Darling were closely aligned as friends with mutual regard. They met in 1928, when Leopold originally surveyed game in Iowa. Over the next years they would play key roles in wildlife conservation.[174] They had mutual respect and admiration for each other's abilities and accomplishments in dissimilar wildlife roles. Each was a potent force in wildlife conservation.

DING DARLING

At Beloit College, in Beloit, Wisconsin, in the H. D. Densmore Department of Biology, hangs the original work for the first "Duck Stamp." Ding Darling (1876–1962) designed that famous iconic stamp in 1934, a blue goose in flight, the icon of the U.S. Fish and Wildlife Service, on all its signs and emblems, including the entrance of all 588 national wildlife refuges throughout the United States. Its artistry highly competitive now, the annual duck stamp competition attracts artists from across the continent for selection of the species of waterfowl on the stamp that must be purchased annually by all waterfowl hunters in the United States and Canada, the proceeds of which support waterfowl habitat acquisition and improvement. (In 2018, the Federal Duck Stamp contest was held at the University of Wisconsin-Stevens Point's College of Natural Resources).

Ding Darling got kicked out of two colleges.[125] In 1894, he started at Yankton College in Yankton, South Dakota, a Congregational college (Ding's father a Congregational minister) where he organized and played football as captain on the college's first football team. But without consent, he and some friends borrowed the college president's horse and buggy. Ding was expelled.

In 1895, he went to Wisconsin and enrolled in Beloit College where he paid his way with his musical talents at funerals and other gigs. He led the glee club, was a member of the mandolin club, managed the track team, was managing editor of the student newspaper, and art director of the yearbook. To sign illustrations in it, for the first time he used the nickname "D'ing," by which he became nationally famous, using the first letter and the last three letters of his last name.

He was in the class of 1899, but with irregularities in class attendance and poor scholarship, and despite his motto his junior year of "I want to be an angel,"[125] he got into trouble. As the art editor of the yearbook for this conservative Congregational college, he illustrated the yearbook with caricatures of Beloit College's president and faculty. As biographer David Lendt[125] put it (p. 13):

> "Darling's skill with the pen was sufficient to make the subjects easily recognizable—whether as the Devil shoveling students into a fiery furnace or as a scrawny male ballet dancer attired in a tutu. The drawings, in fact, were so well done that the members of the small, reserved faculty considered the publication shocking. They did not appreciate the sketch of a revered professor of Latin singing, 'There'll Be a Hot Time in the Old Town Tonight.' They also failed to see the humor in the sight of the president of the college, E. D. Eaton, dancing the Highland Fling in appropriate attire. They did not like seeing the principal of the academy, a devoted soldier of temperance, singing, 'Give Us a Drink, Bartender.' ... The sketch of faculty lined up as chorus girls was too much for their dignity to bear."

For a second time, Ding was suspended, no doubt a humiliation for this son of a Congregational minister, and his father. Ding spent the year milking cows, picking corn, singing in a male quartet, and reporting for his hometown newspaper, the *Sioux City Journal.*

He graduated from Beloit College in 1900 with a degree in biology; 25 years later, 1925, Beloit College conferred on Ding an honorary Doctor of Letters.

Jay Norwood Darling was born 21 October 1876 in Norwood, Michigan, to Diantha and Marcellus Darling, and grew up in Sioux City, Iowa, where his father, a Civil War veteran, accepted a call in 1886 as minister to the Congregational Church. He left home for college at age 18 and returned after college in 1900 to work six years as a reporter for the *Sioux City Journal*. Then at age 30 in 1906 he began his long career with the *Des Moines Register and Leader*, mainly as a cartoonist, syndicated through the *New York Herald* in 1916 for 130 client newspapers, winning the Pulitzer Prize in 1925 for one of his cartoons, and again in 1942. Regularly using conservation themes, his cartoons often said more than a written document on the subject, and were familiar to newspaper readers across the U.S.

In the 1930s, Darling became involved in wildlife conservation. He was instrumental in separating Iowa's conservation activities from political interference. In 1932, the governor of Iowa appointed Darling as the first chair of the Iowa Fish and Game Commission (later the Department of Natural Resources). Recognizing that no scientifically-trained people were available to conduct work in wildlife research and management, Darling met with the president of Iowa State College (now Iowa State University) in Ames to propose a joint tripartite effort to correct this dilemma, with funding provided by the college, the state, and an outside source. Darling turned out to be the outside source, pledging $9,000 over three years (enough to buy a 100-acre farm during these depression years) to help fund in 1932 the Iowa Cooperative Wildlife Research Unit. Darling was the driving force behind the development of Cooperative Wildlife Research Units in the nation (see Cooperative Wildlife Research Unit, in Chapter 3).

In 1934, President Franklin Roosevelt appointed Darling, Aldo Leopold, and Thomas Beck (Chair of the Connecticut State Board of Fisheries and Game, and founder and president of More Game Birds) to the President's Committee on Wild Life Restoration, with a budget of $25 million to buy sub-marginal agricultural lands. Leopold and Darling had known each other since 1928. Only Beck had been a Roosevelt supporter, but this idea was strongly supported by all three committee members.[11]

On 1 March 1934, Roosevelt appointed Darling to direct the U.S. Biological Survey. He originated the idea of the duck stamp (Migratory Bird Hunting and Conservation Stamp). On 16 March 1934 Congress passed and Roosevelt signed the Duck Stamp Act of 1934, requiring $1 for purchase, the money to be used for waterfowl habitat acquisition and improvement.[47]

Darling was an energetic and active man, articulate and outspoken—just what the new wildlife profession of low esteem needed. But wildlife conservation was mostly a hobby for him, not a profession. Except for a BS degree in biology, he was not professionally trained in wildlife ecology, which makes him all the more amazing.

During Darling's 20 months as director of the Biological Survey, the national wildlife refuges greatly expanded by three million acres. In 1935, at almost 60, Darling resigned, frustrated and exhausted with the politics and red tape of it all, his blunt locution and somewhat brash temperament making enemies. He turned the reins over to Ira T. Gabrielson, who would become the first director of the U.S. Fish and Wildlife Service when the name changed in 1940 from the U.S. Biological Survey.

Darling returned to the *Des Moines Register* in 1936. That year in Washington, D.C., at the first annual North American Wildlife Conference, which he had convinced President Roosevelt to arrange, Darling began to organize the National Wildlife Federation, the nation's largest private conservation education organization, and was elected its first president.

In 1937, Darling played a leading role in the passage of the Pittman-Robertson Act, which was the Federal Aid in Wildlife Restoration Act of 1937. This magnificent act provides money to the states through a tax on the sale of sporting arms and ammunition (see WCD to WDNR, in Chapter 4).

In 1939, Darling's son John, a promising medical doctor, sustained brain damage in a car accident. The injury affected John the rest of his life, leading to epilepsy and a nursing home in 1957. It affected his father too, who became despondent and reduced his conservation activities, especially in the early 1940s when doctors advised him to do so. He became disillusioned with many conservation activities and lack thereof.

In 1949, Darling resigned from the *Des Moines Register*. He and his wife Penny lived for many years in Des Moines and on Captiva Island next to Sanibel Island in Florida. In 1950 Jay N. Darling received the first annual Aldo Leopold Memorial Award from The Wildlife Society. In the 1950s his health declined, but he and Penny spent much time traveling. Hospitalized in 1959, and thinking he was dying, he made a farewell cartoon drawing. His secretary kept it until 12 February 1962, when Darling died at age 85; the *Des Moines Register* published it the next day.[125]

The Lake Darling State Park in Iowa is named after him. The Sanibel National Wildlife Refuge on Sanibel Island, Florida, was formed in 1945. In 1967, the U.S. Fish and Wildlife Service renamed it. It is now the popular J. N. "Ding" Darling National Wildlife Refuge.

JOHN MUIR

John Muir (1838–1914) was one of the most famous and influential naturalists in the world. Sometimes referred to as "Father of the National Parks," he was one of the earliest advocates of the national park system, now with 63 national parks (48 in Canada).

Muir gained his early philosophy and formal training in Wisconsin, where he lived for 14 years.[186] Born in Scotland, he immigrated to Wisconsin at age 11 with his parents who farmed near Portage. The farm is now a National Historic Landmark of 80 acres called Fountain Lake Farm, near Montello, and borders John Muir Memorial County Park's prairie, wetland, and hardwood forest. Next to that is the Fox River National Wildlife Refuge (1054 acres).

At age 22, Muir enrolled at the University of Wisconsin in Madison and lived in North Hall from 1860 to 1863. He didn't graduate, but learned enough botany and geology to be useful later in life. He moved to Ontario and then California where he was influential in establishing Yosemite National Park, and involved in establishing Grand Canyon, Kings Canyon, Petrified Forest, and Mount Rainier national parks. He was the first president of the renowned Sierra Club, which he co-founded in 1892. John Muir was 76 when he died.

PAUL ERRINGTON

Like Ding Darling and Aldo Leopold, who had connections to both Wisconsin and Iowa, so did Paul Errington (1902–1962). From South Dakota, Errington wasn't long in Wisconsin, just long enough, from 1929 to 1932, to acquire his PhD. But it wasn't from Aldo Leopold. A wildlife degree was not yet established when Errington acquired his PhD in zoology, having studied bobwhite quail for three years. Errington was a frequent visitor of Leopold, discussing the progress of Errington's bobwhite quail study. Leopold edited Errington's writing in the office and at home. Spending much time together, Leopold honed Errington's future talents.[174]

Errington left Madison for his first and only job with his PhD, joining the zoology faculty at Iowa State University in 1932 and launching a new wildlife research position, Ding Darling providing moral and financial support. The position would develop into the first Cooperative Wildlife Research Unit in the nation, a prototype for the rest of them to follow beginning in 1935, with Errington as the nation's first Unit Leader, where he would remain until his death (see Cooperative Wildlife Research Unit, in Chapter 3).

With his work on predator-prey relationships and publication of several books and over 200 technical articles, in 1961 Errington was featured in *Life* magazine as one of ten outstanding naturalists in North America. In 1962, The Wildlife Society presented him with its Aldo Leopold Memorial Award. Paul Errington was 60 when he died.

HERBERT STODDARD

A close friend and professional associate of Aldo Leopold, Herb Stoddard (1889–1970) would spend 16 years in Wisconsin. Born in Illinois, Stoddard moved to Wisconsin in 1902 and trained, as a taxidermist, on a hippopotamus (no doubt a challenge) from Ringling Brothers Circus in Baraboo, Wisconsin. Then he worked as a taxidermist for the Milwaukee Public Museum (1910–1913), the Field Museum of Natural History in Chicago (1913–1920), and again the Milwaukee Public Museum (1920–1924). He was hired by the U.S. Biological Survey to work on bobwhite quail in Georgia and Florida. His classic study culminated with his seminal 559-page book, *The Bobwhite Quail: Its Habits, Preservation, and Increase*[226] in 1931. It was the first book to examine a game species in detail and use the information to manage and restore the species. Stoddard was instrumental in promoting and using prescribed fire for habitat improvement. He was the first to document the mortality of birds from transmission towers and guy lines. All this from an unusual guy who never finished high school. He was 81 when he died.

JOSEPH J. HICKEY

Joe Hickey (1907–1993) earned his MS degree under Leopold in 1943, was recruited by Leopold to be the second member in the department and stepped into Leopold's position as department chair during 1948–1952 after Leopold died (see University of Wisconsin–Madison, in Appendix 2). He remained a professor of wildlife management (later, wildlife ecology) at the University of Wisconsin for 28 years. Hickey gained national and international recognition with the 569-page book he edited in 1969, *Peregrine Falcon Populations: Their Biology and Decline*.[93] He was instrumental in the activism leading to bans on the organochlorine pesticides, especially DDT, causing eggshell thinning and the decline of peregrines, ospreys, and eagles in North America and elsewhere. With that, those populations recovered.

From New York City, he had studied history at New York University where he was a champion mile runner and track coach. Always interested in birds, he took evening courses leading to a degree in biology, then studied under Aldo Leopold for his MS degree. His thesis, *A Guide to Bird Watching* became a landmark book.[92] He acquired his PhD in zoology at the University of Michigan. In 1972, Hickey received the Aldo Leopold Memorial Award. He retired in 1976, and was inducted into the Wisconsin Conservation Hall of Fame. He was 86 when he died.

EDWARD BIRGE, CHAUNCEY JUDAY, ARTHUR D. HASLER

Edward Birge (1851–1950) from New York, Chauncey Juday (1871–1944) from Indiana, and Arthur D. Hasler (1908–2001) from Utah were professors in Madison at the University of Wisconsin, known as the birthplace of limnology in North America. In Madison, on the shore of Lake Mendota, the most studied lake in the world, is the University of Wisconsin's Center for Limnology established in 1982, with its Trout Lake (field) Station in northern Wisconsin. The Center grew out of almost 100 years of limnology initiated by Edward Birge and Chancey Juday, the pioneers of limnology, further developed by Arthur D. Hasler (my undergraduate advisor). Among decades of other limnological research, Hasler determined that salmon, migrating from the ocean to spawn, locate their natal river via olfaction. Juday was a founder of the Limnological Society of America. The Hasler Laboratory of Limnology (Hasler Lim Lab) and the venerable Birge Hall of biology are buildings on the Madison campus dedicated to Hasler and Birge. Birge was 99, Juday was 73, and Hasler was 93 when they died.

ERNEST (ERNIE) SWIFT

Ernest (Ernie) Swift (1897–1968), from Minnesota, began as a Wisconsin game warden in 1926, a year before the Wisconsin Conservation Department was formed in 1927 and the old Conservation Commission still existed. He rose to prominence. Without a college degree but hard-driving, impatient, and blunt, with formidable administrative skill, in 1927 he became the director of the law enforcement program for the WCD, then in 1947 director of the WCD. As director, he got 79 of 100 bills, written by his department, passed into law. In 1954, he left Wisconsin to become assistant director of the U.S. Fish and Wildlife Service, and in 1955, executive director of the National Wildlife Federation and a writer.[228] In 1959, The Wildlife Society awarded him the wildlife profession's highest honor, the Aldo Leopold Memorial Award. He was inducted into the Wisconsin Conservation Hall of Fame. Ernie Swift was 71 when he died.

LAURENCE (LARRY) JAHN

Laurence (Larry) Jahn (1926–2000), from Jefferson, earned a BS (1949) in zoology and an MS (1958) and PhD (1965) in wildlife at the University of Wisconsin. From 1949 to 1959, he worked as a waterfowl biologist with the Wisconsin Conservation Department. In 1959, he began work with the Wildlife Management Institute in Washington, D.C., retiring as president and board chairperson in 1991. He published numerous wildlife articles. He was President of The Wildlife Society, Chair of the Natural Resources Council of America, Chair of the National Watershed Congress, Chair of the Virginia Game and Inland Fisheries Commission, Chair of the North American Wildlife and Natural Resources Conference, Chair of the Environmental Advisory Board of the U.S. Army Corps of Engineers, and Chair of the Scientific Advisory Board for the Department of Defense, Strategic Environmental Research and Development Program. In 1989, The Wildlife Society awarded him the wildlife profession's highest honor, the Aldo Leopold Memorial Award. He was inducted into the Wisconsin Conservation Hall of Fame. Larry Jahn was 74 when he died.

FRANCES AND FREDERICK HAMERSTROM

They came from Boston, Fran from wealth and Fred from Harvard. They studied under Paul Errington at Iowa State University and then under Aldo Leopold at the University of Wisconsin, Fran (1907–1998) for her MS, in 1940, and Fred (1909–1990) for his PhD, in 1941. As Leopold's only female graduate student, Fran became the first female wildlife biologist in history. This internationally renowned husband and wife team of wildlife biologists worked as researchers: Fred for the Wisconsin Conservation Department and Fran part-time, focusing on prairie chickens. Fran volunteered time on raptors especially harriers (marsh hawks), field voles, and kestrels.[36, 81, 193] They are credited with saving the prairie chicken from extirpation in Wisconsin, with help from some 7,000 observers they hosted over the years in their ante-bellum home in central Wisconsin (see Appendix 5). They published many articles in technical journals and Fran wrote 12 books. Fran made appearances on the *Tonight Show* with Johnny Carson and the *Late Show* with David Letterman. Frederick and Frances Hamerstrom received numerous awards and honors for their wildlife work. They are considered one of the closest and most effective research teams in American ornithological history. Their daughter Elva Hamerstrom Paulson is an accomplished, renowned wildlife artist; she has illustrated Fran's books. Fred and Fran were inducted into the Wisconsin Conservation Hall of Fame. Fran was 91 and Fred was 81 when they died.

JOHN T. CURTIS

A plant ecologist, not a wildlifer, Dr. John T. Curtis (1913-1961) wrote the classic book published in 1959, *The Vegetation of Wisconsin: an Ordination of Plant Communities*,[39] which all wildlifers in Wisconsin use in their wildlife habitat work. In 1937 he received his PhD in botany from the University of Wisconsin and served on its faculty. (I took his plant ecology course from him in 1960.) His 657-page book presents descriptions of the natural communities of Wisconsin and identified the "tension zone" where the interaction of climate, soil type, and fire create a dynamic transition, and where southern and northern species of plants and animals overlap (see Chapter 6). Curtis was instrumental in developing the discipline of restoration ecology, with examples at the University of Wisconsin's Arboretum in Madison where the Leopold Pines and Curtis Prairie are located and studied. He was 48 when he died. In 2013 Curtis was inducted into the Wisconsin Conservation Hall of Fame.

OWEN GROMME

Owen Gromme (1896–1991), from Fond du Lac, is known as the Dean of American Wildlife Artists.[178] Curator of birds and mammals at the Milwaukee Public Museum, he used his reputation as an acclaimed wildlife artist of birds mostly to bring national attention to important conservation issues such as protecting birds by lobbying against use of chemicals, and for the formation of the International Crane Foundation in Baraboo. He helped protect Horicon Marsh from being drained, where a state wildlife refuge and a national wildlife refuge now exist. He was inducted into the Wisconsin Conservation Hall of Fame. Owen Gromme was 95 when he died.

POLITICAL HELP

Leopold and his contemporaries had a little help from legislation passed before the wildlife profession began. The U.S. Lacey Act of 1900 targeted the illegal wildlife trade, to control market hunting. The U.S. Weeks-McLean Act of 1913 prohibited spring migratory bird hunting and cracked down on the feather trade but was promptly found to be unconstitutional for infringing on states' rights. It was replaced by the Migratory Bird Treaty of 1916 and the Migratory Bird Treaty of 1918 between the United States and Canada, and in 1936 with Mexico, prohibiting harvesting, capturing, disturbing, and selling or trading migratory birds and their nests and eggs without permit. The Fish and Wildlife Coordination Act of 1934 provided the U.S. Fish and Wildlife Service with authority to evaluate impacts to fish and wildlife from proposed projects of water resource development. Also in 1934, Congress passed the Migratory Bird Hunting and Conservation Stamp Act, known as the Stamp Act, which requires all waterfowl hunters to buy a hunting license and the stamp, proceeds of which are used to buy, protect, and manage wetlands and other wildlife habitat.

National conservation efforts were already in effect by Theodore Roosevelt's presidency (1901–1909)[26] and his fifth cousin Franklin D. Roosevelt during his presidency (1933–1945).[27] FDR took office as U.S. president in 1933, the same year Leopold began the wildlife profession with formal training.

"The 2 Roosevelts—TR and FDR—are undisputedly America's great revolutionary conservation presidents. While Thomas Jefferson, Abraham Lincoln, Benjamin Harrison, John F. Kennedy, Lyndon B. Johnson, Richard M. Nixon, Jimmy Carter, Bill Clinton, and Barack Obama were likewise outstanding environmental-minded presidents, the Roosevelts made the management of natural resources the top domestic issue during their White House tenures." (pp. 627–628)[27]

President Theodore "Teddy" Roosevelt was the most influential conservationist the nation had seen. His friend John Muir influenced Roosevelt regarding national parks. His friend Gifford Pinchot was the first Chief Forester (1905–1910) for the U.S. Forest Service when it was created in 1905. Pinchot once said that without natural resources, life itself would be impossible. With Henry Graves, Pinchot founded the School of Forestry at Yale University, where Aldo Leopold received his master's degree in forestry.

During his presidency, Theodore Roosevelt established or enlarged 150 national forests (increasing America's national forests by 450%), 51 national bird reservations (which became national wildlife refuges) including the first one at Florida's Pelican Island in 1903, four national game preserves, six national parks, and 18 national monuments.[26] He signed into law the National Monuments Act in 1906.

During his presidency, Franklin Roosevelt established 140 national wildlife refuges in 36 states (Horicon 16 July 1941: 21,400 acres; Necedah 14 March 1939: 43,696 acres; Trempealeau 22 August 1936: 6,226 acres), eight national parks, 21 national monuments, 32 new national forests (Wisconsin's Chequamegon in 1933, Wisconsin's Nicolet also in 1933, but by President Hoover [Public Land, in Chapter 6]), and another 244 adjusted national forests mostly with land added.[27] In 1933, Roosevelt established the Civilian Conservation Corps of young men conducting reforestation and other conservation projects throughout the United States between 1933–42. In Wisconsin, the CCC established 128 camps of 165,000 men (including my uncle).[5]

Today, provincial and state wildlife agencies work with federal wildlife agencies of Canada and the United States to manage birds and their habitats within four flyway councils established in 1952: Pacific, Central, Mississippi, Atlantic. Across the country in recent years, new conservation initiatives have emerged. In 1990, Partners in Flight united wildlife interests of governmental agencies, nongovernmental organizations, educators and scientists, industry representatives, and other groups with the goals of keeping common birds common, and recovering threatened species of birds. The North America Bird Conservation Initiative (1998) and the Wisconsin Bird Conservation Initiative (2001)—as of 2020, the Wisconsin Bird Conservation Partnership—coordinate federal, state, and partner efforts to monitor birds on an ecological scale and to improve bird habitat. Hunters and non-hunters alike benefit from habitat improvements for birds that enhance the environment for wildlife and for human society in general.

2.

WILDLIFER

WILD LIFE, WILDLIFE, WILDLIFER

Wildlifers are professionals who possess a specialized degree in wildlife and are engaged in various aspects of wildlife-related work. They can be wildlife biologists (sometimes called wildlife ecologists or conservation biologists), researchers, professors, consultants, or a combination of these roles. Wildlife biologists with a master's degree in wildlife often work as researchers, managers, or both, specializing in game or nongame species and their biodiversity. Wildlifers who hold PhDs typically work as teachers and researchers, usually publishing wildlife research results in technical journals. Some wildlifers serve as conservation officers (game wardens). Others are involved in dissemination of wildlife information and education. Most wildlifers are civil servants, but many work as consultants for nongovernmental organizations including environmental consulting firms.

"Game" was the word. In the old days it was almost synonymous with "wildlife," but it is far more exclusive than the word "wildlife." The term "game animals," i.e., game species of animals, refers to species such as deer, ducks, and grouse—animals that usually are hunted and eaten, or used as clothing. Sometimes furbearers are considered as game animals because they are sought by hunters and trappers. The term "game bird" was first used about 1866 (*Merriam-Webster's Collegiate Dictionary*). But the word "gamekeeper"[67] (keepers of the game) commonly used in England, goes back to 1671 (dictionary) to describe a person hired with the responsibility to breed and protect game animals on a private preserve.

The words "wild life" were first used for wild animals about 1879 (dictionary) to include only birds and mammals at first, usually game species, then eventually all vertebrates except fish, although the Merriam-Webster's Collegiate Dictionary includes fish in the definition. In early 1932, Leopold made a point of distinguishing the word "game" from the term "wild life" in a paper he published, entitled "Game and Wild Life Conservation,"[132] to include nongame species of vertebrates (except fish) as well as game species. In 1933, he continued using "wild life" as two words in *Game Management*.[133] The words "wild life" were later hyphenated at times; in 1934, Leopold used "wild-life" as an adjective in the "Report of the President's Committee on Wild-life Restoration."[11]

"Wildlife" was first combined into one word sometime around 1935.[174] In 1935, Leopold appears to have first used "wildlife" as one word in "Wildlife Research Rapidly Growing,"[135] although that same year he split it again in "Wild Life Research in Wisconsin."[136] Mostly, the word continues to refer to all vertebrates except fish (e.g., "fish and wildlife"), viz., mammals, birds, reptiles, and amphibians, but in recent years, insects (at least some), are included, e.g., Karner blue butterfly, monarch and other butterflies, dragonflies. Sometimes the word is used so inclusively that it is practically useless if it refers to all animals, both vertebrates and invertebrates.

When Leopold received the first appointment in the nation to a wildlife faculty position at a university in 1933, his title was "Professor of Game Management," the word "wildlife" still ignored. After the university gave him his own department in 1939, Leopold was named "Professor of Wildlife Management."[67]

Not until 1975 did the Wisconsin Department of Natural Resources change the title "game manager" officially to "wildlife manager," to include nongame and endangered species. It is the wildlife manager who comprehensively manages wildlife in the ecosystem—the ultimate goal of the wildlife profession and reason for its existence. But game species still receive priority due to the demand and financial support of the hunting public.

The word "wildlifer" in the wildlife profession is becoming more widely used, but it is less recognized publicly than the more established word "forester" in the forestry profession, and not even found in dictionaries or on computers yet (fisheries has no counterpart to "wildlifer" and "forester." A "fisher" is a unisex term for fisherman and fisherwoman; it also is a species of mustelid).

Foresters are university-educated people in the profession of forestry (sometimes called forest science or forest ecology). They are taught holistic forest management with an emphasis on wood production. The first forestry school was established in 1785 in Germany. The first forestry schools in North America were established in 1898 at Cornell University (New York State College of Forestry) and at the Biltmore Forest School near Asheville, North Carolina, and also at Yale University in 1900. Forest rangers differ from foresters. Forest rangers are technicians, often with university degrees, who patrol, protect, and manage the forest under the direction of a (university-educated) forester.

Like foresters, wildlifers are university-educated people, but in the profession of wildlife (sometimes called wildlife science, wildlife ecology, wildlife management, or wildlife conservation). In 1919, the term "wild lifer" was first used by Leopold as two words in the published paper "Wild Lifers vs. Game Farmers: a Plea for Democracy in Sport."[127] The counterpart to the forest ranger is the wildlife technician. Wildlifers continue to be called wildlife biologists or wildlife managers or conservation biologists or wildlife ecologists or wildlife researchers or wildlife consultants or professors of wildlife.

Not all biologists in wildlife positions are actual wildlifers, for they lack the proper education yet misleadingly carry the title. Hiring someone as a wildlifer without a wildlife degree would be similar to hiring someone as a forester without a forestry degree. Many so-called wildlife biologists have a master's degree in biology, not in wildlife. Such "wildlifers" are missing the important basic university courses of wildlife habitat management, wildlife population dynamics, and wildlife techniques in research and management (wherein the *Wildlife Techniques Manual*[224] is used as a textbook). A trained wildlifer would qualify for certification by The Wildlife Society as a Certified Wildlife Biologist (CWB) and could hit the ground running with a far shorter learning curve and less time spent in on-the-job training, would have stronger knowledge of wildlife research and management techniques, stronger knowledge of the wildlife technical literature, stronger approach to research projects and data analysis, and better writing skills for reports and for publishing results. A trained wildlifer will enhance the credentials and credibility of the associated wildlife program and the wildlife profession.

In addition to the wildlife agency in each of the 60 U.S. states and Canadian provinces, about 35 public agencies and private organizations offer about 100 wildlife-based positions that use a wildlife degree.[89] Not all such wildlife positions use the title "wildlife biologist," although most wildlife field positions do. Becoming a wildlife professional requires intellect, knowledge, enthusiasm, personal commitment, talent, sound technical training, and an array of special skills. Wildlife professionals include wildlife technicians, usually with a bachelor of science degree in wildlife. Historically, most wildlife technicians had farming backgrounds and were good with machinery. Becoming a wildlifer, i.e., a wildlife professional—those with an advanced college degree in wildlife management—involves studying, conserving, protecting, and managing wildlife populations and the land and water environments on which they (and we) depend. This in turn involves learning about the biology and ecology of wildlife, how to manage wildlife populations and their habitats including restoration and disease resolution, how to resolve conflicts between humans and wildlife, and how to understand, conserve, protect, and enhance the biological diversity of ecosystems.

During the 1930s, Aldo Leopold provided qualifications and scientific training to students planning to pursue the new profession of wildlife management he was promoting.[138] The 1940s began to shape the game management profession with the creation of a field management system of game managers. But few such "wildlife managers" existed then because university-trained people were just being produced and often entered World War II before entering the new wildlife profession. The end of the war in 1945 was essentially the beginning of this new, identifiable profession, as wildlife-trained veterans and newly emerging wildlife graduates became available. During the 1950s, the young wildlife profession became involved with an increasing volume of wildlife activities, even as it struggled for identity and acceptance.[67] Both would be slow in coming.

At first, training in wildlife biology at a university produced a game biologist, not a wildlife biologist. The emphasis then was on game species of wildlife, not nongame species. That would slowly change. Today no "game biologist" exists; all are comprehensive "wildlife biologists," for the profession includes game and non-game species now. Sometimes the term "nongame biologist" is used, but seldom, if ever, "game biologist," although "big game biologist," "small game biologist," "waterfowl biologist," and "fur-bearer biologist" (fur biologist) are used. The term "conservation biologist" is sometimes used, which means someone concerned with the biodiversity and interdependence of plants and animals, especially the conservation of nongame and endangered animals and plants. The term is, perhaps, more descriptive than "wildlife biologist," but these days a wildlife biologist is similarly concerned about the conservation and biodiversity of plants and animals, even if working on a single species of wildlife.

Wildlife work can be dangerous. From 1937 to 2000, 91 deaths occurred to wildlife workers in the United States alone, mostly from aviation accidents, drowning, vehicle accidents, and murder.[214z] Two-thirds of the deaths were from aviation accidents, mostly from aerodynamic stalls and power line collisions due to low-level flying for censusing and other low-level work, which defines most aerial wildlife work. Float planes (Cessnas and super cubs, helicopters too but usually too expensive) are used in remote areas because ponds and lakes serve as landing sites and runways. In 2000, one of my former undergraduate students, wildlife biologist Mike Gratson, 48, died in a helicopter crash during a survey of mountain lions in Idaho.[186x]

Two general forms of wildlife management exist: population management and habitat management. Population management generally applies only to game species, e.g., setting hunting season length and quota. It can be done over a broad scale, i.e., over large areas, like an entire state. But population management can be a form of habitat management if, say, the deer population is reduced to prevent habitat destruction of over-browsing in winter that reduces the carrying capacity of the habitat to support more deer—which would also reduce the carrying capacity to support more ground- and shrub-associated birds and other wildlife. Unlike wildlife population management, wildlife habitat management is time-consuming and expensive. It is done to relatively specific, small areas over time, often with the use of fire or heavy equipment, and often in collaboration with other resource management such as forest management (tree cutting) and range management (cattle grazing). Generally, focusing on the management of a single species of wildlife, deer, for example, usually means managing against certain other species of wildlife, canopy-associated songbirds, for example. In a general oversimplification, various species of wildlife are associated with three layers of vegetation—ground layer, shrub layer, and canopy—as edge or interior species of wildlife.[197, 203] (Only a ground layer exists in grasslands, for example.) Usually, managing habitat for one species of wildlife improves habitat for other species of wildlife too, but never all of them.

THE NATIONAL WILDLIFE FEDERATION AND THE WILDLIFE SOCIETY

Started in 1911 by sportsmen/businessmen, The Wildlife Management Institute initially called their organization the Sporting Arms and Ammunition Manufacturers Institute. Since 1936 it has sponsored the huge, comprehensive annual conference called the North American Wildlife Conference, changing the name in 1960 to the North American Wildlife and Natural Resources Conference. Conference transactions are published annually. Both the National Wildlife Federation and The Wildlife Society began during this first conference.

With 51 state and territorial affiliates and ten regional offices across the U.S., The National Wildlife Federation is the largest private, nonprofit conservation education and advocacy organization in the United States,[174] with over six million members. It began in 1936, with Ding Darling its first president. Its mission is to increase America's fish and wildlife populations by protecting and restoring wildlife habitats, advancing wildlife management, fighting for issues such as climate change and wildlife diseases, inspiring the next generation of conservationists, and supporting legislation that advocates saving wildlife. It produces the iconic magazines *Ranger Rick* for children and *National Wildlife* for adults. The Wisconsin Wildlife Federation is an affiliate.

The foremost professional wildlife organization in the world, The Wildlife Society (TWS) is a nonprofit society dedicated to excellence in wildlife stewardship through science and education, objectives achieved best with the guidance of well-educated and experienced wildlifers. At the first North American Wildlife Conference in 1936, the professional wildlife researchers present formed a tentative "Society of Wildlife Specialists," with Aldo Leopold and Herb Stoddard as counselors to its first president, Ralph T. King. In 1937, it became "The Wildlife Society," with the first issue in 1937 of a new journal, the widely respected wildlife science technical publication, *Journal of Wildlife Management*.[190] In addition, The Wildlife Society now also publishes *Wildlife Monographs, Wildlife Society Bulletin, Wildlife Professional*, and various wildlife books.

The Wildlife Society has over 10,000 members in 70 countries. Beginning in 1994, The Wildlife Society's annual conference has been one of the largest gatherings of wildlife professionals and supporters in North America. With its international headquarters in Bethesda, Maryland, The Wildlife Society has eight regional sections and 58 chapters in North America. Student chapters of The Wildlife Society exist at 147 universities (Utah State University the first, in March 1962), with three student chapters in Wisconsin: University of Wisconsin–Stevens Point (1971),

University of Wisconsin–Madison (1997), and Northland College (2014) in Ashland. The Wildlife Society annually presents to an individual the highest award in the wildlife profession: the Aldo Leopold Memorial Award. As the foremost wildlife society in the world, The Wildlife Society assumes responsibility for designating the wildlife profession's certification program, i.e., Certified Wildlife Biologist (CWB) and Associate Wildlife Biologist (AWB).

CERTIFIED WILDLIFE BIOLOGIST (CWB)

A professional wildlife biologist is a person with expertise in the art and science of wildlife ecology. To promote and strengthen professional standards devoted to wildlife resources, and to lend recognition and status to the professionally trained wildlifer, The Wildlife Society has developed a professional certification program designed to evaluate a wildlife biologist's credentials in education and professional experience. Education includes coursework in the biological, physical, and quantitative sciences; humanities and social sciences; communications; and policy, administration, and law.

The certification program, administered only by The Wildlife Society (TWS), began in 1977. In 2008, the Trademark Office's Principal Register officially approved The Wildlife Society's titles of Associate Wildlife Biologist (AWB) and Certified Wildlife Biologist (CWB) for trademark registration, as described in The Wildlife Society's Wildlife Biologist Certification Program *Policies & Procedures Manual* (updated 2021). The TWS Certification Review Board, which reviews qualifications of education and experience, will designate an applicant a Certified Wildlife Biologist (CWB) or an Associate Wildlife Biologist (AWB). The CWB is awarded when the applicant satisfies all educational requirements, usually built into the university's degree requirements for a wildlife degree, and has at least five years of experience. The AWB is awarded to individuals who satisfy university course requirements but lack experience. CWBs and AWBs are expected to adhere to TWS's Code of Ethics. This designation is especially helpful to those wildlife biologists working for consulting firms or providing expert testimony in court cases.

PROFESSIONAL WILDLIFE MANAGEMENT

The wildlife profession has played a lead role in developing approaches integral to all scientific disciplines, contributing substantially to the evolution of methods that assist in decision making.[189x] The impact of Wisconsin on the wildlife profession throughout the world is immense because Wisconsin is where it all started in 1933. Because of the presence of the famed wildlifer Aldo Leopold, Wisconsin has the distinction of being the location for the origin of the profession of wildlife management, with its knowledge and manipulation of our life-sustaining ecosystems, a profoundly comprehensive and complex life-sustaining profession. The profession produces the most comprehensive and unique ecologists in the world because a wildlifer has to relate the sciences of soils, water, plants, landscape, and climate to wildlife. Leopold founded the profession of wildlife management and wrote the first important book on the subject (see Chapter 1).

Formally articulated in 2001, the North American Model of Wildlife Conservation, the most successful such model in the world, is a set of principles that has guided wildlife management and conservation decisions in the United States and Canada so that wildlife populations will be sustained forever.[159x] It has been responsible for the recovery of most of North America's game species in the past 100 years. The model contains seven tenets: 1) Wildlife is a public resource, owned publicly, not privately; 2) Market (commercial) hunting is prohibited; 3) Wildlife is allocated equitably to the public by law; 4) Wildlife should be killed for only a legitimate purpose, viz., food, fur, self-defense, and property protection; 5) Wildlife is an international resource that crosses international borders; 6) Wildlife policy is based on science; 7) Hunting is a democratic pursuit available to all citizens, supporting access to firearms and the hunting industry from which much funding for conservation accrues.

In a sense, North America was ripe for this new profession. The American Ornithological Union (AOU) had begun in 1883,

John Muir's Sierra Club in 1892, the National Audubon Society in 1898, the U.S. Forest Service in 1898, the Canadian Forest Service in 1911, the Wildlife Management Institute in 1911, and the National Park Service in 1911 in Canada and 1916 in the United States. Game departments were extant in the states and provinces, but without university-trained wildlife biologists. They existed only to set seasons and harvest methods, and to enforce game laws. No research and management programs existed.

Now, many universities in North America and other parts of the world offer degrees in wildlife ecology to train professional wildlife biologists for employment with various wildlife government agencies, nongovernmental organizations, and consulting firms. Every state and province in the United States and Canada has a government wildlife agency with trained wildlife biologists. Wildlife biologists also work for federal departments, e.g., the U.S. Fish and Wildlife Service, the U.S. Forest Service, the U.S. Bureau of Land Management, the U.S. Natural Resources Conservation Service (formerly Soil Conservation Service), the U.S. National Park Service, the U.S. Army Corps of Engineers, the Canadian Wildlife Service, the Canadian Forest Service, and the Canadian Park Service. Numerous environmental consulting firms and nongovernmental environmental organizations employ wildifers,[24] e.g., National Wildlife Federation, Wilderness Society, Sierra Club, National Defense Council, Environmental Defense Fund, and the Nature Conservancy.

Professional exchange of research and management ideas began in 1936, with the Wildlife Management Institute and its annual North American Wildlife Conference. The Wildlife Society has done a nice job of briefly describing online the history of the wildlife profession.

Trained wildlifers seeking public or private employment in the wildlife profession will find the names of all federal, state, and private organizations affiliated with wildlife work listed in the comprehensive *Conservation Directory: The Guide to Worldwide Environmental Organizations*. First produced in 1962, and now some 600 pages long, it has information on more than 4,000 government agencies, political committees, nongovernmental organizations, environmental consulting firms, and universities directly and indirectly involved with wildlife. That is a publication that would impress society with how advanced and extensive wildlifers and the wildlife profession have become.

Most people know that the wildlife resource was paramount in the survival of our early hunter-gatherer ancestors throughout the world; absolutely nothing was more important.[235] With subsistence farming in North America and elsewhere, wildlife played a lesser role as food and clothing, but was still important. As the 1900s began, wildlife became mostly unnecessary for food and clothing, although its recreational value was recognized, but not its ecological and economic values until the 1900s advanced. Some wildlife species became extinct (e.g., great auk, Carolina parakeet, passenger pigeon) and others vastly reduced in numbers or extirpated (e.g., bison, deer, elk, wild turkey, wolf, cougar, wood duck, egrets).

Eventually, towards the latter half of the 20th century, some of society began to recognize the importance of wildlife recreationally, economically, and ecologically, and began to identify as critical the maintenance of wildlife populations as part of the vital biodiversity of an ecosystem. But efforts and laws were based mostly on guesswork. Scientific-based management of wildlife was just beginning in the 1930s. Field science of the new profession of wildlife management did not exist before then.[29]

It's arguably the most important profession in the world, for a balanced and healthy ecosystem supports all human endeavor. A healthy ecosystem is the foundation of a healthy society.

It's a noble and inspiring profession for its contribution to the health and well-being of society, the animal community, the ecosystem, and the accompanying satisfaction in doing something worthwhile and useful.

It's a depressing profession, or can be, because it is mostly an uphill battle with human encroachment and "development," pollution, and environmental ignorance. Wildlifers have been playing much more defense than offense.

It's an interesting, exciting, adventurous, and fascinating profession.

It's a fun profession, for observing, investigating, managing, and writing about wildlife and their habitats and teaching others about wildlife.

It's a challenging, difficult profession; much wildlife exists in difficult locations, in difficult weather, at awkward times such as nocturnally (although most wildlife is crepuscular), and various-sized animals often must be located, handled, and data collected and analyzed, often without public support due to environmental ignorance.

It can be a dangerous profession. Animals can bite, kick, scratch, gore, and carry diseases and parasites. Not only animals, but their sometimes challenging habitats can make things dangerous. The weather, the use of low-flying helicopters, super cubs, and Cessnas,[186x] the use of vehicles and small boats, and the use of immobilizing drugs also can make events dangerous.

It's a demanding profession, often requiring weeks in the field away from home, and disciplined field work in all weather and any hour.

It's an intellectual profession due to the biodiversity of complicated ecosystems, sampling design, data analysis, literature search, report writing, and human dimensions, among others.

It's a technical profession with its use of, for example, laboratory, radio telemetry and GPS, satellites, infrared, trail cameras, body cameras, cell phones. computers, trucks, snowmobiles, ATVs, boats, drones, helicopters and fixed-wing airplanes.

It's a broad, complicated profession, one of the most complex in the world. Everything depends on everything else. In order to relate everything, a wildlifer must be familiar with plants, water, soils, geology, geography, and wildlife—all sorts of wildlife—for these things are interdependent in the complex biodiversity of ecosystems. Everything affects everything else. Mess with one thing, and something else is affected. Add to that the variables of weather and people; human encroachment on wildlife habitat is the biggest problem, and now climate change is further complicating things.

It's a rewarding profession emotionally, for the subject matter is fascinating, as revealed by the interest in national parks, wildlife watching, wildlife programs on television, and other wildlife activities including hunting. Society confers emotional values to certain species, especially glamour species like large mammals, or species (e.g., wolves) that prey upon species (e.g., deer) that humans prefer to hunt. The work is interesting, attractive (mostly), and stimulating, with public appeal. But some of society frowns on hunting and fishing and those associated with it.

It is a rewarding profession intellectually because of its complexity, including research and publication.

It's an unrewarding profession monetarily, for most positions are low-paying civil servant (government) positions incommensurate with the responsibility and contribution to society (similar to teaching in this regard), and the essential role of managing society's vital life-sustaining ecosystems.

It's an often-disrespected profession in that an uninformed public is quite willing to tell the informed, trained, and experienced wildlife professional of this complicated profession what to do. Few other new professions have struggled so for acceptance. Most other new professions occur in fields of endeavor in which the public is mostly unfamiliar; experts are more readily accepted. But professional wildlifers deal with a public that tends to think it is "familiar" with the subject because of occasional walks in the woods, hunting or otherwise, including professional hunting guides and hunting outfitters. The wildlife profession deals with the landscape over which people have roamed for ages. Therefore, most folks presume to know a lot more about it than they do. But most folks have no knowledge of biology and thus do no scientific work to support their often misinterpreted observations, leading to erroneous and stubborn conclusions. Misinformed politicians often side with them. The required master's degree in wildlife science and the wildlife biologist's contribution in wildlife management for public benefit were recognized, but not respected; wildlifers were forced to enter low-salaried government positions that much of the public considered frivolous or useless, as revealed by the low pay.

Even today, the attitude persists among many that hunters and trappers know more than the trained wildlife biologists, who so often are disrespected, challenged, and belittled in their research results and recommendations if their recommendations conflict with the public. Underpaid, they are often considered incompetent and untrustworthy, and are often humiliated at public meetings. Hunters and trappers know something about the landscape with which they are familiar. But, unlike most other new professions, limited unscientific knowledge tends to be misinterpreted, and interferes with acceptance of more accurate scientific knowledge, as regional hunter and trapper meetings and naïve letters to the editor readily reveal. As deceased famed comedian Rodney Dangerfield used to say, "I don't get no respect," a wildlifer could say the same thing (see Biopolitics, in Chapter 4). Hunter and trapper education and environmental education of society are the answers for more acceptance by lay people of the scientific community's greater knowledge of wildlife and its ability to manage it.

It's an unending profession. Unlike most other professions, you can never leave it behind after retirement. You are surrounded by the ecosystem about which you know so much and have spent your career studying. You are hunting and fishing in it or bird watching or just observing it. You continue to be surrounded by it all your life and are constantly reminded of it, at times for action, often for pleasure, but often annoyingly and sadly. In *A Sand County Almanac*,[142] Leopold wrote (p. 183), "One of the penalties of an ecological education is that one lives in a world of wounds. Much of the damage inflicted on land is quite invisible to laymen." Because of the knowledge a wildlifer has of the surrounding natural environment, a wildlifer never really retires; for better or worse, you can't walk away from it.

It is the political arena that is now most in need of wildlifers. Other professions are represented there, but almost no wildlifers. That isn't their bent. In today's atmosphere, that's unfortunate; that's where the greatest need is. Politicians with wildlife backgrounds are sorely needed at the county, state/provincial, and federal levels. These days, a wildlifer could accomplish more in the political field than in the outdoor field, especially in view of the concern about global climate change—a tough thing to coordinate worldwide.

Initially, our natural resources were decimated in the quest for Manifest Destiny, as the human population increased and moved westward in the United States and Canada, decimating habitats and wildlife in the process while overwhelming indigenous people. Ultimately the complexities of wildlife management emerged with the new profession. Nonetheless, during hard times particularly, many in society have viewed, and continue to view, conservation of natural resources, especially wildlife, as a luxury, despite all evidence to the contrary including the tremendous value of ecotourism—the number 1 or 2 industry in many countries—and strangely, the mostly unrecognized fact that a healthy society is based on a healthy ecosystem.

3.

WILDLIFE EDUCATION

BECOMING A WILDLIFER

Richard D. Taber wrote, "This pattern of exploiting wildlife populations persisted into the early 1900s and later but has gradually been modified and contained by governmental restraint, husbandry, and restoration, technical goals requiring a new professional—the wildlife biologist."[200]

As early as 1940, Aldo Leopold said that it takes five or six years of college, including a master's degree, to become the type of wildlifer known as a wildlife biologist who works mostly in the field, usually for a resource agency. That is as true today as it was then: a four-year bachelor's degree in biology or wildlife science and a two- to three-year master's degree in wildlife science to include one year of coursework and one to two years of research and thesis. For the type of wildlifer known as a university professor of wildlife science or a high-level wildlife researcher usually with a federal agency, a PhD degree in wildlife science is required. For a PhD, an MS in wildlife science is required plus another year of coursework and three to five years of research and dissertation. (The final research report for an MS is a thesis; for the more comprehensive PhD, it is a dissertation). The 12 chapters in the book *Becoming a Wildlife Professional*[89] provided details.

BS, MS, and PhD degrees in wildlife on the diploma can be written as *wildlife, wildlife management, wildlife biology, wildlife ecology, wildlife science, wildlife conservation, wildlife ecology and management, forestry and wildlife, natural resources*; all mean essentially the same thing.

Bob McCabe wrote (p. 154) that a program in wildlife is viable when "1. The institution gives the new discipline (Wildlife Management) an official status by name; 2. Professors teaching, doing or guiding research are recognized by title that their expertise is indeed in wildlife management; 3. Diplomas for advanced degrees indicate that the education was in the field of wildlife management."[167]

A student with a bachelor's degree in wildlife or biology searching for an MS program in wildlife or a student with an MS in wildlife searching for a PhD program in wildlife must identify: 1) a university with a wildlife program (listed with The Wildlife Society) and 2) a wildlife professor there who has funding for a research project and is looking for and has funding for a graduate student to get paid while taking coursework and then while conducting the research, analyzing the data, and writing the report (MS thesis or PhD dissertation). Such a stipend is called a fellowship. Sometimes the stipend is an assistantship for which the graduate student performs work such as teaching labs to undergraduate students. The professor becomes the major professor (advisor) of the student selected, and usually has just 3 to 5 graduate students. The selected student is then a graduate student and will move to that campus and find a place to stay. The graduate stipend is enough to pay for room and board with some extra (gas money) so the graduate student does not have to go into debt. Graduate student positions are competitive.

The graduate student will select a graduate committee of at least three (for an MS) or five (for a PhD) faculty, with the student's major professor as chair. The graduate committee will approve the student's selection of coursework, the research proposal, and the thesis or dissertation defended orally. The student will take the coursework and then conduct the research study, analyze the data, and draft the thesis or dissertation. Distant research sites require grad students to move there from the campus after the coursework is completed. Usually, the thesis or dissertation yields at least one publication, usually co-authored by student and major professor, and accepted by a peer-reviewed technical journal like the *Journal of Wildlife Management*. For the MS candidate, that first publication (often the only publication of a practicing wildlife biologist) often is a sort of rite of passage into the wildlife profession, although not all MS theses yield a publication, unlike a PhD dissertation.

Of the 13 university campuses in the University of Wisconsin System, only Madison and Stevens Point offer a BS or BA undergraduate degree and an MS graduate degree in wildlife; only Madison offers a PhD in wildlife (see Appendix 2).

Undergraduate and graduate instruction in wildlife ecology at universities is taught by professors of wildlife ecology, with PhDs. Most of the world's research in wildlife ecology is conducted at universities, by professors of wildlife ecology, with PhDs, often in collaboration with state or federal wildlife agencies. Most folks with a PhD in wildlife work at universities as teachers/researchers. Most others work as researchers for federal natural resource agencies, and some as researchers for the state or provincial wildlife agency.

Undergraduate students in the wildlife major should take a minor in political science or economics to prepare themselves for the economic and political challenges they will face—and to prepare some of them for entering politics where they are so sorely needed. This aspect of the wildlife profession is the weakest. Wildlifers are poorly represented in the political arena. Politics so often trumps biology, despite the best science (see Biopolitics, Chapter 4).

COOPERATIVE WILDLIFE RESEARCH UNIT

The mission of the Cooperative Wildlife Research Unit, the Cooperative Fishery Research Unit, and the Cooperative Fish and Wildlife Research Unit is to provide graduate education and research in fish and wildlife, technical assistance in fish and wildlife matters to federal, state, and private conservation agencies, and education in fish and wildlife matters through publication and consultation. In 1932, Paul Errington (see Chapter 1) completed his PhD in zoology at the University of Wisconsin, with studies of bobwhite quail and agreed to start a wildlife research station at Iowa State University. Jay N. "Ding" Darling (see Chapter 1), director of the U.S. Biological Survey in 1934, conceived and initiated the idea and provided his personal financial support for what would become a model for the nation's Cooperative Wildlife Research Unit three years later.

The Iowa Cooperative Wildlife Research Unit, then, was the prototype wildlife unit. In 1935, Darling met with a group of industrialists at the Waldorf-Astoria Hotel in New York, persuading them to support a national program of Cooperative Wildlife Research Unit modeled after the one at Iowa State. Darling persuaded the American Wildlife Institute (now the Wildlife Management Institute) to contribute funding for wildlife units at nine university campuses he had lined up: Alabama, Connecticut, Iowa, Maine, Ohio, Oregon, Texas, Utah, and Virginia. (My MS came through the Virginia Cooperative Wildlife Research Unit at Virginia Tech in Blacksburg, from Unit Leader Burd S. McGinnes, and my PhD through the Utah Cooperative Wildlife Research Unit at Utah State University in Logan, from Assistant Unit Leader J. Juan Spillett.)

Only a few university wildlife programs have wildlife units. Currently, 40 units exist in 38 states. These units added two more faculty members to the faculty: unit leader and assistant unit leader, although they are federal employees with federal salaries. They have no teaching requirement but are members of the wildlife faculty. In 1973 the fish units were combined with the wildlife units into the Cooperative Fish and Wildlife Research Unit. But only in Wisconsin and Montana are the 2 units on separate campuses. Also, California, Hawaii, and Tennessee have fish units only. (In Wisconsin, the wildlife unit for MS and PhD students is within the wildlife program at UW–Madison and the fish unit for MS students is within the fisheries program at UW–Stevens Point.)

In 1993, the unit program was moved from the U.S. Fish and Wildlife Service to the U.S. Geological Survey. Today the partnership of the Cooperative Fish and Wildlife Research Unit consists of the U.S. Geological Survey (staffing), the state fish and wildlife agency (funding), the Wildlife Management Institute (funding), and the host university (office space and secretarial support). Many wildlifers in the United States and Canada have been educated through a Cooperative Wildlife Research Unit or Cooperative Fish and Wildlife Research Unit.

WILDLIFE MANAGEMENT BOOKS FROM WISCONSIN

Few wildlifers have written wildlife books or more than one book about wildlife management. Several books specific to general wildlife management have been written by Wisconsin authors. Only one Wisconsin wildlife book deals with the principles of wildlife management. In the preface of his landmark book *Game Management*,[133] Aldo Leopold wrote then what still applies today, decades later: "Every countryside proclaims the fact that we have, today, less control in the field of conservation than in any other contact with surrounding nature. ...We stand guard over works of art, but species representing the work of eons are stolen from under our noses" (p. vii). The preface stated (p. ix) that the book is 1) a text for students and practicing wildlife managers, 2) an interpretation of the significance of some of the things the thinking sportsman or nature-lover "sees while afield with gun or glass, or does in his capacity as a voting conservationist," and 3) an explanation "to the naturalist, biologist, agricultural expert, and forester how his own science relates to game management."

Supported by 500 references, the far-sighted 481-page book is divided into three parts: management theory with five chapters, management technique with ten chapters (only one involving habitat manipulation), and game administration with three chapters. (In 1960, I took the course "Wildlife Ecology" from Leopold's former graduate student and eventual faculty colleague Joe Hickey who was using a more current text by Purdue University's Durward Allen.[2] In 1961, I took a course at Virginia

Tech in wildlife management taught by Henry Mosby who used Reuben Trippensee's two books.[251, 252])

In 1949, Leopold defined the land ethic by the relationship humans should have with land, including wildlife and the general biota: "A thing is right when it tends to preserve the integrity, stability, and beauty of the biotic community. It is wrong when it tends otherwise"[142] (p. 240). Humans continue to violate that philosophy extensively all the way into the 21st century!

Six general wildlife management books have been written by Wisconsin authors: 1) *Game Management* by Leopold[133] in 1933, 2) *The Way to Game Abundance* by Grange[71] in 1949, 3) *Wildlife and Fisheries Habitat Improvement Handbook* by Payne and Copes[204] in 1986 (reprinted in 1988 and 1990), 4) *Techniques for Wildlife Habitat Management of Wetlands* by Payne[197] in 1992, 5) *Techniques for Wildlife Habitat Management of Uplands* by Payne and Bryant[203] in 1994, and 6) *More Wildlife on Your Land: A Guide for Private Landowners* by Payne[198] in 2002. Supported by 340 figures and 2,200 references, the two-book set by Payne and Payne and Bryant are how-to books of descriptive narrative to enhance biodiversity for edge and interior species of wildlife by improving habitat in wetlands, forestlands, rangelands, and farmlands, not only for Wisconsin but for all the United States and Canada. The two techniques books were reprinted in 1998 with a slight name change: 1) *Wildlife Habitat Management of Wetlands* and 2) *Wildlife Habitat Management of Forestlands, Rangelands, and Farmlands*. Jessop B. Low, Leader, Utah Cooperative Wildlife Research Unit, wrote the foreword to Payne.[197] Richard D. Taber, University of Washington Professor of Forest Zoology, wrote the foreword to Payne and Bryant.[203]

Three other general wildlife books, non-management, by Wisconsin authors described the history of wildlife management: Taber and Payne[235] in 2003, Payne[200] in 2011, and Gjestson[67] in 2013. Taber and Payne[235] traced the changes in treatment of wildlife populations and habitats, and the evolving patterns of human response to wildlife endangerment in industrial societies, from the European and North American Stone Age to contemporary times. Payne[200] described the history of wildlife management in the Canadian province of Newfoundland and Labrador, with its title *Wildlife Delights and Dilemmas*, taken from the second sentence of Leopold's *A Sand County Almanac*.[142]

In *The Gamekeepers: Wisconsin Wildlife Conservation from WCD to CWD*,[67] the cleverly altered initials refer to the early-named Wisconsin Conservation Department (WCD) and the problematic deadly deer disease: chronic wasting disease (CWD). In it, former WDNR wildlife biologist David Gjestson comprehensively and brilliantly described the wildlife history, development, and practice of the Wisconsin Department of Natural Resources, with details, names, and historical photographs.

Wisconsin authors of wildlife books and wildlife-related books are identified in References.

GUY BALDASSARRE

Ducks, Geese, and Swans of North America—all wildlifers know this classic. It began as a book[115] by Francis H. Kortright of Ontario. Aldo Leopold wrote the introduction.[139] The book was first published in 1942, and the second edition[13] was published in 1976 by Frank C. Bellrose of Illinois.

Guy Baldassarre was a 23-year-old MS candidate of Dr. Lyle Nauman at the University of Wisconsin–Stevens Point. I served on his graduate committee and signed his MS thesis in 1978: *Ecological Factors Affecting Waterfowl Production on Three Man-Made Flowages in Central Wisconsin*.[8] Guy's study area was on the Wisconsin Wildlife Bureau's Sandhill Wildlife Area and Meadow Valley Wildlife Area. From Boston, with a BS from the University of Maine, Guy showed up at UWSP in 1976, the year after I did. He was so good that we then hired him to help teach the introductory wildlife labs in 1977–1978. In 1976 and 1977, he taught my two sons, Adam (age 9–10) and Mark (age 6–7), to trap muskrats in the nearby marsh on the Wisconsin River. After running the trapline, the boys were amused to pick leaves and twigs from Guy's afro when he sat for coffee with us. He gave them his 75 traps when he left to pursue a PhD at Texas Tech University.

After serving as editor of the *Journal of Wildlife Management* and co-authoring, with Eric Bolen, *Waterfowl Ecology and Management* [10] in 1994 (revised in 2006) and numerous technical articles, Guy returned to UWSP from his faculty position at the State University of New York to receive the UWSP College of Natural Resources Alumni Award in 1996. Before the ceremony, as he and I sat in the CNR faculty lounge, Adam (age 29 and 6-foot-1) and Mark (age 26 and 6-foot-7) suddenly strolled in with big grins on their admiring, delighted, excited faces. Immediately, Guy returned the grin, arose and said, "I don't recognize these two big guys, but they've got to be Adam and Mark!" Later, Guy told me that the highlights of his trip were receiving the Alumni Award and greeting my two sons.

With his Boston accent, booming voice, enthusiasm, and sense of humor mixed with knowledge, he was an unforgettable character. Dr. Guy A. Baldassarre (1953–2012), wildlifer, died at age 59 from leukemia, leaving his beloved family: wife Eileen (Quinlan) and sons Dan and Adam. Guy Baldassarre was the only wildlifer to produce two comprehensive treatises about waterfowl and their habitats. He had just completed the magnificent, brilliant manuscript, published in 2014—the 1027-page, 2-volume, third-edition classic, *Ducks, Geese, and Swans of North America.*[9]

OTHER WISCONSIN PUBLICATION SOURCES

Many wildlife research results in Wisconsin have been published in two major publications that began in Wisconsin. In 1870, the Wisconsin Legislature enacted the Charter of the Wisconsin Academy of Sciences, Arts & Letters. Its annual publication began then: *Transactions of the Wisconsin Academy of Sciences, Arts & Letters.*

In 1939, the Wisconsin Society for Ornithology introduced its journal *The Passenger Pigeon.* In 1965, the first meeting of the Raptor Research Foundation occurred in Madison, Wisconsin. Their quarterly publication, *Journal of Raptor Research,* first appeared in 1967, then named simply, *Raptor Research.* Established in 1990, in honor of two Wisconsin raptor researchers, the Raptor Research Foundation annually presents the Fran and

Frederick Hamerstrom Award to an individual recognized for significant contributions to the understanding of raptor ecology and natural history (see Frances and Frederick Hamerstrom, Chapter 1).

Since 1976, the Wisconsin Department of Natural Resources has published its magazine, *Wisconsin Natural Resources*, monthly, until quarterly in 2018. The biweekly *Wisconsin Outdoor News*, edited by Dean Bortz, began in 1968; to subscribers it presents informative government, other professional, and layman news, and opinions about Wisconsin fish and wildlife, game species mostly.

WILDLIFE TECHNIQUES MANUAL

In 1961, I entered Virginia Polytechnic Institute and State University, where I was a charter member in January 1963 of the Virginia Tech Student Chapter of The Wildlife Society, its faculty advisor famed wildlifer Henry S. Mosby (1913–1984), grandson of John Mosby of the Civil War's Mosby's Raiders. Co-author of one of the earliest wildlife books (1943),[184] he was the editor of the first (1960)[182] and the second (1963)[183] editions of the iconic *Wildlife Techniques Manual*. I began my MS degree with Dr. Mosby as my teacher. Dr. Burd McGinnes, Unit Leader, Virginia Cooperative Wildlife Research Unit, was my advisor. Burd and Henry were two of the three most influential professionals in my life. I dedicated my first book (1992) "to Burd S. McGinnes, my mentor, and the memory of Henry S. Mosby, my teacher."[197]

In 1939, Associate Professor of Forest Zoology Howard M. Wight at the University of Michigan wrote a 107-page 10-chapter manual named *Field and Laboratory Technic in Wildlife Management*.[261] Ten years after Leopold died, the prototype of The Wildlife Society's august *Wildlife Techniques Manual*, as it is called now, was written in 1958, titled *Manual of Wildlife Techniques*,[181] edited by Henry S. Mosby. It had a paper cover and was held together by a two-piece prong fastener. Two years later it was published for sale in 1960 at $4.50 in a green hard cover, titled *Manual of Game Investigational Techniques*,[182] edited by Henry S. Mosby.

Mosby taught a wildlife techniques course from that first (1960) edition. In 1961, my class of three MS grad students—David Patton, Joe Bachant, Neil Payne—was the second class in history to study from that techniques manual, after Mosby's previous class of three MS students in 1960: my friends Dick Thompson, Charlie Cushwa, and Bob Bellig. Although the wildlife techniques manual was published by The Wildlife Society, checks for the books then were sent to the Virginia Cooperative Wildlife Research Unit in Blacksburg. To package and send out the books, Mosby and the wildlife secretary at Virginia Tech would use the large table in the grad room, where grad students had their desks in the basement of Price Hall. Sometimes we would help.

Although a bit awestruck by our knowledgeable, accomplished, clever, friendly, esteemed teacher, the three of us—Dave, Joe, and I—played a trick on Dr. Mosby one time. Assigned the task of overdosing a cantankerous black bear at the children's zoo in Roanoke, we did so, then returned to campus with it and placed it in Doc's chair behind his desk, with a Smokey the Bear hat, Doc's pipe in its mouth, and a pencil in its paw. The next morning to our amusement, Doc stopped short upon entering his office and coolly said, "What have we here?"

As editor, Henry S. Mosby (recipient, Aldo Leopold Memorial Award, 1978; President of The Wildlife Society, 1965–66) of Virginia Tech was the chair of the Wildlife Techniques Committee for The Wildlife Society, the committee consisting of the seven authors of the new manual. Mosby's unbound prototype copy[181] of 1958 had 17 chapters, paginated independently with literature cited at the end of each chapter, and seven authors: Ian McTaggert-Cowan, David E. Davis, Antoon de Vos, Alexander C. Martin, Henry S. Mosby, Horace F. Quick, and Richard D. Taber (my future boss and book co-author)—the same seven authors and 17 chapters in the first edition in 1960,[182] also with each chapter paginated independently, totaling 368 pages in the book. In 1961, when I was a young, naïve, 22-year-old MS graduate student at Virginia Tech studying Dr. Richard D. Taber's three chapters in the first edition of the wildlife techniques manual, *Manual of Game Investigational Techniques*,[182] I would have been astounded to know then that 40 years later I would co-author a book[235] with this famous wildlifer, a former graduate student of Aldo Leopold!

One of the chapters described developing a personal reprint file of hard-to-get booklets, brochures, reports, etc., about wildlife from state, provincial, and federal agencies. In 1961, the three of us MS candidates divided those agencies among us and sent for three copies to be distributed among us when they arrived. Adding to it my entire career, I thus built a valuable, useful, large, reference reprint file, many of the contents out of print, donating it upon my retirement to the University of Wisconsin–Stevens Point library.

With errors in the hastily published first (green cover) edition, Mosby published the second (red cover) edition only three years later,[183] while I was a grad student at Virginia Tech. (I reviewed the Literature Cited section). Consecutively paginated with 419 pages, it had 16 chapters and three additional authors: Aelred D. Geis, Robert H. Giles, Jr., and Leroy J. Korschgen. In my copy, the inscription reads, "1/29/64 To Neil Payne—May all of your experiences fit neatly into tables and graphs—Henry S. Mosby." (Augmenting the vitally important habitat chapter in the *Wildlife Techniques Manual*, my two comprehensive habitat techniques books published by McGraw-Hill in 1992, *Techniques for Wildlife Habitat Management of Wetlands*,[194] and in 1994, *Techniques for Wildlife Habitat Management of Uplands*,[203] with Fred Bryant, Texas A&M University, met with little apparent notice except from the Texas Chapter of The Wildlife Society.) Over the years, the *Wildlife Techniques Manual* has had 6 title changes. Although the number of how-to techniques figures has been severely reduced, after some 60 years, and now in its eighth edition of two volumes (one on research, one on management), this magnificent work contains 50 chapters and 141 authors[224] (five from Wisconsin) and continues to be used by all wildlife students and professionals.

Wildlife Management

4.

THE DEPARTMENT OF NATURAL RESOURCES AND SUPPORT

WCD TO WDNR

With the origin and development of the wildlife profession in Wisconsin through education and research, the Wisconsin wildlife agency in its Department of Natural Resources has always been one of the best and a standard-setter in wildlife management. By far most of the wildlifers educated at the University of Wisconsin-Madison, the University of Wisconsin-Stevens Point, and elsewhere in the United States and Canada serve with the ten provincial and 50 state wildlife agencies responsible for delivering the wildlife programs to society, augmented by the federal wildlife agencies, mainly the Canadian Wildlife Service and the U.S. Fish and Wildlife Service.

Wildlife exploitation in North America has progressed through three phases since Europeans first arrived on the eastern seaboard five centuries ago: 1) consumptive, 2) recreational, and 3) non-consumptive.[180]

The earliest European immigrants, completely unrestrained, looked upon wilderness as an adversary to be conquered. The first phase of exploitation of New World wildlife was for consumptive use: subsistence, the market, and pest control. Wildlife continued to decline over the centuries with use of progressively more sophisticated, and destructive, weapons. The intoxicating profusion of natural resources of North America enticed people to think in terms of resource infinity, encouraging market hunting. But it was fiction rather than fact, and has been referred to as the Myth of Superabundance.[235] It took some 300 years to figure that out; the inadequate and short-sighted nature of North American wildlife practices were dead wrong. By the late 1800s, stocks of many species were decimated and others extirpated,[185] bison a shocking example[64x, 97x, 212y] (see Bison, in Chapter 5)! Adversarial approaches to nature mellowed as wilderness was "conquered" through exploitation and habitat alteration.

As the 1900s began, market hunting continued. But the main value of wildlife exploitation was changing to "sport," the second phase of North American wildlife exploitation. This phase was characterized by legislation that first curtailed then eliminated utilitarian efforts such as market hunting and emphasized recreational values (sport hunting and fishing). Hence, "game" species received most of the conservation attention and policies. Sport hunters replaced market hunters and saved North American wildlife, particularly game species, because sport hunters generated substantial revenue through licensing that was used for wildlife protection and management. Much hunter influence is economic and political (with lobbying). But hunting is important to many folks because it provides the only legal use of weapons beyond target practice and self-defense[155] (see Appendix 4). Moreover, a potent symbol of the independent North American is portrayed by the hunter's image of self-sufficiency.[180]

Toward the latter part of the 1900s, although sport hunting continued albeit with declining interest, many conservationists became preservationists who valued wildlife for aesthetic, ethical, and ecological reasons of non-consumptive purposes: birdwatching, wildlife photography, natural history, etc. With this third phase of wildlife exploitation, biodiversity was considered by some folks as a vital part of the human ecosystem and an indicator of environmental quality. The term "game" was replaced with "wildlife" in legislature and vocabulary (although it still persists in the name of some state wildlife agencies). The voluminous writings of the earliest natural resource conservationists—Lapham[122] in 1844, von Humboldt[259] in 1845–47 and 1850–58, Darwin[43] in 1859, and Marsh[163] in 1864—clearly emphasize that wildlife conservation is a direct result of land conservation of unpolluted soil, water, and air for natural, undisturbed ecosystems and habitats.[2, 142, 180] Many private and government practices blatantly threaten the integrity of these life-sustaining natural resource components. Such practices, for example, include industrial pollution and waste; housing and other building developments and accompanying infrastructure; forestry and agriculture and their massive applications of fertilizers and toxic pesticides to maintain those artificial monocultures; filling, draining, dredging, and diking wetlands—among the most productive ecosystems in the world—and now, global warming with climate change. Habitat conservation is becoming an important societal concern as anthropogenic global climate change threatens environmental balance. Society has little knowledge of the necessity of biodiversity; environmental ignorance is rampant and particularly disturbing at this environmentally critical time in human history (see Epilogue).

Long before anyone thought about a conservation department, Increase Lapham (1811–1875) is credited with founding Wisconsin's conservation movement.[67, 122, 123] University of Wisconsin geologist Charles Van Hise wrote an early book in 1910 on the conservation of natural resources in the United States, although wildlife was not included.[257]

In 1908, Governor James Davidson appointed seven unsalaried men to Wisconsin's first Conservation Commission, chaired by Van Hise. The Commission included forests, soils, and waterpower, but not fish and wildlife. In 1915 a three-man salaried Conservation Commission was appointed, and for the first time, fish and wildlife were included.

In 1927, Senate Bill 404, the Conservation Act, was passed and the WCD was born—the Wisconsin Conservation Department, with five major divisions within it—administration, forestry, parks, wardens, and fisheries—and a budget of $245,675. The WCD was authorized to set hunting seasons and bag limits, among other regulations. The Conservation Commission would continue as a board ultimately to become the NRB, i.e., the Natural Resources Board.

In 1928, a Game Division was included in the department. The first Research Bureau was attached to the Game Division in 1929, but consisted of volunteers. Until 1930, wildlife "management" consisted of hunting regulations, (generous) quotas, predator control for preserving game species, artificial feeding, game refuges, stocking, closed seasons, and law enforcement. No habitat improvement was done. Wildlife habitat management and sophisticated wildlife population management were unknown. Nothing was based on scientific data. No research was done. Thus, with the lack of scientific facts for guiding critically important decision making, expensive time-consuming mistakes were made.

One good appointment that occurred during 1928 was Wallace Grange as the first superintendent of the newly established Game Division within the Conservation Department.[73] He was a staff of one. In 1962, he would sell to the Wisconsin Conservation Department his 9000-acre deer-proof fenced area in central Wisconsin, now known as the Sandhill Wildlife Area—the only fenced state wildlife area authorized, and thus uniquely qualified for special research projects,[116] demonstrations, and education.

In 1928, conservation-minded Walter J. Kohler was elected governor, and immediately appointed Paul Kelleter as director of the new WCD. He had been a professional forester and former forest extension director at New York College in Syracuse. In 1934, Kelleter was replaced by former chief warden Harley MacKenzie, who professionalized the warden force, initiated sports licenses for revenue to manage wildlife and fish, and established the state game farm and conservation education center named after him.

In 1930, Wallace Grange left as director of the Game Division and was replaced by William Grimmer, a graduate and later assistant commandant of St. John's Military Academy in Delafield, Wisconsin. Grimmer was such a good administrator that when he died in 1955, he was honored with the establishment of the Grimmer Award presented annually to Wisconsin's best wildlife manager and best wildlife technician of the year.

In 1937, the federal Pittman-Robertson Act was passed[171] when legislation drafted by Carl Shoemaker, a conservationist from Oregon, was promoted by sportsmen and industry to authorize a tax on the sale of sporting arms and ammunition to aid states in wildlife restoration (and in 1950, for sport fishing, when the Dingle-Johnson Act taxed sport fishing tackle). Shoemaker got U.S. Senator Key Pittman (Nevada) and Congressman A. Willis Robertson (Virginia) to sponsor it. Robertson added: "...and which shall include a prohibition against the diversion of license fees paid by hunters for any other purpose than the administration of said state fish and game department." With that, the Pittman-Robertson (P-R) Act was authorized in the United States. As they came to be called, P-R funds provided substantial financial support to state wildlife agencies—from consumptive users (e.g., hunters), but nothing from non-consumptive users (e.g., bird watchers) unless they pay park fees to enter for non-consumptive activity.

Under the P-R rules, Robertson's 29 words gave state wildlife agencies exclusive use of game funds raised by license sales in order to receive P-R funds as well. The P-R Act prevents state governors and legislators from raiding these state wildlife funds for various purposes unrelated to wildlife conservation. The P-R Act also requires the states receiving this federal funding to contribute state money for wildlife on a 3-to-1 federal-state match, federal funds allocated by a simple formula: 50% based on the amount of land area of a state relative to other states and 50% based on the number of hunting license holders in a state relative to other states. Thus, the state game agencies now had two channels of assured support from basically the same group—the sportsmen. (See Consumptive vs. Non-consumptive Use of Wildlife, in Chapter 8).

The State Wildlife Grants (SWG) Program, which began in 2001, provides federal funds to state fish and wildlife agencies for developing programs that benefit game and nongame fish and wildlife and their habitats. Funds are apportioned based on a formula that considers each state's geographical area and human population. The Wildlife and Sport Fish Restoration Program of the U.S. Fish and Wildlife Service administers the SWG funds.

Compared to other state and provincial agencies, which had to go begging to the legislature every year for funds and hence were in constant competition with each other, state wildlife agencies were in the enviable position of raising and controlling their own budgets. Their loyalty to their sportsmen clientele is understandable, for the ability of administrators to conduct activities under authority of legislation depends on the level and predictability of funding. Unfortunately, as hunting becomes less popular, fees from the sale of hunting licenses and the associated P-R funds are declining, and thus the budget for wildlife, used for both game and nongame species.

Most of the terrestrial wildlife management in the United States and Canada is conducted by the wildlife agency in each of the 50 states and ten provinces. The 15 chapters in the book *State Wildlife Management and Conservation* [214] provide details of state and provincial wildlife management. The 16 chapters in the book *International Wildlife Management* [114] provide international perspective.

In 1943, the WCD's Conservation Commission (future NRB) got a boost when one of the most renowned wildlifers was appointed to it, one of the few wildlifers ever on it. Aldo Leopold would serve until his death in 1948.

Wisconsin has always been on the cutting edge of natural resource technology. Its wildlife management program has been admired and emulated by many such programs nationally and internationally. Its deer management system has been considered the best in the country.

When Wisconsinites want to refer to the government aspect of wildlife, they simply say "DNR," as though DNR (Wisconsin Department of Natural Resources) and wildlife are synonymous. They are not, of course, the DNR being much more comprehensive. In fact, what people really mean is the Wildlife Division, i.e., the Fish, Wildlife and Parks Division, and the Law Enforcement

Division—all being parts of the DNR, a complex department that includes wildlife, fisheries, forests, and parks.

The term "game" used to be synonymous with the term "wildlife," and the name "game department," still called that in some states, reflected that view. The game department focused on game species of wildlife then. Although some hangers-on wildlife departments in the U.S. still retain the word "game" in their title, for the most part the word "wildlife" prevails in the titles, and has for decades; it encompasses all wildlife, not just game species. All wildlife agencies now have a nongame wildlife program, with nongame wildlife biologists employed. Many more nongame species of wildlife exist than game species. Regardless of title, game species received priority in state conservation programs because of the nature of their funding (exclusively from hunters and trappers), the interest, expensive equipment needs, clout of hunters, and the long tradition of agency focus on game management.

In 1967, the name, Wisconsin Conservation Department, changed to Wisconsin Department of Natural Resources (the Game Division or Wildlife Bureau part of it) when the Conservation Department merged with the Department of Resource Development. It is led by the Secretary of the DNR who is appointed by the governor and confirmed by the state senate. The Natural Resources Board (NRB) was organized in 1968 with seven members, usually non-natural resource types, appointed by the governor to represent seven parts of the state; each member is approved by the state senate and serves a six-year term. In accordance with state laws, the NRB has authority over and responsibility of the DNR, sets policy, and reviews the biennial budget, i.e., the NRB directs and supervises the DNR. The Secretary of the DNR directs statewide programs for environmental protection, natural resource management, outdoor recreation, and law enforcement, i.e., the Secretary administers the DNR. The DNR implements federal and state laws that protect and enhance Wisconsin's natural resources: air, water, land, forests, parks, wildlife, fish, plants.

In 1974, the Fish and Wildlife Management Bureau was formed within the DNR; in 1976 it separated into two bureaus. In 1975, game managers were renamed wildlife managers to reflect an expanded role with nongame. In 2000, wildlife managers were called wildlife biologists.

Unlike nongame species, game species are relatively easily managed because hunting is controlled and research information can be obtained from hunters' submission of measurements of their kill, etc., to augment that obtained from wildlife managers. Thus, most threatened and endangered species are nongame species. In 1978, the Wisconsin Department of Natural Resources established an Office of Endangered and Nongame Species, which became the Bureau of Endangered Resources (BER) in 1982 and in 2013, ambiguously, the Bureau of Natural Heritage Conservation.

During the next 20 years, the DNR was reorganized three times, as though they couldn't quite get it right despite decades of existence and experience. Times were changing, and apparently things needed tweaking.

In 1993–94, the DNR was reorganized. It had four divisions: enforcement (three bureaus), environmental quality (five bureaus), management services (four bureaus including Information and Education), and resource management (seven bureaus). The Bureau of Wildlife Management was in the Division of Resource Management, along with the Bureau of Fisheries Management, the Bureau of Research, the Bureau of Natural Heritage Conservation, the Bureau of Forestry, the Bureau of Parks and Recreation, and the Bureau of Property Management. It thus becomes clear that referring to, say, deer management as "the DNR's" responsibility was hardly accurate; more accurate would be "the Wildlife Bureau's" responsibility.

The DNR worked well with an NRB-appointed secretary from 1929 to 1995. In 1995, legislation was passed that made the Secretary of the DNR subject to appointment by the governor as part of the governor's cabinet instead of appointment by the Natural Resources Board. The Secretary of the DNR was subject to direction by both the governor and the NRB, with the governor taking precedence.

In 2006, the DNR was reorganized again. This time it had six divisions: Division of Air and Waste, Division of Land, Division of Forestry, Division of Water, Division of Enforcement and Science, Division of Customer and Employee Services.

In 2014–15 the DNR was again reorganized into six divisions:

Environmental Management Division
External Services Division
Internal Services Division
Forestry Division
Fish, Wildlife and Parks Division
Public Safety and Resource Protection Division

The Fish, Wildlife and Parks Division contains six programs:

Wildlife Management
Fisheries Management
Natural Heritage Conservation
Parks and Recreation Management
Office of Applied Science
Office of Business Services

Instead of appreciating and sustaining or building on the elite wildlife program inherited, for 2017–2019, Governor Scott Walker and the legislature reduced the number of employees in the DNR by 50. Between 2000–2001 and 2017–2019, staffing decreased by 15%, including most of the research scientists. The two-year budget for 2023–2025 is $1.2 billion, which supports the WDNR with its 2,500 employees.

Of all the talented folks who worked at length for the Wisconsin Department of Natural Resources (WDNR), two received the Aldo Leopold Memorial Award: Ernie Swift in 1959, and Larry Jahn in 1989. From the WDNR, 20 have been inducted into the Wisconsin Conservation Hall of Fame at the University of Wisconsin–Stevens Point.

The 21st century has seen the DNR's wildlife program increase collaboration and cooperation with other public and private agencies to increase expertise, stretch budgets, and improve grant acquisition. Innovations such as the creation of endangered resources car license plates help offset loss of revenue from decreasing hunting license sales. Wildlife diseases such as chronic wasting disease in deer have caused the wildlife program to expand its personnel and involvement in wildlife health investigation and management; it has ready access to the National Wildlife Health Center in Madison. Satellite radio transmitters, GIS, and computer modeling are examples of the DNR's wildlife program's increased use of technology to manage wildlife.

The WDNR uses modern management techniques and a commitment to environmental protection to provide stewardship for Wisconsin's natural resources. Partnered with the efforts of Wisconsin sportsmen, the wildlife program within the WDNR has developed and maintained quality populations of wildlife for viewing and hunting, while enhancing the natural world in which society lives and on which it mostly unknowingly depends for survival. Thus, the department of natural resources in all 50 states of the United States and ten provinces of Canada—and worldwide—has a *vital* responsibility in maintaining the biodiversity of the ecosystem, now complicated by global climate change, that supports all of society. Regrettably for the uninformed society, few people seem impressed thus far.

THE BIG THREE

Any wildlife agency, state and provincial or federal, develops three areas of expertise for a successful program: research and management, protection and enforcement, information and education. Gjestson[67] and Kahler and Zani[107] presented a comprehensive historical treatment of the development of the Wisconsin Department of Natural Resources, especially its wildlife program.

RESEARCH AND MANAGEMENT

In 1929, a research bureau was established and attached to the Game Division of the Wisconsin Conservation Department (WCD). It consisted of unpaid volunteers! None of them at this time had special education in wildlife science. The first researcher was Dr. Alfred Gross of Bowdoin College in Brunswick, Maine, who studied Wisconsin prairie chickens. In 1930, he produced the first research report: "Progress Report of the Wisconsin Prairie Chicken Investigation." In 1932, the prairie chicken research was continued by Aldo Leopold's first graduate student, Franklin Schmidt (see Chapter 1).

Until 1946, the college graduate was rare in the field ranks of the WCD. Throughout the WCD, the few employees with college degrees tended to have them in chemistry, pathology, administration, and biology. At the end of World War II, though, the WCD's *Conservation Bulletin* mentioned an influx of surveyors, engineers, foresters, and "game men" to the WCD. In 1938, Aldo Leopold's former graduate student Art Hawkins was hired by the Illinois Natural History Survey as the world's first university-trained wildlifer in the new profession of wildlife management.[87] Graduating in 1939, Irven Buss was Aldo Leopold's first wildlife graduate to be hired by the Wisconsin Conservation Department, in 1940.[67, 169] The rest of the world followed. Thus began a new generation of wildlife managers in the task of building a new profession.

In 1945 and 1946 at the end of World War II, the Wisconsin Game Management Division hired 30 men[67]—a milestone for the game management profession, although few had a master's degree in game management. Ralph Conway resumed his position as supervisor of Refuges and Public Hunting Grounds after returning from the army; in 1945, he was given the first title of "Game Manager," arguably the first time the vocation had an identity. Nonetheless, not until the late 1940s did wildlife work move from protection to biological management.[262]

In 1946, a new wildlife research section was created. Cyril Kabat in 1946, and Donald R. Thompson in 1947, became wildlife researchers for the WCD, both men former graduate students of Aldo Leopold. They remained in wildlife research with the WCD their entire careers. The next two people hired in research by the WCD, in 1949, were the husband-and-wife team of Fred Hamerstrom, who graduated with a PhD in 1942, and, perhaps surprisingly for those days, a woman in this chauvinistic profession, Fran Hamerstrom.[83, 84] She graduated in 1940 with an MS as the only woman who had Aldo Leopold as a major professor. Fran was the first woman trained in wildlife ecology in the world, but it took decades before female wildlife biologists became common in this male-dominated profession.[159] Not only were women much less common in the wildlife profession, but to this day the wildlife profession is dominated by European Americans in far greater proportion than occurs in the general population relative to Asian Americans, Latino Americans, African Americans, and Native Americans.[111x]

By 2000, the Wildlife Bureau of the Wisconsin Department of Natural Resources employed some 80 wildlife biologists as wildlife managers and researchers. These scientifically-trained (university-trained) wildlifers are assigned to various district offices and to the state wildlife areas in Wisconsin to manage wildlife via population manipulation mainly through hunting and trapping, and via habitat manipulation on state land. Wildlifers also work for the national forest and the four large national wildlife refuges in Wisconsin. As the conservation era grew in Wisconsin and North America, Wisconsin relied increasingly on science-based decision-making in wildlife management, generating a national reputation in wildlife research for the state. While species-specific wildlifers continue to perform (e.g., deer biologist, small game biologist), ecosystem management to conserve biodiversity is gaining increasing importance.[23]

PROTECTION AND ENFORCEMENT

In 2019, four Wisconsin men were convicted under the federal Lacey Act of illegally hunting bobcats in Wisconsin and selling them in Minnesota, fined $65,000, and forfeited a pickup truck, rifles, binoculars, etc.[22] That the enforcement of wildlife laws is still necessary, and even hazardous, is clear.

Ninety years earlier, on 16 May 1929, Game Warden Einar Johnson, who survived World War I as a 2nd lieutenant in a tank corps, and his partner Allen Hanson, encountered Amio Maisio, from Minnesota, poaching beaver near Ladysmith. Maisio drew his Colt .45 and began shooting. Hanson was unarmed, but Johnson drew his own .45. Johnson and Maisio were hit, Johnson in the abdomen and Maisio in the chest. Both men were taken to the hospital. Johnson told the nurse that his experience in WWI indicated gunshot wounds in the stomach tended to be fatal. He gave a deathbed statement about the shootout and died the next day. He was 27. Maisio lived and was convicted of murder. Over a beaver.[277]

But Neil LaFave was the only Wisconsin game warden (actually a game technician with warden credentials) stalked and killed. On 24 September 1971, his 32nd birthday, on Sensiba Wildlife Area in northwestern Wisconsin in Green Bay, he was stalked, shot, and killed by revengeful poacher Brian Hussong, who then decapitated LaFave and buried head and body separately. Hussong was caught, imprisoned, escaped, and shot and killed by a Wisconsin game warden.[50]

Since 1928, seven Wisconsin Conservation Wardens have died in the line of duty, four of them shot.

In the early days, before a research and management division and trained wildlife biologists were established, game wardens were considered the wildlife experts, despite their limited knowledge of wildlife ecology. As early as 1851, the first wildlife regulation was passed, closing hunting for part of the year for deer, prairie chicken, quail, woodcock, and pheasant (although no pheasants existed in Wisconsin until 1910[67]). But the first explicit enforcement of the regulation was in 1879, when Rolla Baker of Bayfield was appointed as Wisconsin's first game warden.[33,34] For decades, the few such appointees that followed had little impact in protecting the wildlife and fish resources from poaching across the state. Most enforcement of the few game laws still fell to local sheriffs and police who did not bother much with it. Even later, when a warden with a poacher and dead grouse or bobcat in hand was right behind a sheriff with a thief or murder suspect in hand, the judge often merely slapped the hand of the poacher and released him.

By 1913, 74 game wardens were employed, at $2.50/day. By 1950, 100 wardens were employed, a gain of only 26 in 37 years. By 2022, about 220 existed in Wisconsin. Duties included enforcing the game laws, inspecting wildlife damage complaints, supervising winter feeding of deer and game birds, surveying winter deer yards, investigating bounty claims, and attending conservation club meetings and public schools to educate folks about wildlife conservation. In 1962, a law enforcement division existed in the Wisconsin Conservation Department. In 1967, when the Wisconsin Conservation Department expanded and became the Wisconsin Department of Natural Resources, the traditional fish and game duties expanded to include environmental law enforcement, thus creating an environmental warden. A game warden now is referred to as a conservation officer (CO) because the work is broader, although much of it still involves enforcing game laws, and "game warden" is still commonly used by the public.

INFORMATION AND EDUCATION (I&E)

In 1911, the Education and Publications Division was established within the Wisconsin Conservation Commission, the first formal effort in the agency to educate the public about conservation.

In 1935, Wisconsin passed a landmark law requiring conservation education be taught in all the state's public schools. The basic problem was, and remains, educating the public, rather than training professional managers. In 1949, the *Guide to Conservation Education in Wisconsin Schools* was published by the WCD. But none of this has seemed to influence or inform society much about environmental awareness, as explained in the book *The Failure of Environmental Education (and How We Can Fix It)* [215] (see Epilogue).

To help educate the public regarding wildlife and natural resources, from 1919 to 1922, the Wisconsin Conservation Commission published *The Wisconsin Conservationist* bimonthly. In 1936, the monthly black-and-white *Wisconsin Conservation Bulletin* began (bimonthly in 1961). In 1976, it was replaced with the color magazine *Wisconsin Natural Resources*, published monthly until 2018. Unfortunately, for the first time in 100 years, in 2018, the magazine was reduced from a monthly publication to a seasonal publication (quarterly), despite its expenses being self-sustained via subscription rate, i.e., no taxpayer money is used.

By 1949, a Division of Information and Education (I&E) existed within the DNR, separate from the Game Management Division and the four other divisions. In 1956, the DNR designed and produced radio and television shows about conservation. In 1960, Information and Education acquired the Poynette wildlife exhibit and picnic grounds from the Game Management Division. Named after Harley MacKenzie, it became the MacKenzie Environmental Education Center (next to the Poynette Game Farm), which offered outdoor education opportunities to school groups and the public. Four state wildlife areas served as the beginning of a wildlife educational center: Crex Meadows, Horicon Marsh, Mead, and Sandhill. With a budget cut in 2005, the DNR considered closing the MacKenzie Environmental Education Center, but the Wisconsin Wildlife Federation agreed to establish its headquarters there to help support the Center, along with the Friends of the MacKenzie Center.

Owned and operated by the Wisconsin Department of Natural Resources, the 285-acre MacKenzie Center is located near Poynette, Wisconsin in Columbia County. The Center has a wildlife exhibit of injured or orphaned native wildlife, a conservation museum, a logging museum, interpretive trails, and programming for school and youth groups. The area has an arboretum, a picnic area and shelter, and an observation (fire) tower. Interpretive trails run through woodland, prairie, and near a pond. Each spring a grove of maple trees produces 35 to 40 gallons of maple syrup.

Connected to the MacKenzie Center is the Poynette Game Farm where 110,000 pheasant chicks are hatched annually, 60,000 to be sold as chicks to conservation clubs in Wisconsin and 50,000 raised for release on state public areas for hunting. The popular (and expensive) operation began in 1928 in Peninsula State Park, Door County, and moved in 1934 to Poynette, Columbia County.

In 1983, a national program entitled "Project WILD" was initiated by the Association of Fish & Wildlife Agencies and then in 1985 by the Wisconsin Bureau of Wildlife Management after DNR wildlife biologist Dave Gjestson was instrumental in getting the Wisconsin Natural Resources Board to approve it. It is designed for state teachers to teach students not "what" to think about wildlife but "how" to think about wildlife. Hundreds of elementary teachers soon were trained in the program that reached tens of thousands of students over the next ten years. Moreover, Wisconsin initiated a program of "Watchable Wildlife," identifying key wildlife viewing locations around the state,[3, 94, 95, 106] a program that then spread nationwide. Various educational publications were produced.

The DNR has done a marvelous job of publishing research results in some 200 technical bulletins and some 200 research reports on fish and wildlife, starting in 1950, as well as publishing research results in technical journals such as the *Journal of Wildlife Management*.

BIOPOLITICS

As applied to wildlife management, the term biopolitics normally refers to the negative influence politics has on biological decisions for wildlife management. Before 1937, the Wisconsin legislature established all fees, seasons, bag limits, and regulations. Today, all regulatory decisions for wildlife management must be approved by the governor-appointed Secretary of the DNR and the governor-appointed Natural Resources Board. Although the NRB sets policy for the DNR, Wisconsin's legislature and governor still retain considerable authority to get involved with and alter conservation recommendations from Wisconsin wildlife biologists in the DNR. First, state wildlife laws (statutes) are developed in the legislature and, if approved, must then be signed by the Governor. Second, all administrative rules for wildlife conservation rules developed by the DNR and approved by the NRB must be approved by both the Governor and the relevant legislative committees. Wildlife conservation regulations, especially if they are controversial with the public, face political scrutiny if deemed politically incorrect or contrary to important constituencies, thus affecting an election. Wildlifers and the public must be aware of this reality.

The NRB and the Secretary of the DNR rely on their wildlife staff for management decisions, many of which involve hunting and fishing regulations. If hunters, anglers, and trappers strongly disagree with sound management decisions, wildlife managers often find their recommendations unapproved. That's why a strong information and education section of the DNR is so important to inform and educate stakeholders better, along with a strong environmental education program in schools throughout the state (see earlier in this chapter, and Epilogue).

In 2022, Wisconsin's Green Fire, a nongovernmental organization of retired Wisconsin wildlifers, produced a 32-page publication,[270y] *Imbalance of Power: How Wisconsin is Failing Citizens in Conserving Natural Resources and Protecting Our Environment.* Between the 1960s and 2010, Wisconsin was recognized as a national leader in conservation and environmental protection, a reputation built on innovative and progressive approaches to new policies and legislation. Since 2011, "the collective effects of state legislative actions, court rulings, and political practices… has produced a shift in power from the executive branch to the legislative branch…" [resulting in] "failure to conserve natural resources in a range of areas including management of fish, wildlife, and forests, protection of public lands, and protection of clean air and water."[270y]

And now we have climate change that is affecting plants, animals, and ecosystems—a biological and political problem (biopolitics) despite the best science (see Epilogue).

In 1934, the State Conservation Commission, predecessor of the NRB, created the Wisconsin Conservation Congress, legally recognized by state statute in 1972, an independent organization of Wisconsin citizens to serve in an advisory capacity to the NRB. The Conservation Congress is comprised mainly of hunters, anglers, and trappers—not wildlifers. During its nearly 90 years, the Congress and other concerned citizens have regularly voiced concern on DNR conservation proposals, most notably deer management policy. Even though DNR proposals were developed by trained wildlife biologists, instead of relying on these wildlifers, opponents often think erroneously that the proposal is not based on sound science or that it threatens long-standing traditions.[67] The Congress often has not been supportive of the DNR when both the DNR and the Congress want the same result but differ in how to achieve it. Other times the Congress has been fully supportive. The Congress' review of DNR proposals has a major impact on NRB and legislative approval. Conservation Congress support for DNR proposals is helpful in gaining NRB and legislative approval.

The two problems with biopolitics are 1) not educating the public and politicians about wildlife biology in the first place (inadequate environmental education), and 2) not giving the professionals, the experts—the wildlife biologists—the authority, without political interference, to make sound biological decisions based on science (see Epilogue). Always go with your best science.

KNOWLES-NELSON STEWARDSHIP PROGRAM

The Knowles-Nelson Stewardship Program was named after two former Wisconsin governors: Warren Knowles, a Republican governor (1965–71), and Gaylord Nelson, a Democratic governor (1959–63). Approved by the Wisconsin legislation in 1989, this sound program is designed to fund the acquisition of ecologically important land and water in Wisconsin. The government program matches state funding with that from nonprofit organizations. Through funding to the DNR, local governments and communities, and nonprofit conservation organizations like land trusts, to date about 879,000 acres of land have been protected. Funding was cut in 2010 from $86 million a year to $60 million, then to $33 million. In 2021, Governor Tony Evers raised it to $70 million. The program must be re-authorized every ten years. A great source to locate these public lands is the DNR's Public Access Lands Atlas of Wisconsin and the DNR's Public Access Lands Publications.

WILDLIFE ORGANIZATIONS

NATIONAL WILDLIFE HEALTH CENTER

The only national center dedicated to wildlife disease detection, control, and prevention is the National Wildlife Health Center. When established in 1975, the National Wildlife Health Center was part of the U.S. Fish and Wildlife Service. Its job was to assess the impact of disease on wildlife. In 1981, the National Wildlife Health Center moved to Madison, Wisconsin, with Dr. Milton Friend at the helm, the Milton Friend Building named after him. Friend had been a graduate student of Dan Trainer at UW–Madison, where Trainer got his PhD and worked for a while before being hired by the University of Wisconsin-Stevens Point as dean of its College of Natural Resources. Milton Friend became founding director of the National Wildlife Health Center in Madison, Wisconsin. Now under the auspices of the U.S. Geological Service, the Center provides technical assistance, research, and information on national and international wildlife health issues.[60] That includes determining ecological relationships leading to disease, assessing the impact of disease on wildlife populations, and providing training, on-site help, and guidance to reduce wildlife losses from disease. The National Wildlife Health Center's location in Wisconsin strengthens Wisconsin's wildlife leadership reputation worldwide.

IZAAK WALTON LEAGUE, WISCONSIN DIVISION

Founded in Chicago in 1922, the Izaak Walton League (the Ikes) promotes outdoor recreation and protection of natural resources. The Wisconsin chapter of the Izaak Walton League is an affiliate.

The Wisconsin Division of the Izaak Walton League was established in Appleton in 1923, now with chapters throughout the state. Aldo Leopold served on the Ike's Board of Directors and thus was instrumental in drafting and creating the Conservation Commission structure that became law and the foundation for the Wisconsin Conservation Department.

ALDO LEOPOLD FOUNDATION

In 1935, Aldo Leopold looked for a weekend retreat from Madison and located a worn-out farm with an old chicken coop on it. He bought it all, cleaned up the chicken coop for human occupation, referred to it as The Shack, and wrote much of *A Sand County Almanac*[142] here, on the shore of the Wisconsin River (see His Shack and His Book, in Chapter 1).

In 1982, the five children of Aldo and Estella Leopold established in Baraboo, Wisconsin, what would become the Aldo Leopold Foundation,[213] a conservation organization that works to inspire an ethical relationship between nature and people. The Foundation hosts programs promoting a land ethic, and owns The Shack, the Leopold Legacy Center, and holds rights to the Leopold Archives housed at the University of Wisconsin-Madison.

In 2007, the Leopold Center, or Aldo Leopold Legacy Center, an award-winning "green" building, opened to the public. It is the visitor center and meeting place, and the headquarters of the Aldo Leopold Foundation. Surrounding the Leopold Foundation is the 16,000-acre Leopold-Pine Island Important Bird Area (IBA) managed by the Wisconsin Department of Natural Resources, the U.S. Fish and Wildlife Service, nonprofit organizations, and private families. It is a mosaic of upland forest, grassland, savanna, marsh, and floodplain that straddles the Wisconsin River in Sauk and Columbia counties.

In 2009, the National Park Service designated The Shack and farm a National Historic Landmark.

INTERNATIONAL CRANE FOUNDATION

The world's only collection of all 15 crane species, 11 of which face extinction, is at the International Crane Foundation in Baraboo, Wisconsin, near Wisconsin Dells.[176] Privately owned and operated, the Foundation's global headquarters started in 1973 and now consists of 300 acres and about 100 cranes. The site features live crane exhibits, visitor center, research library, guided and self-guided tours, and four miles of nature trails. The Foundation has collaborated with, and led effective community-based conservation programs with, important research projects, and innovative captive breeding and reintroduction efforts, all of which has inspired international cooperation (see Chapter 5).

Born in 1946 in Nova Scotia, and founder in 1973 of the International Crane Foundation, director Dr. George Archibald received a BS from Dalhousie University in 1968, and a PhD in ornithology from Cornell University in 1975. One of his innovative techniques to rear cranes in captivity was the use of crane costumes by human handlers. In 1982, on Johnny Carson's *The Tonight Show*, Archibald entertained the audience by describing his technique of dressing like an endangered whooping crane and acting like a male crane performing before a female crane by walking, calling, and dancing in order to shift her into reproductive condition and inseminate her artificially. Archibald has won awards for his work.

WISCONSIN WILDLIFE FEDERATION

The Wisconsin Wildlife Federation (WWF) began in 1949 as an affiliate of the National Wildlife Federation (1936). With the bold and accomplished leadership of conservationist George Meyer as Executive Director, 2003–2021 (and former DNR Secretary, 1993–2001), the Wisconsin Wildlife Federation represents 207 hunting, fishing, trapping, and other affiliated sporting conservation groups in Wisconsin. It is the state's largest private conservation organization dedicated to protecting fish and wildlife habitat, hunting, fishing, and other outdoor recreational opportunities statewide. It is dedicated to conserving Wisconsin's natural resources and outdoor sporting heritage through conservation education and advocating strong state and national conservation policies. Located in the village of Poynette, the Wisconsin Wildlife Federation produces the informative monthly newspaper *Wisconservation*.

THE NATURE CONSERVANCY, WISCONSIN CHAPTER

Founded in 1951, The Nature Conservancy (TNC) is the largest environmental non-profit organization in the Americas. The Wisconsin Chapter of The Nature Conservancy began in 1960, with several of Leopold's students as founders. With its scientific and legal team, it buys imperiled, ecologically important land (about 236,100 acres in Wisconsin) and assists state and federal natural resource agencies to obtain land for preservation and outdoor recreation. Besides land acquisition, TNC also has programs that address climate change, invasive species, and freshwater including the Great Lakes.

WISCONSIN LAND AND WATER CONSERVATION ASSOCIATION

The Wisconsin Land and Water Conservation Association was established in 1953, its present name established in 1997 (during my son Adam Payne's tenure as executive director). It works toward protecting, conserving, and enhancing Wisconsin's natural resources by advocating for and supporting the conservation efforts of the Land and Water Conservation departments in Wisconsin's 72 counties. The Association provides training, promotes youth conservation education, builds conservation partnerships, facilitates conservation standards, and advocates for members. The Association is headquartered in Madison.

WISCONSIN'S GREEN FIRE

The name comes from "Thinking Like a Mountain," one of Aldo Leopold's essays in *A Sand County Almanac*,[142] in which he described his thought transition about predator control by the green fire in a dying wolf's eyes. Wisconsin's Green Fire began in 2017 as a group of retired biologists from the Wisconsin Department of Natural Resources, other Wisconsin-based wildlife and fishery organizations, and University of Wisconsin wildlife professors interested in delivering scientific information at legislative hearings on behalf of working DNR personnel who are no longer allowed to testify at such hearings. Membership has now expanded, as have the objectives.

THE WILDLIFE SOCIETY, WISCONSIN CHAPTER

Founded in 1973, The Wisconsin Chapter of The Wildlife Society is an educational and scientific organization of wildlife professionals, retirees, and students interested in conserving Wisconsin's wildlife resources to benefit society by exchanging wildlife information through publications, conferences, and working groups. Its mission is to help wildlifers sustain wildlife populations, manage wildlife resources, and conserve biological diversity. Its newsletter, *Intelligent Tinkering*, is published three to four times a year. The name comes from *A Sand County Almanac*,[142] viz, "To keep every cog and wheel is the first precaution of intelligent tinkering" (p.

177). Each state and provincial chapter supports the mission of the parental Wildlife Society, with its own officers, by-laws, and events. The Wisconsin Chapter of The Wildlife Society is an affiliate member of The Wildlife Society (1937).

NATURAL RESOURCES FOUNDATION OF WISCONSIN

Because declining budgets severely compromised critical programs of the Wisconsin Department of Natural Resources, the Natural Resources Foundation of Wisconsin (a nonprofit 501c3) was formed in 1986. Through its grant-making programs, the Foundation has boosted private sector involvement and investment to support the efforts of those working to protect Wisconsin's natural resources.

WISCONSIN SOCIETY FOR ORNITHOLOGY

Established in 1939, with members throughout Wisconsin, the United States, and the world, the Wisconsin Society for Ornithology promotes the study, conservation, and enjoyment of Wisconsin birds. It offers research grants and publishes the quarterly journal, *The Passenger Pigeon*. It also publishes the *Wisconsin's Favorite Bird Haunts*[245] and the *Atlas of the Breeding Birds of Wisconsin*[40] in collaboration with the WDNR's wildlife program.

WILDLIFE REHABILITATION

Wildlife rehabilitation has little impact on wildlife populations, especially compared to habitat rehabilitation. Wildlife rehabilitation affects only a single animal usually. Habitat rehabilitation, manipulation, protection, or acquisition involves entire populations of several species of animals, and that's where the money should go if a choice must be made. But no one wants to see an animal suffer or die unnecessarily. Too many young animals are scooped up by well-intentioned but ill-informed people when these young animals, such as fawns and rabbits, should be left alone where their mothers can find them. And many urban folks illegally feed and habituate wildlife, thus causing nuisance problems. Other animals are injured, often by vehicles. The Raptor

Education Group, Inc. in Antigo, Wisconsin, educates people about the problems associated with lead ammunition and fishing baits. Such groups have been helpful in partnering with the WDNR on the Keep Wildlife Wild campaign.

The WDNR's Wildlife Program has a *Wildlife Rehabilitation Directory* listing licensed wildlife rehabilitators and facilities in the state. The WDNR lists sites for the Wildlife Rehabilitation Council, Wisconsin Wildlife Rehabilitation Association, National Wildlife Rehabilitation Association, and International Rehabilitation Council. The Wisconsin Humane Society also offers assistance and advice.

OTHER WILDLIFE ORGANIZATIONS

Many wildlife or wildlife-related organizations began before the wildlife profession began in 1933. Their leaders had no formal wildlife education, of course, and thus much less scientific direction than eventually.

The U.S. Commission on Fish and Fisheries began in 1871, with its name changed in 1903 to the U.S. Bureau of Fisheries. In 1885, the U.S. Division of Economic Ornithology and Mammalogy was established, with its first chief C. Hart Merriam (a founding member of the National Geographic Society and the American Ornithologists' Union). That became the U.S. Division of Biological Survey in 1896. In 1934, it was renamed the U.S. Bureau of Biological Survey, with its first director Jay N. "Ding" Darling (see Chapter 1). In 1940, the U.S. Bureau of Fisheries and U.S. Bureau of Biological Survey were combined into the U.S. Fish and Wildlife Service.

The year Aldo Leopold was born, 1887, Theodore Roosevelt and other hunters founded the Boone and Crockett Club to conserve America's big game and their habitat. Its iconic book, *Records of North American Big Game*,[124] is updated regularly.

One of the earliest wildlife-related nongovernmental organizations is the International Association of Fish and Wildlife Agencies (IAFWA).[12x] It began in 1902 as the National Association of Game and Fish Wardens and Commissioners, with membership from provincial, state, and territorial wildlife agencies in Canada and the United States, and eventually Mexico. The commitment to wildlife and fish has remained unchanged, viz., protecting and supporting state, provincial, and territorial authority for fish and wildlife conservation and preventing overexploitation of natural resources on public and private lands and waters. Its presidents from Wisconsin were W. E. Barber (1919–21), L. P. Voigt (1964–65), and C. D. "Buzz" Besadny (1983–84). The University of Wisconsin–Stevens Point's College of Natural Resources is an affiliate member.

The U.S. Fish and Wildlife Service's National Wildlife Refuge System began in 1903, with President Theodore Roosevelt's establishment of Florida's Pelican Island National Wildlife Refuge. Now, 588 national wildlife refuges and wetland management districts of more than 850,000,000 acres exist in the U.S. (for national wildlife refuges in Wisconsin, see Chapter 6).

Other nongovernmental wildlife organizations in Wisconsin include Citizens Natural Resources Association of Wisconsin, River Alliance of Wisconsin, Wisconsin Lakes Partnership, Wisconsin Chapter of the Sierra Club, Wisconsin Conservation Voters, Wisconsin Wetlands Association, Wisconsin Conservation Congress, Wisconsin Conservation Corps, Wisconsin Chapters (17) of the Audubon Society, Bird City Wisconsin, Wings over Wisconsin, Wisconsin Purple Martin Association, Bluebird Restoration Association of Wisconsin, Wisconsin Chapter of Ducks Unlimited, Wisconsin Waterfowl Association, Wisconsin Chapter of the Ruffed Grouse Society, Wisconsin Sharp-tailed Grouse Society, Wisconsin Chapter of the National Wild Turkey Federation, Pheasants Forever and Quail Forever, Society of *Tympanuchus cupido pinnatus* (prairie chicken), Dane County Conservation League, Wisconsin Trappers Association, Wisconsin Deer Hunters Association, Whitetails Unlimited (National Headquarters in Sturgeon Bay, Wisconsin), Rocky Mountain Elk Foundation, Wisconsin Bowhunters Association, Wisconsin Bear Hunters Association, Daniel Boone Conservation League, Wisconsin Bird Conservation Partnership, Driftless Area Land Conservancy, The Prairie Enthusiasts, and others.

5.

WILDLIFE EXPLOITATION, REDUCTION, AND RECOVERY

The Wisconsin Department of Natural Resources (DNR) has done a stellar job in recovering most populations of wildlife formerly overexploited or otherwise decimated through habitat loss and chemical contamination. The two most contentious species to manage have been deer and wolves. Five species have been reintroduced: fisher, marten, turkey, trumpeter swan, and whooping crane (in collaboration with the U.S. Fish and Wildlife Service). But before a DNR was around (way before), losses occurred.

DINOSAURS

So where are the dinosaur skeletons like those found in South Dakota but not in Minnesota or Wisconsin? They probably were here, but no skeletons have yet been found partly because the rocks that would have preserved them were eroded away during the 66 million years since the massive collision of a meteor off Mexico's Yucatan Peninsula caused the massive extinction.

MASTODONS AND MAMMOTHS

If you visit the University of Wisconsin-Madison Geology Museum, you will see the Boaz mastodon, a composite skeleton

97

of bones (about 12,200 years BP) found in 1897 near Boaz, a small town off Highway 14 in southwestern Wisconsin, and another set (about 12,900 years BP) found in 1898 near the extinct town of Anderson Mills, also in southwestern Wisconsin's Driftless Area. It was an estimated 18 feet long, 9 feet high, and 6–8 tons. Other skeletal remains of a mastodon, found near Deerfield in eastern Dane County, are housed in the UW–Madison Zoological Museum in Noland Hall. Male mastodons weighed 8–11 tons. Mastodons disappeared from Wisconsin about 9,000 years ago. Other skeletal specimens of extinct megafauna include a bison from Polk County, a larger species of our present bison (buffalo). Also, found in Johnson Creek is the mandible from a giant beaver which might have weighed 350 pounds, larger than present-day adult beaver at 35–65 pounds (same family Castoridae but different species and genus).

Not only the American mastodon, a browser, but also the woolly mammoth, a grazer, were present in Wisconsin in the late Pleistocene until the end of the Ice Age 11,000 years ago. Skeletons of woolly mammoths dating 14,500 years ago were found in Kenosha Co. and are displayed in the Kenosha Public Museum; a replica is in the Milwaukee Public Museum. Weighing 7–8 tons, the mammoths showed signs of butchering. The oldest known site of butchered mammoths in North America, this site places humans in Wisconsin earlier than thought.

So, what happened to the megafauna? Cro-Magnon humans (*Homo sapiens*), our species, developed in Africa 150,000 years ago. They emigrated out of Africa by way of the Sinai, the only route into Eurasia about 100,000 years ago (the 15 km across the Mediterranean Sea between Morocco and Gibraltar not being used). They overlapped with Neanderthal humans (*Homo neanderthalensis*) in Europe (procreating with some, as DNA analysis shows) until the last Neanderthal died 28,000 years ago, and maybe overlapped with *Homo erectus* in Asia.[229] As they emigrated, a wave of extinction of large-bodied, slow breeding mammals ensued, including the Neanderthals.[165]

Currently, experts differ whether the first human immigrants to North America and South America walked across the land bridge of Beringia (Aleutian Islands between Alaska and Russia) when sea water was locked in ice during the Ice Age, or boated along the western shoreline of North America 40,000 or 50,000 years ago (evidence made difficult by encampments now under water), or both, or even crossed the North Atlantic pack ice. DNA studies indicate that Asian origins for four lineages account for more than 95% of Indigenous Americans, but that a fifth DNA lineage, mostly in Canada's Ojibwe people, occurs in Europeans. Moreover, experts say that North America needed over 50,000 years to become one of the most linguistically complex areas in the world[235] (see Chapter 6).

When modern humans entered North America, 78 slow-breeding species that weighed over a ton vanished, including mammoths and mastodons which went extinct about 13,000 years ago. The record indicates that humans were responsible; extinction was facilitated by climate and landscape change causing a reduction in grasses and sedges and an increase in deciduous trees.[273] Reproduction of these slow-breeding megafauna could not keep pace with unsustainable exploitation with better weapons.[118] In some places, this trend continues with modern extinctions and extirpations, especially of large, long-lived, slow-breeding mammals (e.g., whales, walrus, elephants, rhinos).

Other large mammals that occurred in Wisconsin and became extinct or extirpated in prehistoric times include woodland musk ox, stag-moose, shrub ox, ground sloth, dire wolf, saber-toothed cat, and short-faced bear.

EXTIRPATED

An increase of human population from immigrants in the 1800s, the so-called Era of Exploitation, in Wisconsin and elsewhere, then resulted in the unlimited take of wildlife and destruction of its habitat. Extirpation and extinction followed.[67, 104, 148, 150, 218] In Wisconsin, the last buffalo was shot in 1832, the last caribou in 1844, Carolina parakeet in 1844, elk in 1875, wild turkey in 1881, whooping crane and cougar in 1884, trumpeter swan in 1893, passenger pigeon in 1899, fisher and moose by 1921, wolverine in 1922, marten by 1925, and gray wolf by 1950. White-tailed jackrabbits seem to be gone (late 1980s). Other species of wildlife have been extirpated from Wisconsin but have been reintroduced. Some species are close to being extirpated and are endangered or threatened.[148] Concerned citizens pressured the Wisconsin legislature to do something.

ENDANGERED AND THREATENED

Scientists estimate that one-third of all U.S. wildlife species are either vulnerable or imperiled, and risk extinction, according to the National Wildlife Federation. The NWF also says that the nation's fish and wildlife agencies have identified 12,000 species in need of proactive conservation efforts to maintain vital biodiversity of ecosystems.

More than 1,267 animals and plants are threatened or endangered in the United States. In 1972, Wisconsin became the first state to pass its own state endangered species law. By developing Habitat Conservation Plans, the Bureau of Natural Heritage Conservation (NHC) within the Wisconsin Department of Natural Resources directs all the endangered and threatened animal, plant, and habitat work in Wisconsin. The U.S. Endangered Species Act lists 23 animals and plants endangered (E) or threatened (T) in Wisconsin: two mammals, viz., Canada lynx (T), and northern long-eared bat (T); two birds, viz., piping plover (E) and red knot (T); one reptile, viz., eastern massasauga (T); seven mussels (E); four insects including Karner blue butterfly (E); and seven plants (T). For example, Fassett's locoweed (*Oxytropis campestris* var. *chartacea*), with its beautiful purple flower, is known from only eight sites in Wisconsin and nowhere else on the planet.

The Wisconsin list of endangered (E) or threatened (T) animals and plants is much longer than the federal list.[268] It contains 233 species: five mammals, viz., American marten (E), big brown bat (T), little brown bat (T), northern long-eared bat (T), and eastern pipistrelle bat (T); 11 birds (E) and 13 birds (T); six reptiles (E) and one reptile (T); one amphibian (E), viz., Blanchard's cricket frog; ten fish (E) and ten fish (T); 11 mussels (E) and eight mussels (T); two snails (E) and two snails (T); 19 insects (E) and four insects (T); 72 plants (E) and 58 plants (T). More than 400 other animals and plants are of "special concern." The Wisconsin Department of Natural Resources[266] listed the birds, mammals, reptiles, amphibians, fish, and invertebrates of greatest conservation need.

A plant or animal is considered "at-risk" when (1) it is proposed for listing as threatened or endangered under the Endangered Species Act, (2) it is a candidate species for listing, or (3) it has been petitioned by a third party for listing. The number of native species in Wisconsin (and those at risk in parentheses) are as follows:[65] 70 mammals (13), 284 birds (68), 37 reptiles (20), 19 amphibians (4), 148 fish (26), 50 mussels (24), 153 butterflies (19), 162 dragonflies (28), 20 bumblebees (8), and 2,336 plants (320).

Many of Wisconsin's wildlife species are the glamour, often huntable, species of particular appeal to the public, usually by size or appearance, and thus carefully managed for sustainability. Wisconsin's human population of 5.9 million has placed huge demands on the state's ecosystems. Of course the reason for the status of endangered, threatened, and special concern is human-caused, viz., habitat—habitat fragmentation and habitat destruction from human encroachment, especially in a state like Wisconsin where 82% of it is privately owned. The pattern of exploiting wildlife populations by hunting and trapping persisted into the 1900s and later, but is generally no longer a concern, for it has gradually been modified and contained by governmental restraint, husbandry, and restoration—technical goals requiring wildlife management by a relatively new professional: the wildlifer.

PASSENGER PIGEON

Here we aren't talking extirpation, but extinction—in the "modern" era! The largest nesting ever documented was in Wisconsin in 1871, when hundreds of millions of pigeons nested in almost every tree in 850 square miles of Central Wisconsin. In 1899, the last passenger pigeon in Wisconsin died, and 15 years later the entire species in the world went extinct when the last one died in 1914 at the Cincinnati Zoo.[75]

In 1947, the Wisconsin Society for Ornithology erected a monument in a public display of sorrow over the selfish extinction.

Aldo Leopold gave a stirring speech at the Wisconsin Society of Ornithology (WSO) convention in 1946, when the plaque was unveiled, revealing a passenger pigeon drawn by famed Wisconsin bird artist Owen Gromme, with the inscription composed by A. W. Schorger: "Dedicated to the last Wisconsin passenger pigeon shot at Babcock, Sept. 1899. This species became extinct through the avarice and thoughtlessness of man." The part of Leopold's speech entitled, "On a Monument to the Pigeon," is reproduced in *A Sand County Almanac*.[142] The plaque now sits as a stone monument in Wyalusing State Park overlooking the confluence of the Wisconsin and Mississippi rivers.

Given the passenger pigeon's prodigious appetite for mast and maize, early indigenous peoples (before 1492) should have kept their numbers under control through hunting so that the maize crops would survive and wild nuts would have been available for collecting. And the pigeons would have been an important source of meat. But few pigeon bones occur in archeological sites. Thus, passenger pigeons were not so numerous before Columbus. Europeans altered the ecosystem such that passenger pigeons found it highly desirable, and proliferated then[161] to numbers so massive that the bird would be considered an agricultural pest now. The definitive account of the pigeon's life history and extinction can be found in the book *The Passenger Pigeon: Its Natural History and Extinction*.[220]

MOURNING DOVE

Wisconsin might be unique as the only state which hunts its Bird of Peace. The mourning dove is one of the most abundant and widespread birds in North America and is hunted in many states. From public pressure that involved the Supreme Court, the Wisconsin legislature gave it the status of Bird of Peace in Wisconsin in 1971 to protect it from hunting. Thirty years later, in 2001, the state proclaimed it a legal game species; the first hunting season occurred in 2003. In addition to resident mourning doves, some 4,000,000 to 5,000,000 doves migrate through Wisconsin; some 100,000 to 150,000 doves are taken annually in Wisconsin.

SONGBIRDS

Songbirds need help. Since 1970, the songbird population of North America has decreased 30%. Although complications, such as pesticides, contribute to the decline, mostly it has to do with habitat reduction both in breeding areas and in wintering areas for migrant birds. Our neotropical migrant songbirds are affected by the destruction of South America's Amazon rainforest, which is much in need of financial aid from the United States and Canada. This situation has major economic impact, not only for farmers who rely on insect-eating birds, but also for others. The U.S. Fish and Wildlife Service reports that Wisconsin is a birdwatching hotspot, ranked second behind Vermont in the percentage of residents (33%) who regularly observe, feed, and/or photograph birds. Half of the 440 bird species in Wisconsin are neotropical migrants to Mexico, Central America, and South America; 243 species nest in Wisconsin. Of these 440 bird species, 91 are classed as accidental, 34 as casual, 53 as rare, and eight as introduced. Since 1900, Christmas bird counts have been conducted throughout Wisconsin and the world; data is compared annually. In Wisconsin, the WDNR has acquired public land to protect special areas including bird-nesting areas (see Chapter 6).

The comprehensive atlas of Wisconsin's breeding birds[40] reveals where and how that has changed over the years. This knowledge will help guide present and future bird conservation efforts. The WDNR published *The Ecological Landscapes of Wisconsin*,[267] which identifies the best state areas to manage native plants and animals in key habitats of natural communities. The DNR also developed a *Public Access Lands Atlas* that can be downloaded from the internet. Both publications would facilitate locating suitable sites for outdoor activities including bird counts.

Other valuable books about Wisconsin birds also are available.[76, 212x, 240, 244, 245]

KIRTLAND'S WARBLER

The rare Kirtland's warbler has been brought back from the brink of extinction in Wisconsin, Michigan, and Ontario. Now at about 2,300 pairs, in 2018, it was removed from the federal Endangered

Species List but remains on the Wisconsin list. It is found in Bayfield, Marinette, Adams, and Jackson counties. The WDNR and its partners set traps to remove brown-headed cowbirds, a nest parasite that lays an egg in other birds' nests, its fast-growing chick then raised by the foster bird, to the detriment of the other nestlings. The partners also improve habitat by maintaining and expanding the mix of 5- to 20-year-old jack pine and red pine stands desired by the birds. In 2007, only 11 Kirtland's warblers and three nests were found in Wisconsin. Ten years later, 53 birds and 20 nests were found—not many, but better.

PIPING PLOVER

The endangered piping plover has increased from just two (one pair) in 1948 to 140 (70 pairs) in 2019. Habitat restoration of large, isolated cobble beach and dunes, and protection along the Great Lakes are responsible. The goal of the DNR and its partners is 150 pairs in the Great Lakes region.

COMMON TERN

Of the four endangered species of tern in Wisconsin—common tern, black tern, Caspian tern, Forster's tern—the common tern fledged 510 chicks in 2020, a state record high, but hardly enough to get it out of trouble. The improved reproduction resulted from development of islands as breeding habitat.

MASSASAUGA RATTLESNAKE

Wisconsin is home to 37 species of reptiles. The timber rattlesnake and the state-endangered massasauga rattlesnake are the two venomous snakes in Wisconsin; until 1975, it had a bounty on them. The massasauga occurs in only nine sites in the state, and now is being threatened with snake fungal disease. By using radiotelemetry, the first intensive study of the massasauga[42] to determine habitat use and movement patterns occurred in Juneau and Monroe counties in 1994 and 1995. Relatively sedentary, adults avoided upland forests but used upland meadows; neonates used upland and lowland meadows more than adults did.

The Natural Heritage Conservation Program of the WDNR has improved habitat for the snake which has expanded its range into Jackson County.

AMPHIBIANS

Wisconsin has 19 species of amphibians: 11 frogs, one toad, and seven salamanders. Every spring during courtship when the males call, the toad and frogs are censused.[192] Begun in 1981, Wisconsin's toad and frog survey is one of the longest-running amphibian surveys in North America. Calls of each species are counted for five minutes; results are compared annually. In Wisconsin, the WDNR has acquired public land to protect special areas including those used by amphibians (see Chapter 6).

BATS

All four cave species and the other four species of bats in Wisconsin are threatened by the disease known as white-nose syndrome. The disease first appeared in the United States (New York) in 2006, and was first observed in Wisconsin in 2014. The disease has reduced populations of bats in Wisconsin by 72–97%. A vaccine is being developed by the WDNR's Natural Heritage Conservation Program in collaboration with the USGS National Wildlife Health Center and the University of Wisconsin-Madison. These insect-eaters, pollinators, and fertilizers are a vital part of the ecosystem.

BISON

The story of this animal belongs, almost, with the passenger pigeon. Once the most abundant large mammal in the world, at 30–60 million in the Great Plains, bison were recklessly extirpated from North America in the 1800s.[64x, 97x, 212y] It took just 30 years. By the late 1800s, less than 1,000 remained. Bison, or American buffalo, occurred in southern and southwestern Wisconsin on prairies and savannas.[150, 217] In 1832, the Sioux apparently killed the last two in Wisconsin, of undoubtedly thousands in the state previously.[104] A mere dozen or so "wild" bison now occur on

Sandhill Wildlife Area near Babcock, and about 7,000, probably containing cattle genes, on several game farms. First it was overexploitation. Now it is habitat. Bison no longer have the expansive open unfenced public range they need, even though their presence increases plant biodiversity.

MOOSE

Originally moose were distributed over most of Wisconsin north of latitude 44 degrees, which runs through southern Bayfield Co. in northern Wisconsin.[104] It was extirpated by 1921. Moose now occur sparsely in northern Wisconsin from the population in Minnesota and the Upper Peninsula of Michigan. Some breeding occurs; cows with calves have been seen in Forest and Ashland counties. A population of 20–30 is estimated.[150] Except for protection, no management efforts are geared for moose. The brainworm that deer have and tolerate is lethal to moose. To have moose, probably until they developed immunity to brainworm, the deer population probably would have to be reduced to less than ten per square mile, politically untenable.

ELK

Elk were widespread in Wisconsin, with records in 50 counties. By 1875, they were reported to be extirpated,[104] but a photo was taken of 12 elk running across a field near Woodruff in 1952, with no subsequent evidence of elk.[67] In 1917, 32 cows and eight bulls were shipped from Jackson Hole, Wyoming, to Trout River in Vilas County, Wisconsin. The little population slowly increased, but ultimately disappeared.

Two sites in Wisconsin now contain elk. In 1995, 25 elk from Michigan were released in the Clam Lake area in Ashland County, the last one of these a cow, dying in 2019 at age 25, evidently and extraordinarily of old age. Another 91 elk were introduced there from Kentucky in 2017 and 2019. The herd in the Clam Lake area contained 355 elk in 2023. The DNR's eventual population goal for northern Wisconsin is 1,400 elk. The first modern—modest—elk hunt occurred there in 2018.

Kentucky provided 23 elk in 2015 and 50 elk in 2016 to Jackson County forests. In 2017, 31 elk were added from Kentucky, and in 2019, 108 more. Numbers grew as pregnant cows gave birth. About 160 elk resided in Jackson County in 2023. The population goal for Jackson County is 400 elk.

Both the Michigan herd and the Kentucky herds have their genetic roots from western elk herds. Predators are wolves and black bears preying on calves; a cow elk has just one calf each year, unlike deer does with one to three fawns annually.

WHITE-TAILED DEER

Wisconsin is the highest producer of Boone and Crockett-ranked whitetails. The deer population in Wisconsin is worth well over $2 billion annually in hunting and tourist observation, $2.2 billion from deer hunting alone. Over 500,000 deer hunters buy a license for the annual nine-day gun deer hunt in Wisconsin; 2021 was the 170th gun deer season in Wisconsin. But license sales have declined with the advent of chronic wasting disease among deer and fewer younger folks interested in hunting. The DNR reported that the average age of Wisconsin deer hunters in 2022 was 60.

To manage the deer population through hunting, the DNR determines population size and huntable surplus by taking population measurements with the sex, age, kill ratio (SAK) coupled with fawn/doe counts for recruitment. The Deer Management Assistance Program encourages private landowners to improve their habitat and management of deer.

With a decrease in interest in hunting, and especially the concern about chronic wasting disease in deer, the Wisconsin deer harvest has declined from its peak of 600,000 in 2000. In 1934, Wisconsin held the first archery season ever conducted in the United States,[170] a five-day season for deer in Sauk and Columbia counties; one spike buck was taken.[67] Now, hunters (about 10% female and 5% non-resident) take about 100,000 deer by archery, including crossbows, and about 200,000 deer with muzzleloaders and rifles in the four zones of Southern Farmland, Central Farmland, Central Forest, and Northern Forest. In 2023, 434,817 hunters from all 50 states and 27 countries bought a Wisconsin gun deer-hunting license, taking 173,942 deer (83,390 antlered, 88,552 antlerless; 40% success) during the traditional 9-day gun deer season around Thanksgiving—down 17.6% from 2022 and 11% from 5 years ago.

In 1951, wardens picked up 448 car-killed deer. That number more than doubled by 1954, passed 2,000 in 1956, and 3000 in 1960, indicating an increase in the deer herd and traffic volume. By 1970, 11,688 road kills were picked up, doubling in number by 1980 and surpassing 30,000 by 1984. Some 20,000–40,000 deer have been reported killed annually by vehicles in Wisconsin[262] (see Gray Wolf). Since 2007 the number of vehicle-killed deer has ranged 15,000 to 20,000.

Originally deer were found commonly throughout Wisconsin, more plentiful in the south than the north.[104, 219] By 1860, deer had become nearly extirpated south of latitude 40 degrees north, which runs through Vilas Co. in northern Wisconsin. In 1925, the deer season was closed for the first time, then opened alternate years during 1926–36.[67] Logging improved brushy habitat for deer.[17, 41, 227] About 1.5 million deer now live throughout Wisconsin.

Wisconsin has now compromised its $2.2 billion deer resource. Deer management and its huge value are now complicated and threatened by the presence of chronic wasting disease (CWD). The DNR first identified it in 2002, perhaps introduced by the state's authorizing 376 deer/elk farms, controlled by the Wisconsin Department of Agriculture, Trade and Consumer Protection, not by the Wisconsin Department of Natural Resources. The unnatural assemblage of deer brought in from outside the state and confined with local deer, then sold and distributed elsewhere, has resulted in many incidents of CWD. Broken fences have allowed confined deer with CWD to escape and mix with wild deer, distributing CWD to the wild herd. In 2023, 62 of 72 counties had deer with CWD. Like elsewhere, deer management in Wisconsin is difficult because of its importance to hunting and non-hunting tourism, the charisma of the animal, public emotion involved, and strong interest by hunters and by resort and tavern/supper club owners who want many deer to show their customers.

BLACK BEAR

Originally occurring throughout Wisconsin and the Upper Peninsula of Michigan, the black bear was extirpated from southeastern Wisconsin by 1860 and central and western Wisconsin by 1890.[150]

Now it is common in forests of northern and central Wisconsin, with an estimate of 25,000 bears. In 1957, bear trapping was outlawed. From 1930 to 1973, bears could be hunted with a small game license. In 1974, bears were elevated to big game status with a hunting license specific for bears, hunted with or without use of dogs.[113] Some of the biggest bears in the country (700–800 pounds) occur in Wisconsin. About 130,000 hunters apply for about 12,000 permits to take about 4,000 bears annually in Wisconsin.

PRAIRIE CHICKEN

Market hunting severely decimated the once abundant but now threatened prairie chicken in Wisconsin and elsewhere. By the 1850s, scarcities were noticed and hunting restrictions were passed to limit the season to about three months, further restricted in 1905 and 1907, and starting in 1917 with a four-year ban (8-year ban in Portage County). A short hunting season was allowed from 1921 to 1955—the last year of prairie chicken hunting. An estimated 600 prairie chickens remain in Wisconsin, shockingly lower than the estimated 2,500 in 1950 and 55,000 in 1930.

The population is restricted to the Buena Vista Wildlife Area, Leola Marsh, Paul J. Olson[7] Marsh, and Mead Wildlife Area in central Wisconsin. Managed by the WDNR, the Buena Vista Wildlife Area is one of four properties that constitute the Central Wisconsin Grassland Conservation Area Project, established in 2004 to protect native grassland wildlife of Wisconsin, prairie chickens included. Over the years, some 30,000 acres of land were acquired, most of it (over 11,000 acres) in Buena Vista, and habitat management was conducted (controlled burning, controlled grazing, brush cutting). Grassland acquisition and management practices for prairie chickens also apply to the state's threatened upland sandpiper, a long-range migrant that winters in Argentina. Still, despite being studied since the late 1920s, the involvement of the Dane County Conservation League, the Society of *Tympanuchus cupido pinnatus,* the work of famed prairie chicken biologists Fred and Fran Hamerstrom,[79] and other WDNR efforts over the decades, the prairie chicken in Wisconsin remains in trouble due to habitat loss and increasing genetic isolation.

Beginning in 2006, 110 hen prairie chickens from Minnesota were released into central Wisconsin to bolster the gene pool and thus stimulate flock vitality and range expansion. No native wildlife species in Wisconsin has been in such a well-documented and well-understood decline for so long. Beginning in 1950 with a count of 782, counts of male prairie chickens reached a high in 1981 of 1,121. With just 264 males counted on 34 booming grounds in 2023 (and presumably another 264 females), the bird is listed as threatened in Wisconsin.

Decades of non-consumptive use of these prairie chickens has involved the placement of a viewing blind beside each booming ground (courtship display areas) so people can observe and record data regarding the fascinating display of the cocks, from sunrise to 8:00 a.m. in April (see Appendix 5). It began in 1950, with the WCD (WDNR now); the Wildlife Discipline at the University of Wisconsin–Stevens Point now coordinates it. This has become so popular, attracting folks from as far away as Chicago and Minneapolis, that a fee is charged, and reservations must be made.

Another form of non-consumptive use is less non-consumptive. The Amateur Field Dog Trials Championship in America has been held on horseback on six courses on the Buena Vista grasslands in September annually for decades. About 50 dogs have been used to flush prairie chickens; riders have shot blanks over the dogs and birds, disturbing and doubtless stressing this threatened species, perhaps reducing survival.

The Covid pandemic of 2020 and 2021 temporarily suspended the activities of viewing and dog trials.

SHARP-TAILED GROUSE

Sharp-tailed grouse remain a concern, although a limited hunting season exists sometimes, and hunter permits might be issued. That depends on the population estimate, normal 50% mortality, and previous hunter success. Populations are small and the Wildlife Division fights to maintain them. Core range is in the northwest barrens and brush prairies of Wisconsin, with potential in central Wisconsin. Timber harvest and brush maintenance are the main habitat management procedures. The Wildlife Division is working with counties and the national forest to create a mosaic of habitat conditions that sharptails need.

SPRUCE GROUSE

Wisconsin's over-harvested forest that fell by 1900 contained more spruce grouse over a wider range than it does now. Forest regrowth resulted in some recovery of the spruce grouse population. Now they are located in a 50-mile-wide strip across part of northern Wisconsin, and in larger numbers in Michigan's Upper Peninsula. Spruce grouse use swamps of tamarack and black spruce of the boreal forest. An estimated population of about 5,600 spruce grouse exists in Wisconsin, where no hunting season for them occurs. They are hunted in adjacent Minnesota.

BOBWHITE QUAIL

An extremely popular game bird in southern U.S., bobwhite quail are on the northern edge of their range in southern and western Wisconsin with its winters of deep snow and cold. Their numbers have declined over the years due to habitat reduction, mostly from more row crops, larger, cleaner fields, and fragmentation of other land. No county or state laws exist requiring landowners to provide winter cover in fields for bobwhites or other wildlife, even though they are public resources. Hunters take about 1000 bobwhites a year.

TURKEY

Reintroducing turkeys into Wisconsin has been a huge wildlife success story. Extirpated by excessive hunting, the last wild turkey seen in Wisconsin was in 1881.[221] Between 1929 and 1939, more than 3,000 game farm turkeys were released in Grant and Sauk counties with no success.[67] In 1954, 69 wild turkeys from Pennsylvania were released in the Meadow Valley Wildlife Area. In 1955, turkey broods were seen, so in 1956, another 217 turkeys were purchased from Pennsylvania and another 460 in 1957. But they were killed off by the severe winter of 1957–58 and inadvertent introduction of blackhead disease from game farm stock from Pennsylvania.

An exchange of three Wisconsin ruffed grouse for one Missouri turkey resulted in 45 wild turkeys from Missouri released in Vernon County in January 1976. Eventually 334 turkeys were released into Buffalo, Iowa, Trempealeau, Jackson, La Crosse,

Vernon, and Dane counties. They reproduced. Turkeys then were live-trapped in Wisconsin for relocation elsewhere so that 49 counties had them in Wisconsin. Turkeys found their way by themselves to the other 23 counties. Turkeys now occur throughout the state including urban areas in an estimated population of 350,000. The first spring season hunt was in 1983, the first fall hunt in 1989. Now, Wisconsin hunters take about 45,000 turkeys annually, about 40,000 in the spring hunt, a lost skill which had to be relearned with blinds, decoys, and turkey calls.

PEREGRINE FALCON

A peregrine is the fastest animal in the world, flying 240 miles per hour in a dive. Native to Wisconsin, peregrine falcons had vanished by the 1960s due to habitat loss—and extremely low production of young due to pesticides, mainly DDT, which caused eggshells to thin and eggs to crack during incubation.[93] In 1970, Wisconsin became the second state to ban the use of DDT (after Michigan) two years before the federal government.[15] (In 1986, Wisconsin passed the first acid rain control law in the nation.) In 1975, reintroduction of peregrine falcons began in Wisconsin along the Mississippi River. In summer 1987, 14 peregrine eggs from Alaska, Mexico, Canada, and Scotland were placed in hack boxes on the U.S. Bank building in downtown Milwaukee. Ten chicks survived. From 1987 to 1992, 103 captive-raised peregrines were released in Wisconsin forming the basis of the population in the state today. Now, Wisconsin averages more than 30 nests and produces some 100 chicks per year.

OSPREY

Catching fish in 25–70% of their dives, ospreys are the only hawk that can dive three feet underwater to catch fish and then fly out shaking water off like a dog. Due to habitat loss and DDT, which thinned eggshells, by 1972 Wisconsin had less than 90 osprey pairs when it was listed as endangered. By banning DDT in 1970,[15] and installing more than 200 nesting platforms from 1972 to 1993, Wisconsin went from a low of 82 breeding pairs in 1974 to a record 600 in 2018. In 2019, 535 occupied nests occurred in 60 of Wisconsin's 72 counties.

BALD EAGLE

By 1900, the state's breeding population of bald eagles was virtually eliminated due to year-round market hunting, egg stealing, and habitat destruction. Due to habitat loss and DDT, which thinned eggshells, Wisconsin had only 108 occupied nests of bald eagles in 1973. With the banning of DDT in 1970,[15] surveyors in 2019 counted 1,695 occupied nests in all 72 counties (i.e., 3,390 adult [nesting] eagles). Including juveniles, which do not get the white head and tail or breed until age 4, this is one of the largest populations in any state. The bald eagle ceased being an endangered species in Wisconsin in 1997, and in the U.S. in 2007—a magnificent recovery.

WHOOPING CRANE

The jury is still out on this one, this iconic internationally endangered species. In Wisconsin in 2023, 71 cranes occurred (38 females, 31 males, two unknown), of which only 17 were wild-hatched, the rest captive-reared.

At 5 feet tall, it is the tallest bird in North America, with a wingspan of 7.5 feet and a long life (22-24 years). Whooping cranes have been a fixture in North American skies and wetlands for millions of years, but were on the verge of extinction in the 1940s due to hunting and habitat loss. The last one seen in Wisconsin was in 1884. Only 20 whooping cranes were alive in the entire world then; now some 850 exist in the wild and captivity. That's not a lot, but it sure beats 20.

The White River Marsh Wildlife Area, a 12,000-acre state property managed by the WDNR's Wildlife Division, is in the northeast corner of Marquette County and the northwest corner of Green Lake County. Beginning in 2011, that's where whooping cranes, raised at the International Crane Foundation in Baraboo, Wisconsin, have been released in Wisconsin (see Chapter 4). The project began in 2001 at Necedah National Wildlife Refuge in central Wisconsin, but blackflies tormented the cranes to abandon their nests there. (The drainage ditches dug there in the late 1800s to convert the marsh into agricultural land failed in that regard but produced black fly habitat.) To learn the migration route, for

15 years (2001–2016) juveniles followed an ultralight airplane to Chassahowitzka National Wildlife Refuge and to St. Marks National Wildlife Refuge in Florida to winter. Although success has been small, enough adults are now available for juveniles to follow. Whooping cranes also winter in northern Alabama and western Indiana.

A resident flock of whooping cranes is being developed in Louisiana. The only other flock of whooping cranes migrates between Aransas National Wildlife Refuge in Texas and Wood Buffalo National Park in northern Alberta and the Northwest Territories of Canada. That flock numbers about 500 cranes.

SANDHILL CRANE

The Wisconsin Society for Ornithology estimated that only about 25 breeding pairs of sandhill cranes existed in the 1930s, due mainly to over-hunting. Since then, due to increased enforcement of the Migratory Bird Treaty of 1918, an estimated 40,000 cranes occur in the Mississippi Flyway, with about 13,000 in Wisconsin, the largest breeding population of the Eastern population—one of the most inspiring conservation success stories of the last century. Now a hunting season is being considered, as in 18 other states and four Canadian provinces, partly because sandhill cranes have reached nuisance status in some areas where they feed on corn sprouts in farmers' fields. One of six subspecies of sandhill crane recognized by ornithologists, Wisconsin cranes are greater sandhill cranes.

At 16,000 acres, the Leopold-Pine Island Important Bird Area straddles the Wisconsin River in Columbia and Sauk counties west of Portage and provides arguably the greatest wildlife spectacle in Wisconsin during late fall when thousands of migrant sandhills stage there. In late afternoon to sunset they descend with 6-foot wings and 3-foot legs extended towards an inelegant but secure landing amidst a cacophony of loud calling. Other large staging areas in Wisconsin include Horicon Marsh, Necedah National Wildlife Area, and Crex Meadows State Wildlife Area. The Wisconsin sandhills winter in areas from southern Indiana to Florida.

TRUMPETER SWAN

In 1893, the largest species of waterfowl in North America, the trumpeter swan, was extirpated from Wisconsin. It was reintroduced 100 years later. Of 385 eggs collected in Alaska by Wisconsin biologists and transported by the private funding of Terry and Mary Kohler of Sheboygan during 1989–1997, 356 (92%) hatched at the Milwaukee County Zoo, were reared in captivity, and placed in marshes with enough success that 29 years later they were removed from the Wisconsin endangered species list in 2009. In 2023, an estimated 13,643 trumpeter swans occured in Wisconsin.

CANADA GOOSE

By 1900, the Canada goose population was virtually eliminated in Wisconsin due to year-round market hunting, egg stealing, and habitat destruction. The early controversy of harvest quotas for the state and the dramatic explosion of the giant Canada goose population from extirpation to its presence on every golf course and boat dock in Wisconsin surprised the state's wildlifers! The population—giant and interior subspecies—increased because of habitat management such as controlled water levels and plantings on public lands, acquisition of additional state wildlife areas for migrating geese, and managed hunts. In 2022, the statewide breeding population was estimated at 180,000—a remarkable success. But even with a liberal hunting season now, geese have reached nuisance status in urban areas particularly, especially with their droppings in parks and elsewhere. To reduce the number of goose-use days in Wisconsin, geese have been hazed to hasten their migration south.

WOOD DUCK

The beautiful wood duck, with its whistling voice, was abundant and an important food source for early Wisconsin settlers, along with the other two important nesting ducks in Wisconsin: mallards and blue-winged teal. During the mid-1800s and early 1900s, wood ducks had been over-hunted in Wisconsin and elsewhere and their habitat drastically reduced from logging and elimination of beaver ponds due to beaver trapping. In 1901, the U.S. Biological Survey reported the wood duck facing extinction.

"Passage of the Migratory Bird Treaty Act (MBTA) in 1918, between the United States and Canada, probably saved this species from near extinction. Prior to the MBTA, waterfowl seasons usually extended from September to April, bag limits were either nonexistent or so large as to be meaningless, market hunting abounded, and enforcement was almost unknown. In the early 1900s, ornithologists and conservationists were so alarmed by the virtual disappearance of wood ducks that several voiced fears of their extinction." (p. 280)[9]

The wood duck population in Wisconsin and elsewhere has recovered through federal and state laws protecting it, improvement of nesting habitat with the maturing of second-growth forest, the management of beaver and beaver ponds, and establishment of wood duck nest boxes. The wood duck, with its clawed toes for grasping tree branches, nests only in tree cavities, which means larger trees that can accommodate a mature wood duck and eggs. Now, wood ducks are one of the four most abundant ducks in Wisconsin's fall hunting harvest, the others being mallards, green-winged teal, and blue-winged teal. Most of the ducks in the harvest breed in Wisconsin. In 2022, the wood duck population in Wisconsin was an estimated 175,000.

COMMON LOON

The common loon, a species of Special Concern in Wisconsin, occurs in the northern third of Wisconsin where the five-year census in 2020 indicated 4,115 territorial pairs nested, one pair per lake unless the lake is large. They winter in the Gulf of Mexico mostly from Gulf Shores, Alabama to Tampa Bay, Florida. Long-term studies have produced innovative live-trapping and telemetry methods. Problems for the loon population include shoreline "development" and associated power boat use, reduction of wetlands, monofilament fishing line entanglement, lead poisoning from ingesting fishing sinkers, and mercury poisoning from coal-fired electric power plants that release mercury in soot that drifts and settles in lakes and bioaccumulates in fish eaten by loons. Other problems include predation, nest abandonment from black flies and fluctuating water levels, poor water quality, Great Lakes botulism outbreaks from invasive species released from ballast tanks of ocean-going ships, and climate change.

DOUBLE-CRESTED CORMORANT

By 1965, double-crested cormorants were nearly extirpated from Wisconsin, with only 30 pairs remaining. In 20 years, this cormorant was removed from the endangered and threatened species list because of successful efforts to establish nesting platforms at Mead Wildlife Area and elsewhere in the state. By 1985, more than 2,200 pairs existed. Now cormorants require control at certain facilities like fish hatcheries.

RING-NECKED PHEASANT

Although not a native bird, the male ring-necked pheasant is highly sought by hunters and birdwatchers who appreciate the striking appearance and call of the pheasant rooster particularly. It was introduced to Wisconsin in 1910.[67] The pheasant stamp, required since 1991 for pheasant hunters, generates about $350,000 annually. It is used to maintain existing habitat, lease grassland nesting cover, grow grass on former cropland, share costs of keeping grasslands idle, and plant winter food plots. The U.S. Department of Agriculture's Conservation Reserve Program (CRP) greatly benefited wild pheasant populations in Wisconsin by paying landowners to take marginal farmland out of production. Then wildlife cover would be established on the property for a ten-year period. CRP enrolled hundreds of thousands of acres in Wisconsin (and elsewhere), which resulted in rising pheasant populations.

So popular are pheasants that for decades the Wisconsin Wildlife Division has sold day-old pheasant chicks to conservation clubs in Wisconsin and has raised and stocked pheasants for hunting, although such stocking does not increase wild populations. Now, about 60,000 day-old chicks are sold and about 50,000 pheasants are raised and stocked from the Wildlife Division's (expensive) Poynette Pheasant Farm.

FUR TRADE

A continent was explored, an indigenous race of people degraded, and its culture crushed, and many people died—in part because beaver fur produced better felt than any other fur did.[16] When the fur trade is mentioned, it is the beaver trade that is really meant. Other furs were taken incidental to beaver. Some, especially the rich sea otter, were far more valuable. But the root and core of the trade was indisputably beaver. The beaver felt hat, "the beaver," as the hat was called, was fashionable in Europe from about 1550 to 1850, and responsible for much of the beaver fur trade.

The fur trade was once one of the largest commercial enterprises in the world. Native tribes played a vital role in the fur trade, but almost always as trappers, almost never as merchants.

In Wisconsin, 20 species of furbearer exist (16 carnivores, three rodents, one marsupial), divided into long-haired furbearers (e.g., bobcat, wolf, fox) and short-haired furbearers (e.g., beaver, muskrat, otter, mink). The first Europeans were attracted to Wisconsin because of the fur trade, especially beaver.[64] They were the French from Montreal and Quebec, Jean Nicolet to be precise, in 1634 at Green Bay. Then Wisconsin was included in the territory known as New France, a vast area stretching through Labrador, Quebec, Ontario, Ohio, Indiana, Illinois, and Wisconsin. For more than a century from 1634 to 1763, the French controlled the fur trade in Wisconsin and elsewhere. At the end of the French and Indian War (1754–1763), France ceded all its land in Canada, even French-speaking Quebec, and all its land east of the Mississippi to Britain. The British took control of Wisconsin from 1763 to the end of the Revolutionary War in 1781, but stayed until 1814, when the Treaty of Ghent ended the War of 1812. Until then, the fur trade comprised most of Wisconsin's history, with most of the voyageurs still the same French-Canadians (from Quebec), although the fur trade was in decline in Wisconsin after 1778. During this entire time, the myriad of rivers and lakes bordering and crisscrossing Wisconsin facilitated travel for Native Americans, fur trappers and traders, missionaries, and settlers.[212]

As with lumbering, the fur trade was full of hardship and peril. It became less so with fur farms. By the 1920s, Wisconsin, Michigan, and Minnesota produced half the nation's commercial fur. By the 1940s, Wisconsin had twice as many fur farms, mostly mink and fox, as any other state. The Fromm Bros. had reportedly the largest fox farm in the world.[210] In 1936, TIME magazine reported 6,000 foxes on the Fromm Bros. ranch near Milwaukee and 2,000 foxes on their ranch near Wausau, all valued at about $1,500,000. In 2018, Wisconsin was the top mink farm producer in the U.S., producing more than 900,000 mink pelts, 1/3 of the nation's total. But fur prices have declined in recent years. Now, ranched mink are dying of Covid, and fur prices have fallen in recent years (571,750 Wisconsin mink pelts produced in 2022). And an anti-fur extremist group known as the Animal Liberation Front illegally releases mink from mink farms (3,000 from one farm in Wisconsin in 2023).

Even the government of Wisconsin got involved with fur farming. In 1934, the state built a fur farm near Poynette beside the state game farm that raised pheasants and other such critters. The state intended to stock annually 500–1,000 raccoons and 25–50 silver foxes and blue foxes (both color phases of the red fox), as well as mink, marten, fisher, muskrat, otter, and even the exotic and invasive nutria. Problems involved genetics, disease, and nutrition, including a carp-feeding project for mink. The Experimental Game and Fur Farm ceased operation in the late 1950s, and is now called simply the State Game Farm, raising pheasants for annual stocking.

BEAVER

At 35–65 pounds, the beaver is the largest rodent in North America and second largest in the world (after the nutria of South America). But the largest beaver on record was caught in 1921 in Iron County, Wisconsin—at 110 pounds. It is the only animal that can alter its environment to suit its needs, which affects other wildlife both positively and negatively.[111] Beaver are colonial and territorial, with one colony per pond. Beaver can be located easily by the presence of their cut trees, dams and ponds, lodges, and browse piles, lending themselves to aerial censusing in fall when lodges with adjacent winter browse piles can be spotted and counted.[196] Its habitat widely available, its abundance was high. The vulnerability of beaver stemmed from the obvious sign of its presence and its sedentary colonial lifestyle. For that reason, coupled with the demand for beaver fur, trappers systematically extirpated beaver from sections of North America, and moved on into new areas to trap.

By 1825, beaver were extirpated from southern Wisconsin, and by 1890 from the center of the state.[104] When beaver fur was so valuable, the beaver population in Wisconsin, as elsewhere in North America, had been exploited unsustainably. By 1900, an estimated 500 beaver existed in isolated colonies in northern Wisconsin. With a closed season in 1903, the beaver population increased.

Nuisance beaver are those interacting with humans in a negative way: cutting ornamental trees, flooding roads, flooding timber,[209] all of which occurs more often when pelt prices are low and fewer are therefore trapped. In the 1920s, nuisance beaver were live-trapped and moved to areas in Wisconsin unoccupied by beaver, thus expanding the population. By 1954, 56 of 72 Wisconsin counties had beaver again.

A beaver is time-consuming to catch (especially through the ice), to pelt (every bit must be cut off, unlike most furbearers), and to prepare the pelt for sale (scraping off all flesh and fat and then stretching by sewing to a hoop with loops every inch or by nailing on a board with nails every inch), so pelt price must be good for profit. (Stretching on a board is faster than on a hoop but the pelt dries flatter on a board, with less value.[194y]) From an estimated population of roughly 70,000 beaver in Wisconsin, during a managed trapping season about 3,000 trappers trap about 15,000–20,000 beaver annually,[150] depending on fur prices.

OTTER

The river otter was nearly extirpated from Wisconsin by 1900. So in 1915, otter trapping was illegal for 12 seasons. It has been seasonally opened annually since 1927, except for 1954. Periodic aerial surveys of otter tracks in snow help managers adjust season length and quota. Considered a secure population now, with about 10,000 in the state, about 1,400 are taken annually.

FISHER

Fur trapping and habitat loss extirpated fishers from Wisconsin by 1921. In 1956, ten fishers from New York and 20 from Minnesota were released into Nicolet National Forest in northeastern Wisconsin. In the next decade, until 1966, Ontario and New York contributed another 120 fishers released in Wisconsin. During 1966–67, at least 60 from Minnesota were released into

Chequamegon National Forest in Ashland and Bayfield counties. In 1985, a restrictive trapping season was opened. Fishers now occur in the northern half of the state,[67, 112, 150] with a population of about 5,000.

MARTEN

Through habitat deterioration and trapping, American marten became extirpated in Wisconsin by 1925.[67] During 1975–83, 172 marten from Ontario and Colorado were released into Nicolet National Forest. During 1987–90, 139 marten and during 2008–2010, 90 marten, all from Minnesota, were released into Chequamegon National Forest. Marten have spread into ten northern counties, but success has been minimal and no trapping season has been declared. Fisher, reintroduced before marten instead of the other way around, apparently prey on marten[150] and thus might suppress growth of an introduced marten population.[272] In 2020, the American marten remains Wisconsin's only endangered mammal. Another species of marten, the invasive stone marten from Europe, has established itself in southeastern Wisconsin after escaping from a fur farm in Burlington in the 1950s.[150]

WOLVERINE

In 1922, the last wolverine in Wisconsin was trapped in Sawyer County. The increasing human population with more roads and other habitat loss, coupled with the wolverine's large home range, have kept them extirpated, with little hope of recovery.

BADGER

Although uncommon, the badger is the state symbol and University of Wisconsin-Madison mascot (Bucky Badger). It is expanding its range where it had been extirpated, even spreading into state areas where it had been previously unknown.[104, 150, 151] Its normal range was the prairie and savanna of southern and sandy central Wisconsin where burrowing and foraging is easier for them. Now they occur in all 72 counties of the state. They were legally trapped from 1927 to 1955, from a high of 4,597 taken in 1938–39 to a low of 128 in 1954–55. Since 1955, no harvest of badgers has been allowed. Its estimated population in Wisconsin is 10,000.

BOBCAT

The bobcat was heavily trapped and shot for its fur. The bobcat was distributed throughout Wisconsin, but agriculture, trapping, and hunting mostly eliminated it from southern Wisconsin. Its prey base is confined mainly to forested regions, so most of the bobcats in Wisconsin occurred in the northern part of the state. In 1988, 1,300 were estimated to be in Wisconsin. Now 3,500 are estimated in the state. Through analysis of its annual fur returns and adjustment of seasons, the bobcat population has been managed carefully for sustained yield. Once again bobcats can be found throughout Wisconsin. The harvest goal is to take 550 bobcats in northern Wisconsin and 200 in southern Wisconsin. About 70% are shot over dogs and about 30% are trapped.

GRAY WOLF

Through habitat loss but mainly persecution including bounties from 1839 to 1957, wolves were extirpated from Wisconsin by the 1950s.[246, 247] An estimated 3,000–5,000 lived throughout Wisconsin in the early 1800s.[150] Unlike predators such as the reintroduced fisher and marten, wolves provoke animosity from some humans, especially some deer hunters. Beginning in the 1970s, wolves introduced themselves from Minnesota. In 1985, only 14 wolves were detected in the state. The over-winter population for 2021–2022 was estimated at 812–1193 wolves (average = 972) in 288 packs (average = 3.4 wolves/pack) in the northern and central forested regions of Wisconsin, and another 600 wolves or so in the Upper Peninsula of Michigan. In the continental United States, Wisconsin has the highest human density in any wolf-recovered area and the second highest number of wolves in the Lower 48 states.

In 2012, a hunting and trapping season on wolves was authorized. That year 117 wolves were taken, 257 in 2013, and 154 in 2014, before wolves were again restored to the U.S. Endangered Species List. After wolves were released from it in January 2021, a lawsuit required the Wisconsin Wildlife Division to set a wolf harvest season in February 2021, rather than waiting until

November as the WDNR wanted. A harvest goal of 200 was set to stabilize the population, with 119 for state-licensed hunters and trappers and 81 to Native tribes, which hold wolves sacred and generally do not kill them. The hunt was to occur over seven days, 22–28 Feb, but was ended in two days when 218 wolves were reported killed, 99 (83%) above the quota of 119. Trappers took 5%, hunters calling or baiting took 9%, and hunters with dogs took 86%.

This is an example of biopolitics interfering with wildlife management, of ignorance trumping science—in the 21st century (see Chapter 4). Of some 245 wolf packs outside Native reservations in Wisconsin, the WDNR's Wildlife Division estimated a 24–40% decline in reproduction due to loss of bred females and alpha males. The wolf hunt for fall 2021 was complicated by lawsuits from the Chippewa in Wisconsin, a coalition of wildlife advocacy groups in Wisconsin, a hunter advocacy group—and incompatibility on the issue between the Wisconsin Wildlife Division and the Wisconsin Natural Resources Board.

Humans love dogs. Maybe the general human dislike of wolves stems from the fact that wolves and dogs are the same genus and many breeds of dogs, e.g., huskies and German shepherds, are similar in appearance to wolves but that wolves can be dangerous to humans physically and monetarily through damage to livestock and pets; thus, they might be considered disloyal and untrustworthy *dogs*.[248] That notion might be reinforced by the villainous *big bad wolf* in childhood stories such as "Little Red Riding Hood" and "The Three Little Pigs." And some folks don't like wolves because they eat deer (thus competing with human hunters), as though wolves therefore do not belong in the ecosystem. But wolves suppress the coyote population, which increases fawn survival and the fox population in our complicated ecosystem. Wolves can cause agricultural damage; from 2012 to 2022, an annual average of 29 farms has had verified wolf depredation, paid for by Wisconsin taxpayers through the WDNR.[270] A controversial species, if wolves had not dispersed into Wisconsin on their own, the Wisconsin legislature is unlikely to have authorized them for reintroduction to its ecosystem. Wolves also have cultural status with some Wisconsin Indian tribes. All of this makes wolves difficult to manage—not biologically, but socially and culturally, even in the 21st century.

In May 2021, an article by agricultural and economic researchers reported that a study conducted in Wisconsin between 1988 and 2010 found that deer/vehicle collisions were reduced 24%, with reduced injury and death and a savings of $10.9 million each year.[211w] That's because wolves use human paths like roads and rights-of-way to facilitate predation on deer; deer respond to it and avoid those areas—a human societal benefit of having wolves in the ecosystem. That makes the economic value of wolves greater than the costs of verified wolf predation on livestock. Wolves also might slow the spread of CWD (see White-tailed Deer).

In February 2022, wolves were again restored federally as a threatened species under the Endangered Species Act. That means no hunting or trapping of wolves. In late winter 2022, the DNR estimated Wisconsin had 972 wolves in 288 packs. Its status is under constant discussion and review by the DNR and private wildlife groups in Wisconsin, and even the legislature! In 2023, the Wildlife Division completed developing a plan for wolf management[270] written by many Wildlife Division writers with input from several nongovernmental organizations—and the legislature—all struggling with a management plan for a fascinating but controversial native animal in the biodiversity of the Wisconsin ecosystem. Approved in 2023,[270] the plan calls for maintaining a flexible population of about 800–1,200 wolves in the state. A success story, wolves have recovered in Wisconsin.

Wildlife Biologist Neil Payne, Newfoundland and Labrador Wildlife Division, measuring and injecting extra Sernylan to tranquilize and tag a nuisance large male Newfoundland black bear (a distinct race) for transport to Long Island in Terra Nova National Park, 1969. (The bear returned 9 miles by swimming 1.25 miles of ocean).

left: Neil Payne with saber, captain of U. Wisconsin fencing team, 1960–61; *right*: 1st Lt. Neil Payne, USMC, with M14 rifle, .45 pistol, and Ka-Bar knife in Vietnam, Christmas 1966.

Great Possessions (on wall of Payne's house in Newfoundland; in lower left corner of frame is a pin with 424, house number of Aldo Leopold's office, given at Leopold's centennial celebration in 1987 at the University of Wisconsin–Madison). Photo by Bruce Paddock.

Left to right, Row 1: Fred Hamerstrom, Fran Hamerstrom, Dick Taber, Bob McCabe, Alice Harper Stokes (secy), Joe Hickey. Row 2: Dan Q. Thompson, Tony deVos, Don R. Thompson, Jim Hale, Doug Wade, Allen Stokes. Row 3: Lyle Sowls, Cy Kabat, Fred Greeley, Al Hochbaum, Art Hawkins, Bob Ellarson. (Not pictured: Harold Hanson, Irv Buss, Steve Richards, Orville Lee.) Photo from McCabe 1987.

Aldo Leopold's Graduate Students (from McCabe 1987).

Fred (1909–90) and Fran (1907–98) Hamerstrom (courtesy Elva Hamerstrom Paulson for Hamerstrom Family Collection, Ruth Hine).

Aldo Leopold family at The Shack. Back row: Aldo, Estella Bergere Leopold, Luna, Starker; Front row: Nina, Estella Jr., Gus; Photographer: Carl; 1939 (courtesy Aldo Leopold Foundation and University of Wisconsin-Madison Archives).

Gaylord Nelson (1916–2005)

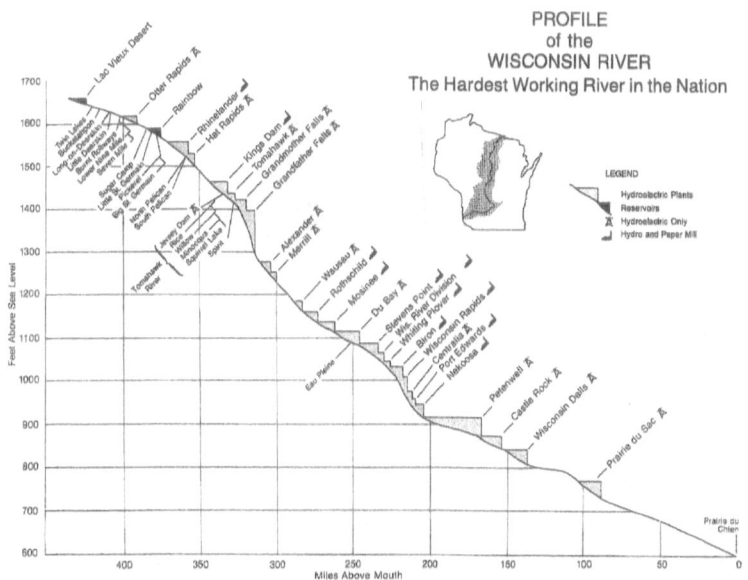

The Wisconsin River

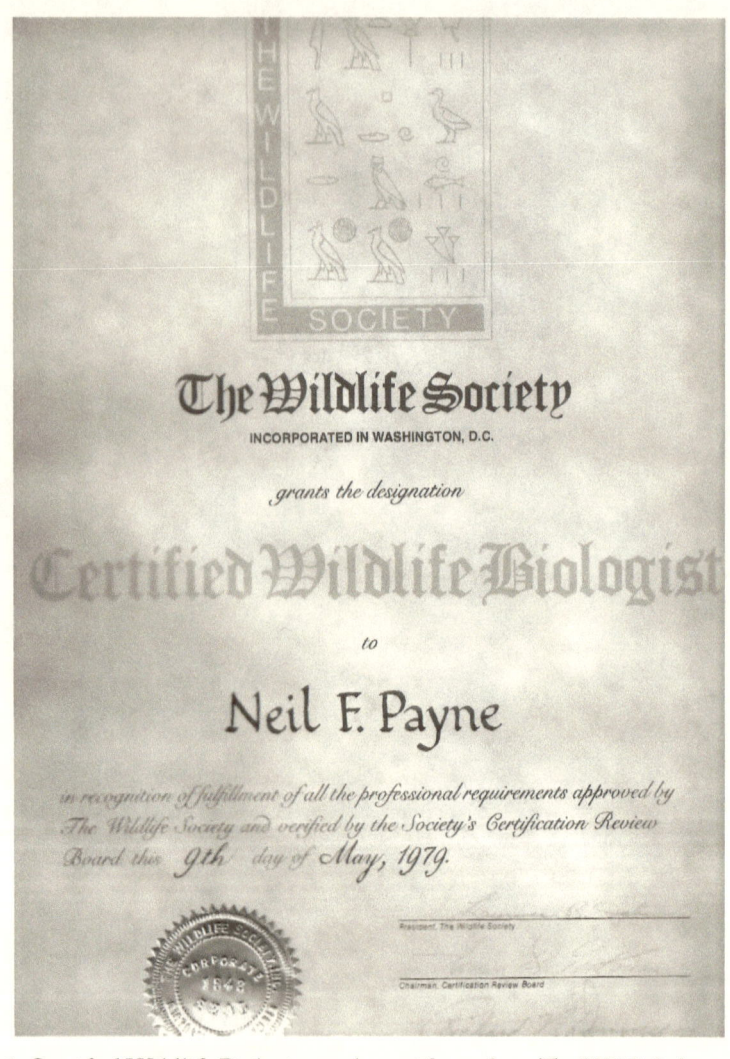

The Wildlife Society
INCORPORATED IN WASHINGTON, D.C.

grants the designation

Certified Wildlife Biologist

to

Neil F. Payne

in recognition of fulfillment of all the professional requirements approved by The Wildlife Society and verified by the Society's Certification Review Board this 9th *day of* May, 1979.

President, The Wildlife Society

Chairman, Certification Review Board

left: Certified Wildlife Biologist, early certificate from The Wildlife Society. (1979); *right, top*: Charter members, January 1963, Virginia Tech Student Chapter of The Wildlife Society (from *Virginia Tech Forester*, Volume XV, June 1963). **Back row** (L-R): W. Alan Guthrie, Tom Hearn, Chris Martin, Edward Folson, Neil F. Payne, Fairfax H. Settle, Joseph P. Bachant; **Middle row** (L-R): Joe Bobb, Claud Oleyar, Donald R. Guthrie, Joe Via, Dr. Henry S. Mosby (Faculty Advisor), Frank Hollis; **Front row** (L-R): Gene W. Wood, David R. Patton (President), Joseph S. Larson (Vice President); *right, bottom*: prototype *Wildlife Techniques Manual* (1958)

Manual of Wildlife Techniques

Wildlife Society

Wildlife Techniques Committee

I. McT. Cowan
David E. Davis
Alexander C. Martin
Horace F. Quick
Richard D. Taber
Antoon de Vos
Henry S. Mosby, Chairman

Published by
The Wildlife Society

1958

The late Guy Baldassarre with Neil's sons, Adam and Mark.

A classic book and revisions: *Ducks, Geese, and Swans of North America* (Kortright 1942, Bellrose 1976, Baldassarre 2014).

Aldo Leopold Memorial Award recipient Richard D. Taber (*left*) in 2008, with Neil F. Payne at the Annual Conference of The Wildlife Society in Miami.

Last surviving Leopold grad student dies in Montana

Richard D. Taber

Richard D. Taber, "Last Surviving Leopold Grad Student, Dies in Montana" (courtesy *Wisconsin Outdoor News*)

Wildlife, Conservation, and Human Welfare (Kreiger 2003)
by Richard D. Taber and Neil F. Payne

May 1967. Neil Forrest Payne, future Professor of Wildlife Ecology at the University of Wisconsin–Stevens Point; his son, Adam Neil Payne, future Secretary of the Wisconsin Department of Natural Resources.

Neil and Adam Payne, present day.

Wildlife Professor Neil Payne presenting BA diploma to his daughter Erin, UWSP, 1998.

Passage of time—three generations deer hunting: son Mark, grandson Forrest (Adam's son), son Adam, Neil Payne

6.

WILDLIFE HABITAT DIVERSITY

ECOLOGICAL DIVERSITY

The ecological diversity influencing wildlife in Wisconsin is exceptional.[267] Wisconsin's landscape inspired Aldo Leopold, John Muir, Gaylord Nelson, and Wisconsin's other great conservation leaders of our nation (see Chapter 1). All plants depend upon soils and climate—and that of course influences wildlife. The vast variety of geology[48, 164] and plant associations[19, 39, 56, 57] in Wisconsin influences the location and produces the vast variety and abundance of animal communities.[212x, 260] Accordingly, Wisconsin's wildlife management program is comprehensively diverse and thus complex (see Chapters 4 and 5).

MAJOR HABITAT TYPES

In Wisconsin, three natural frontiers of the North American landscape merge: dry grasslands sweep in from the west, the great hardwood forest advances from the east, and the boreal forest extends from the north. Wisconsin has 99 natural communities grouped into eight major habitat categories: northern forest, southern forest, oak savanna, barrens, grassland, wetland, aquatic, and miscellaneous.[266] These major habitat types are divided into 16 ecological landscapes. The Wisconsin Department of Natural Resources[267] provided an ecosystem management perspective

133

with a description of Wisconsin's landscape before European settlement and how it has changed.

Major geologic landscape features in Wisconsin that affect wildlife habitat and associated wildlife are 1) Baraboo Hills, 2) Gogebic and Trap Ranges, 3) Blue Hills, 4) margin of the northern ice lobes, 5) Northern Highlands, 6) Central Sand Plains, 7) Lower Wisconsin River valley, 8) Blue Mounds, 9) drumlins of the southern Green Bay Lobe, 10) Kettle Moraine, 11) Green Bay and Fox River lowland, 12) marginal ridge of the Green Bay Lobe, 13) Niagara Escarpment, and 14) Driftless Area.

Before European settlement, Wisconsin was at least 95% forested with magnificent virgin forests: in the north, pine, hemlock, spruce, tamarack, birch, maple, elm, ash, aspen, and cedar; in the south, ash, basswood, oak, cherry, elm, aspen, hickory, maple, and walnut. Oaks predominated in the southern 15 million acres of hardwood forest. The northern 20 million acres were in mainly coniferous forest dominated by white pine but with many deciduous tree species. By 1924, the pine had been cut in the north and agriculture covered most of the south.[67] As of 2023, Wisconsin has 17.1 million acres of forest, covering nearly half the state (46%). As to old-growth forest—essentially a nonrenewable resource—unfortunately the greedy lumber barons destroyed it, and the wildlife dependent on it. Sadly, the largest stand of old growth remaining in Wisconsin, Cathedral Pines in Chequamegon-Nicolet National Forest, is just 40 acres. Wildlife associated with old growth in Wisconsin has taken a severe hit (see Chapter 7).

Only 0.5% (13,000 acres) of fragmented prairie remains in Wisconsin of the original 2,600,000-acre grassland (prairie) ecosystem, with few remaining prairies exceeding 50 acres. In the 1800s, more than 5,000,000 acres of oak savanna existed, compared to only a few thousand acres now, mostly privately owned. Less than 1% of pre-settlement oak and pine barren habitat remains.

Before Columbus arrived in 1492, indigenous peoples used fire extensively to set back succession on prairie and in forest, knowing that most game species of wildlife are associated with early successional stages or with habitat edge. In many if not most terrestrial landscapes, fire is a dominating factor, from lightning and humans. Prairies were lush with fresh grass after the old dead grass was burned off, encouraging bison in southern Wisconsin and elsewhere. Many forests recovering from fire tended to be park-like or brushy in appearance, with little old growth. As Mann[161] observed: "When Indian societies disintegrated from disease and mistreatment, forest invaded savanna in Wisconsin.... Europeans forgot what the landscape looked like before and why.... Indians retooled ecosystems to encourage elk, deer, and bear. Constant burning of undergrowth increased the numbers of herbivores, the predators that fed on them, and the people who ate them both" (p. 283).

It was the same throughout the Americas. Even today, controlled burns are used to improve prairie, savanna, forest, and wetland.[197]

TENSION ZONE

Wisconsin is uniquely and bizarrely divided by an ecotone called the Tension Zone, identified and named by plant ecologist John Curtis.[39] It is 10 to 40 miles wide extending diagonally in an S-shape through the state southeast to northwest from Milwaukee County to Polk County. In it, southern and northern species of plants and animals overlap, from the southern broadleaf forest of southern Wisconsin and beyond and the northern mixed forest of northern Wisconsin and beyond (e.g., southern flying squirrel and northern flying squirrel[55]). The tension zone has to do with climate, i.e., a climate gradient in the zone, with warmer, drier conditions to the south and relatively cooler, moister conditions to the north. Global warming, i.e., global climate change is changing things, probably moving the Tension Zone north.

THE WISCONSIN GLACIER AND THE DRIFTLESS AREA

The glaciers and meltwater streams of the Ice Age have left Wisconsin a landscape of great diversity and beauty. The most recent glacier to flow into Wisconsin began 75,000 years ago, retreating 11,000 years ago. Nowhere is the glacier's mark upon the land more impressive than in Wisconsin, which has lent its name to it. The Wisconsin Glacier, an incredible mile high at least, covered much of Canada and the United States including two-thirds of Wisconsin, leaving river valleys, lakes, gently rolling hills, and ridges, with kames, drumlins, moraines, striations, eskers, kettles, and erratics—all in six lobes in Wisconsin: Superior Lobe, Chippewa Lobe, Wisconsin Valley Lobe, Langlade Lobe, Green Bay Lobe, Lake Michigan Lobe. Southwestern and part of central Wisconsin were untouched by the massive ice sheets of the Pleistocene Epoch and is referred to as the Driftless Area. This area has no glacial drift, i.e., no rocky debris deposited by glaciers. The Driftless Area is a landscape of deep valleys, rolling hills, flat land, and steep cliffs, much of it carved by water as the glaciers melted. The Driftless Area in southwest Wisconsin contains isolated hills, bluffs (especially along the Mississippi River), mesas, buttes, pinnacles, and coulees (river valleys). About 19,000 years ago, the Green Bay Lobe extended to four miles east of The Dells of the Wisconsin River, on the extreme eastern margin of the Driftless Area.

Wisconsin's rocks, boulders, and cliffs consist mostly of sandstone, limestone, granite, and 1.7-billion-year-old quartzite. This variety produces diverse waterfalls such as Tyler Forks Cascades, Big Manitou Falls, Willow Falls, Lost Creek Falls, Copper Falls, Grandfather Falls, and Now and Then Falls, with associated fish and wildlife. The highest point in Wisconsin, at 1,951 feet above sea level, is Timms Hill in Timms Hill County Park, near Ogema in north-central Wisconsin, with Rib Mountain a close second at 1,942 feet above sea level, in Rib Mountain State Park near Wausau in central Wisconsin.

Ecologically unique in the Midwest, the Baraboo Hills of Sauk and Columbia counties are all that remain of one of the most ancient rock outcrops in North America. Located within an agricultural landscape, the Baraboo Hills rise 700 feet with piles of broken rock called talus on the slopes of the bluffs. The Green Bay Lobe of the glacier deposited moraines that block each end of an ancient valley that now contains Devil's Lake and Devil's Lake State Park. The forest covering the hills is the largest block of upland forest still standing in southern Wisconsin.

With more than 1,800 species of animals and plants, the Baraboo Hills provide important breeding and nesting habitat for songbirds, such as Acadian flycatchers, Canada warblers, and hooded warblers, which require large unfragmented blocks of forest. The Baraboo Hills support one of the most important communities of forest-interior birds in the Midwest.

Two miles south of the Baraboo Hills is Natural Bridge State Park, with the Leland Natural Bridge archway 35 feet long and 25 feet high at center. About 35 miles south of the Baraboo Hills, just east of Blue Mound State Park, is Cave of the Mounds, 70 feet deep and about a half mile long, a natural National Landmark. A tourist attraction, it opened in 1940 with its handsome stalagmites and stalactites. Some 250 caves exist in Wisconsin.

Established in 1971 and containing 32,500 acres, the Ice Age National Scientific Reserve in Wisconsin includes landforms of the Wisconsin glaciation. It contains nine sites, mostly Wisconsin state parks or other protected areas, to preserve geological evidence of glaciation: 1) Campbellsport Drumlins State Park (Campbellsport), 2) Chippewa Moraine State Recreation Area (New Auburn), 3) Cross Plains State Park (Cross Plains), 4) Devil's Lake State Park (Baraboo), 5) Horicon Marsh State Wildlife Area (Horicon), 6) Interstate State Park (St. Croix Falls), 7) Kettle Moraine State Forest, Northern Unit (Glenbeulah and Kewaskum), 8) Mill Bluff State Park (Camp Douglas), 9) Two Creeks Buried Forest State Natural Area (Two Creeks). Some of these are connected by the Ice Age National Scenic Trail. Ice Age National Scientific Reserve is affiliated with the National Park Service and administered by the Wisconsin Department of Natural Resources.

In some areas the terrain is flat where glacial meltwater carried and dropped sand and other fine soils, accommodating huge agricultural fields of mostly corn, potatoes, and beans watered with circular irrigation units pumping groundwater. The terminal moraine of the glacier is clearly visible. Just behind the terminal moraine, in the tilled fields of the glaciated area can be seen the last of the stone fencerows and the stone piles in the center of large fields where farmers piled rocks from "picking stone," i.e., picking rocks out of fields in order to till them, a periodic duty in glaciated areas as new rocks are brought to the surface via frost heave. Difficult to move or otherwise disturb, these rock piles and fencerows provide crevices for burrowing animals and nesting sites as herbaceous and woody vegetation develop in and around the piles to make good wildlife cover.

Niagara Falls in Ontario and New York, and the Door Peninsula in Wisconsin, have something in common. Both are part of the Niagara Cuesta, or Niagara Escarpment, a cliff, bluff, or ridge which runs prominently between them and includes them. The Niagara Escarpment is a UNESCO World Biosphere Reserve Escarpment. Soils are glacial: gravel, sand, and clay over limestone. The escarpment extends 230 miles along the Door Peninsula through the Bayshore Blufflands and then more inland along the western coast of Lake Michigan and Milwaukee ending northwest of Chicago near the Wisconsin–Illinois border. Within High Cliff State Park, on the northeast corner of Lake Winnebago, are various geometric and animal effigy mounds and the remains of an early limestone quarry and kiln, indicating the use that prehistoric and modern humans made of the escarpment, culturally and economically. Just east of Fond du Lac, the Niagara Escarpment contains a prominent feature known here as "The Ledge." Cliffs along the Niagara Escarpment contain the oldest forest ecosystem in eastern North America.

FRESHWATER HAVEN: RIVERS, LAKES, WETLANDS

Wisconsin borders the largest surface freshwater system in the world—the Great Lakes. Wisconsin has Lake Superior to the north, Lake Michigan to the east, the Mississippi River to the west, the Wisconsin River in the center, 7,446 streams totaling 56,884 miles, 15,074 lakes, and scattered wetlands of bog, fen, marsh, and swamp throughout. Nearly all the natural lakes in Wisconsin have resulted from glaciers. Wisconsin contains 11,188 square miles of water, more freshwater than all but two other states (Michigan and Florida; Alaska too, ten times larger than Wisconsin), and 147 species of fish.

Lake Winnebago and its supporting waters—the Wolf River and Lake Butte de Morts, Lake Winneconne, and Lake Poygan—support the largest concentration of lake sturgeon in the world, with spring spawning concentrations a tourist attraction at the Wolf and Embarrass rivers where sturgeon first spawn at age 25, then every four years. The lake sturgeon is a prehistoric relic (200,000,000 years ago), the oldest-living (about 150 years) and largest (up to 250 pounds) fish species in the Great Lakes area.

The 120-mile Baraboo River is the longest restored free-flowing river in the United States. The heavily used Fox River is one of the few rivers in the U.S. that flows north. The Upper Mississippi River National Wildlife and Fish Refuge is the longest river refuge in the nation, at 261 miles. The fourth highest waterfall east of the Rockies is 165-foot Big Manitou Falls on the Black River in Pattison State Park, Douglas County. And with its 28 lakes, the Eagle River chain of lakes is the largest in the world. The deepest lake in Wisconsin is Green Lake (236 feet). Madison's Lake Mendota is the most studied lake in the world. The largest lake in Wisconsin is Lake Winnebago (137,708 acres).

Wisconsin has destroyed almost half (47%) of its original 10,000,000 acres of wetlands (24% of the state) through draining and filling; only 5,300,000 acres remain. In 1971, more than 160 countries met in Ramsar, Iran, to identify and protect the world's most important wetlands. Wisconsin is home to five of these worldwide Wetlands of International Importance: 1) Chiwaukee Prairie Illinois Beach Lake Plain (3,914 acres straddling the Wisconsin and Illinois state lines), 2) Door Peninsula Coastal Wetlands (11,443 acres and 22.55 miles of Lake Michigan shoreline), 3) Horicon Marsh (33,000 acres), 4) Upper Mississippi River Floodplain Marshes (302,000 acres), 5) Kakagon and Bad River Sloughs (10,760 acres along Lake Superior's south shore).

TWO GREAT LAKES

Of the five Great Lakes—Superior, Michigan, Huron, Ontario, and Erie—Wisconsin borders the two largest: Lake Superior and Lake Michigan. By total area, the Great Lakes are the largest group of freshwater lakes on Earth. The Great Lakes have been called inland seas because of their sea-like characteristics such as sustained winds, rolling waves, strong currents, great depths, and distant horizons. They are connected to the Atlantic Ocean via the St. Lawrence River. Wisconsin has 153 miles of shoreline along Lake Superior and 850 miles along Lake Michigan. Wisconsin shorelines of these two Great Lakes contain a variety of geologic habitats including large and small sandy beaches, rocky beaches, rock cliffs, sand dunes, and wetlands, some of which are in state, county, and city parks. They support a commercial fishery mainly for lake trout and whitefish, the value of which is $22.5 million annually in the U.S. The lakes also support an active sport fishery for stocked salmon and trout and in localized places, muskellunge and walleye. Early season hunting occurs for dabbling ducks and late season hunting for diving ducks. During migration, 35 species of shorebirds use the lakes to maintain and to build up fat reserves.

The world's largest freshwater estuary is Green Bay in Lake Michigan, where the Fox River flows into it through the city of Green Bay, the oldest city in Wisconsin. The bay is confined by the Door Peninsula on the east and the Wisconsin and Michigan mainland on the west. Here is where beaver were first trapped in the 1600s for European hat makers. Jutting into Lake Michigan, Door County has more shoreline (250 miles) than any other county in the nation. The Door Peninsula has five state parks and some ten county parks. Its picturesque villages nestled in harbors between bold headlands have been compared to the coastal retreats of New England. The oldest lighthouse in Wisconsin is the Potawatomi Lighthouse, built in 1836 and rebuilt in 1858, in Rock Island State Park.

The Kakagon/Bad River Sloughs at the eastern end of Lake Superior's Chequamegon Bay contain 16,000 acres of wild rice, wetlands, streams, and open water, the largest and healthiest estuary system remaining in the upper Great Lakes region. Stretching across Ashland, Bayfield, and Iron counties is a 700,000-acre watershed that feeds the sloughs and contains 28 different plant communities, 72 rare and endangered animals and plants, and an intact forest community important to many breeding and migratory neotropical songbirds. At the extreme west of Lake Superior, between Duluth, Minnesota and Superior, Wisconsin, Superior Bay contains the largest freshwater port in the world, the Duluth-Superior Harbor (its accompanying water/soil pollution being cleaned up).

Wisconsin is second to Michigan in the length of its Great Lakes coastline. Wisconsin would have been first if Michigan hadn't become a state in 1837 before Wisconsin in 1848, with that part of the Wisconsin Territory, the so-called Upper Peninsula of Michigan, or UP, given to Michigan by the U.S. government to compensate Michigan for its lost territorial dispute with Ohio. Bordered by Lake Michigan and Lake Superior, and also by Wisconsin rather than the rest of Michigan, the UP is 16,377 square miles and 90% forested, with 1,700 miles of Great Lakes shoreline, more than 4,300 lakes, and 12,000 miles of streams. (When the border between Minnesota and Wisconsin was formed politically in 1846 for Wisconsin's statehood in 1848, if the border had continued along the Mississippi River north and then east to Lake Superior, as discussed then, instead of veering off along the St. Croix River, Wisconsin could have had two capitals: Madison and St. Paul. The Mississippi River separates the Twin Cities of Minneapolis and St. Paul.)

MISSISSIPPI RIVER

The Mississippi River and its branch the Missouri River comprise the fourth longest river combination in the world (after the Nile, Amazon, and Yangtze rivers). The Mississippi River drains a watershed of 1,151,000 square miles between the Rocky Mountains and the Appalachian Mountains. The 2,320-mile Mississippi River has 235 miles of it separating Wisconsin from Iowa and Minnesota. It runs from the southern border of Wisconsin to Minnesota's Twin Cities where it meets the St. Croix River. The Wisconsin stretch of the river has 4 locks and dams and numerous wing dams that facilitate river travel and back the river into reservoirs covering once shallow water and sand bars. Along it runs Wisconsin's portion of the National Scenic Byway, part of the Great River Road running along the river through ten states.

The portion of the Mississippi River in Wisconsin contains the Upper Mississippi River National Wildlife and Fish Refuge and Trempealeau National Wildlife Refuge.

The Upper Mississippi River (extending south to St. Louis) and its floodplain provides habitat for 45 species of mammals, 37 species of reptiles and amphibians, 260 species of fish, 37 species of freshwater mussels, and is a globally important flyway for 60% (326 species) of North American birds including 40% of North American waterfowl. The Mississippi River's main problem is agricultural pollution from fertilizer, pesticide, and sediment loads which cause a dead zone of hypoxic water 6,000–7,000 square miles at its mouth in the Gulf of Mexico where few organisms can live and massive fish die-offs can occur.

Various organizations try to balance the needs of wildlife and fish with recreation, agriculture, industry, and navigation. The Upper Mississippi River (from Minneapolis to the confluence with the Ohio River) supports not only hunting and trapping but also recreational and commercial fishing. Recreation and tourism employ 143,000 people in the Upper Mississippi River corridor. Recreational visits to the Upper Mississippi River exceed that of most national parks including Yellowstone, resulting in huge economic value.

TWO CONTINENTAL WATERSHEDS

Wisconsin is connected to the Gulf of St. Lawrence and to the Gulf of Mexico. The St. Lawrence River Divide cuts through the state, extending from the Laurentian Divide in Minnesota north of the headwaters of the Mississippi River, through Wisconsin north of the Wisconsin River headwaters to just south of Lake Michigan in Illinois, then across northern Indiana, Ohio, northern New York, Vermont, New Hampshire, Maine, New Brunswick, and through Nova Scotia. Rivers in eastern Wisconsin drain east and north to Lake Michigan and Lake Superior, 577 feet above sea level, through the Great Lakes, and ultimately out the St. Lawrence River through Canada into the Gulf of St. Lawrence in the Atlantic Ocean between the Maritime Provinces and Newfoundland and Labrador. That river is now the St. Lawrence

Seaway, opened in 1959, with a series of 15 locks and dams that permit commercial ship traffic from the ocean to cities like Milwaukee and Chicago (bringing with it in the ballast tanks such invasive species as sea lampreys and zebra mussels).

Rivers in western Wisconsin are in the Continental Divide that traverses the Rocky Mountains. These Wisconsin rivers flow into the Wisconsin River and the Mississippi River. The Mississippi Watershed drains streams between the Rocky Mountains and the Appalachian Mountains into the Gulf of Mexico at Louisiana. The Mississippi River drops about 1,000 feet from Minnesota to sea level through its 29 locks and dams.

A portage through Portage, Wisconsin, of 1.4 miles between the Fox River and the Wisconsin River, connected these two watersheds of the Great Lakes (to the Gulf of St. Lawrence) and the Mississippi River (to the Gulf of Mexico), and accommodated the fur trade so heavily exploited in Wisconsin. The Ho-Chunk charged a fee for this portage. To avoid this fee and to facilitate transporting boats, people, and goods between the Fox and Wisconsin rivers, a canal was dug, starting in 1838, but, due to much difficulty, not completed until 1876 by the U.S. Army Corps of Engineers. As the closest point in Wisconsin between the Fox River and the Wisconsin River, the Portage Canal, through present-day Portage, connects the St. Lawrence River Divide and the Continental Divide. The Portage Canal connects the North Atlantic Ocean and the Gulf of Mexico via the St. Lawrence River, the Great Lakes, and the Mississippi River. It was 2.5 miles long, 75 feet wide, and 7 feet deep. The canal closed to commercial traffic in 1951, but is visible today and restored for tourism, and is a leg of the Ice Age Trail in Wisconsin. The Portage Canal is on the National and State Register of Historic Places. (The town of Portage was once in Portage County, a large county created in 1836 in the Wisconsin Territory. The name was changed to Columbia County, created in 1846 in the Wisconsin Territory two years before Wisconsin became a state in 1848, with Portage its county seat. Portage County is now a smaller, northern part of the original county, with Stevens Point the county seat.)

WISCONSIN RIVER

In Portage County of central Wisconsin, just a few miles north of the Buena Vista Marsh where the Hamerstroms gained fame with their prairie chicken work, I live on the shore of the Wisconsin River. It begins its journey from the headwaters at Lac Vieux Desert bordering Wisconsin and Michigan, and passes my dock and Leopold's Shack en route to the Mississippi River and the Gulf of Mexico. This major river lies solely within the state,[45, 49] cutting through the middle of it before heading west in southern Wisconsin to the Mississippi River. It has 27 dams[68] and 60 bridges: 38 highway bridges, 21 railroad bridges, and one foot bridge.[45]

Four distinct types of drainage, and associated plants and wildlife, make the Wisconsin River system unique.[45, 49] First, in northern Wisconsin, almost 1,500 lakes and ponds cause the river to widen over a region of the most recent glacial drift and then over older glacial drift in the Merrill area. Second, the river winds through a comparatively recent sandy plain from Stevens Point to Wisconsin Dells. Third, the river flows through the glacial drift region from Wisconsin Dells to Sauk Prairie, the nickname for the adjacent villages of Sauk City and Prairie du Sac. Fourth, the river then flows to the Mississippi River through the driftless limestone region of few swamps and lakes.

The Wisconsin River is 430 miles long, traveling through three geographic provinces: Northern Highland, Central Plain, and Western Upland. From Lac Vieux Desert the river drops 1,050 feet to its mouth in the Mississippi River near Prairie du Chien. The Wisconsin River watershed is 12,280 square miles and drains nearly 25% of Wisconsin into the Mississippi River.

The upper Wisconsin River (338 miles) runs through glaciated area and has many dams and reservoirs (see Chapter 7). The lower Wisconsin River (92 miles) runs through unglaciated (driftless) area. Like Everglades National Park in Florida, the Lower Wisconsin Riverway was recognized, in 2020, as a Wetland of International Importance by the United States and the Ramsar Convention on Wetlands, one of six in Wisconsin and 40 in the U.S. (Signed in Ramsar, Iran, in 1971, the Ramsar Convention on Wetlands is an international treaty for the conservation and sustainable use of wetlands.)

Since 1989, about 45,000 acres of land on both sides of the lower Wisconsin River running west have been designated the Lower Wisconsin State Riverway, managed by the WDNR; the Riverway's special scenic performance standards are administered by the Lower Wisconsin State Riverway Board (a separate state agency). The longest free-flowing stretch of the river, it flows 92.3 miles unimpeded by any man-made structure from the dam at Prairie du Sac downstream to its mouth at the Mississippi River, which it enters about three miles south of Prairie du Chien. Human activity on private land within the Waterway has restrictions. The Riverway contains 98 species of fish, 38 species of reptiles and amphibians, 45 species of mussels, 140 species of birds, and 39 species of mammals.

The massive Glacial Lake Wisconsin was eight times the size of Lake Winnebago. It was formed during the last Wisconsin Glacier when the Green Bay Lobe of the Laurentide Ice Sheet blocked the Wisconsin River at the outlet at Baraboo Hills, backing water up to Wisconsin Rapids. As the glacier melted, it left Glacial Lake Wisconsin about 150 feet deep and more than 1,800 square miles, the size of Utah's Great Salt Lake—until the ice dam broke 14,000 years ago. A flood was released that carved out stunning geologic wonders of exposed sandstone cliffs and tall rock formations, such as iconic Stand Rock, along five miles of the Wisconsin River at Wisconsin Dells. As a result, this area, called the Dells, has developed into a heavy tourist destination where obsolete military amphibious ducks and other passenger boats are used to view the formations.

PUBLIC LAND AND PROTECTED PRIVATE LAND

NATIVE LAND

Of 574 federally recognized Native American tribes in the U.S. and some 50 in Canada, about 300 languages were spoken. Another 80 were spoken in Mexico and Central America, and about 500 in South America. Thus, rather than the 10,000 to 25,000 years ago archeologists say the first immigrants came to

North America, linguists say that more than 50,000 years were needed for North America and South America to become two of the most linguistically complex areas in the world.[235]

At least 24 Native American tribes have occupied Wisconsin at various times,[18,149] ten of them when Europeans first arrived in 1634: Mascoutin, Kickapoo, Fox (Meskwaki), Sauk, Ho-Chunk (Winnebago), Menominee, Chippewa (Ojibwe), Potawatomi, Ottawa, and Dakota Sioux. Other tribes that have moved in before passing on or stayed are the Santee Sioux, Miami, Huron, Illinois, Petun, Oneida, Stockbridge, Munsee, Mohican, and the tribes consolidated into the Brothertown (Mohegan, Pequot, Narragansett, Montauk, Delaware).

This whole era was marked by trade-related aggression. The Iroquois (the Five Nations Confederacy) sought a middleman position through a monopoly of their fur trade in the East with the Dutch, and by 1700 were able to force the Chippewa (Ojibwe) westward into present day Wisconsin, upper Michigan, and Minnesota. That brought the Ojibwe into conflict with the Sioux who were driven westward into conflict with still other tribes (and ultimately George Custer). Lack of unity, organization, cooperation, and invention (of wheel, firearms, etc.) among and between Native tribes, lack of the horse, and no immunity to European diseases, left them susceptible to European incursion. And so the development of the new nation combined the shameful treatment of the indigenous people already here with that of the slaves brought here (Indian Wars and decimation of bison populations, Civil War).

Presently, the Native American tribes in Wisconsin are the Ho-Chunk, Menominee, Potawatomi, Oneida, Stockbridge-Munsee band of Mohicans, Brothertown (five tribes), and six bands of Chippewa (Ojibwe): Bad River, Lac Courte Oreilles, Lac du Flambeau, Red Cliff, Mole Lake (Sokaogon), and St. Croix. These tribes have 644,000 acres in reservation varying from 1,700 acres (Mole Lake Chippewa) to 234,000 acres (Menominee), in 11 reservations. The Ho-Chunk and Brothertown tribes have no reservation. Some 86,000 Native Americans live in Wisconsin.

The Great Lakes Indian Fish & Wildlife Commission[74] (GLIFWC) formed in 1984 to represent 11 bands of Chippewa (Ojibwe) in Wisconsin, Michigan, and Minnesota. The treaties in Wisconsin of 1837, 1842, and 1854, between the Ojibwe and the United States, ceded land to the U.S. but maintained for the Ojibwe the hunting, fishing, and gathering rights off reservation in the northern half of Wisconsin.[74] Between 1985 and 1991, the courts agreed that the tribes could exercise these rights finally. Despite the treaties, off-reservation use of natural resources in the ceded area has caused European Americans to view it as special treatment for Indigenous Americans, with occasional hassle.

GLIFWC employs wildlife biologists and other natural resource types to provide natural resource management expertise, conservation enforcement, legal and policy analysis, and public information services for off-reservation seasons throughout the treaty-ceded territories. To ensure conservation, GLIFWC cooperates with the DNR to regulate a sustainable harvest of treaty resources and ensure conservation. Bag limits in northern Wisconsin for fish and deer have not changed dramatically, and Native American hunting and spearfishing have not affected tourism. Moreover, the six Ojibwe bands in Wisconsin annually stock, from their own fish hatcheries, more fish than they remove from lakes.

In 1959, the Menominee Reservation became Wisconsin's 72nd county, with 235,000 acres. Of the 72 counties in Wisconsin, only Menominee County has no public land, but 98% of its land is held in trust by the Menominee Tribe, which has the oldest forest management program in Wisconsin and one of the world's best and oldest examples of sustainable forestry. This sound forest management benefits wildlife.

Wisconsin contains many Native burial mounds and effigy mounds. Three miles east of Necedah National Wildlife refuge, near New Miner, Wisconsin, is 675-acre Cranberry Creek Archeology District, a state natural area of 300–500 Indigenous burial mounds from circa 100–800 AD, one of the larger mound groups in Wisconsin. Near Baraboo is Man Mound Park, in 2016 designated a National Historic Landmark, with its human effigy in an area that once contained the richest concentration of effigy mounds in North America.

The inaccurate term "Indian," first applied in 1492 by a disoriented Christopher Columbus in the "West Indies," is often applied to all Aboriginals as a group in North America and South America. The name is unacceptable to some tribes, acceptable to others. The inclusive term "Indian" has been described as something like the term "European," that is, peoples with a wide variety of culture, language, and sociopolitical organization who occupy a contiguous geographic area. Referring to North America and South America, the term "Indian" certainly can be confused with the Indians of India. The search for an alternate term has been awkward, even confusing. Unlike all other people who live in North America, Aboriginals have no recent immigrant experience and have cultures that predate societies of present-day Canada and the United States.

PUBLIC LAND

Wildlife is most readily managed on public land, where university-trained wildlifers hold sway mostly on public wildlife areas. Wisconsin has 5,000,000 acres of public hunting land.

Alaska ranks first among the 50 states in the percentage (96%) of land in public ownership; Rhode Island ranks last (1.5%). Wisconsin ranks 20th with 18% of its land in public ownership. Public land is in 71 of Wisconsin's 72 counties, with the most public land (464,673 acres) in Bayfield County. Of public land, 12 counties have less than 10,000 acres, 20 counties have more than 100,000 acres.

To meet conservation and recreation needs, Wisconsin has been acquiring land for public use since 1876. Excluding military bases, government buildings, college/school campuses, cities, and roads, more than 5.7 million acres (16.5%) are publicly owned, of the approximately 34.8 million acres of land in Wisconsin. That land is in parks, forests, wildlife areas, trails, and other protected natural areas. About 1.5 million acres (4.4%) is federal land, with almost all in forest land located in Chequamegon-Nicolet National Forest. About 1.6 million acres (4.6%) is state land, managed by two agencies—the Board of Commissioners of Public Land, ratified in 1848 and the oldest state agency (which manages lands granted by the federal government) and the Department of Natural Resources (which manages land owned by the state). About 2.4 million acres (7.5%) is county land.

Wisconsin has five ocean-like beaches on its two Great Lakes: 1) North Beach in Racine on Lake Michigan, 2) Kohler-Andrae State Park on Lake Michigan near Sheboygan, 3) Point Beach State Forest on Lake Michigan near Two Rivers, 4) Schoolhouse Beach on Washington Island in Lake Michigan off the Door Peninsula, 5) Big Bay Beach at Town Park on Madeline Island in Lake Superior.

Beginning at the confluence of the St. Croix and Mississippi rivers near the Twin Cities of Minneapolis and St. Paul, 125 miles of the 169-mile St. Croix River National Scenic Riverway separate Wisconsin from Minnesota. The Riverway joins the Mississippi National River and Recreation Area (72 miles long, 54,000 acres) in Minnesota near the town of Prescott, Wisconsin. The Lower Wisconsin State Riverway, 92 free-flowing miles of Wisconsin River from Prairie du Sac to the Mississippi River, contains 45,000 acres of land on each side of the river (see Wisconsin River).

Along the Mississippi River in Wisconsin, eight scenic overlooks occur: 1) Nelson Dewey State Park near Cassville, 2) Wyalusing State Park near Bagley, 3) Larson Bluff near Lynxville, 4) Grandad Bluff near La Crosse, 5) Sunny the Sunfish near Onalaska, 6) Perrot State Park near Trempealeau, 7) Buena Vista Park near Alma, and 8) Freedom Park near Prescott.

Wisconsin has 93 Important Bird Areas totaling over 3,000,000 acres on federal, state, municipal, tribal, and private lands. Using science-based criteria, the IBA program in Wisconsin identifies the most critical habitat for birds and maintains and improves those habitats through voluntary stewardship and collaborative conservation.

County and School. Wisconsin has 30 county forests of 2,400,000 acres, the largest public ownership in the state, and some 600 county parks. The first county forest was created in 1928 in Langlade County.

A school forest is land used for environmental education and natural resource management that is registered through the state community forest program and owned or controlled by a public or private school. The first school forests began in 1928 for schools in Laona, Crandon, and Wabena. Now more than 340 school forests exist, totaling some 25,000 acres. In addition, the Wisconsin Board of Commissioners of Public Lands oversees 77,000 acres of school trust lands.

State. The Wisconsin Department of Natural Resources owns 1,517,454 acres and has almost 400,000 acres in easements. Its state parks, forests, recreation areas, and trails are listed in the Wisconsin Bureau of Parks and Recreation's *Wisconsin State Park System.* In addition, more than 113,000 acres of farm and forest land in the state have been protected by The Conservation Fund in collaboration with the state; such land is kept on the tax rolls.

Wisconsin has 14 state forests totaling 471,329 acres, ranging from Havenwoods State Forest of 237 acres in Milwaukee County to Northern Highland-American Legion State Forest of 223,283 acres in Iron, Vilas, and Oneida counties. The first state forest was Brule River State Forest in 1907, site of Cedar Island Lodge, "the Summer White House," where American presidents have vacationed.

Although Wisconsin was the first state to create a state park (in most of Vilas County), in 1878, powerful lumber barons bought most of that land at $8 per acre, and cut it heavily, thus defeating the purpose of a state park. The first state park in Wisconsin, in 1900, and the first interstate park in the nation, is Interstate State Park in Wisconsin (1,330 acres) and Minnesota (298 acres) on the St. Croix River at the Dalles of St. Croix Falls. The Dalles is a deep basalt gorge with glacial potholes and other rock formations. Interstate Park on the Wisconsin side is within the St. Croix National Scenic Riverway and the Ice Age National Scientific Reserve. Wisconsin has 66 state parks and seven state recreation areas totaling 60,570 acres, and 44 state trails. The largest state park, in south central Wisconsin, is Devil's Lake State Park, at 9,217 acres. Baraboo Range National Natural Landmark is 50,000 acres, including Devil's Lake and the largest contiguous forest in southern Wisconsin. The Elroy-Sparta State Trail, at 32 miles, opened in 1965 as the first rails-to trails project in the nation, converting unused rail corridors to public use. The National Register of Historic Places contains 23 listings in 15 Wisconsin state parks.

Wisconsin's State Natural Areas Program, the nation's oldest and largest statewide system of natural areas, highlights and protects areas with outstanding natural, geological, or archaeological resources. These state natural areas number 693, containing 406,000 acres, which protect natural communities for research, threatened or endangered species, and biodiversity.[1] The Wisconsin State Natural Areas Program was created in 1951 as the first such state-sponsored program in the U.S., with Parfrey's Glen State Natural Area in Sauk Co. the first one, in 1952. The natural areas range in size from less than one acre to more than 7,700 acres. Many of the natural areas are on state-owned land; others use easements or cooperative agreements on land owned by the National Park Service, U.S. Forest Service, and county or private conservation organizations such as The Nature Conservancy.

Wisconsin has 240 state wildlife areas totaling about 500,000 acres, but most wildlife areas are less than 3,000 acres. The largest state wildlife area is George W. Mead Wildlife Area of 33,000 acres in central Wisconsin. In central Wisconsin, Sandhill Wildlife Area is 9,150 acres, and next to that is Wood County Wildlife Area of 21,000 acres. Next to that is Meadow Valley Wildlife Area of 58,000 acres, owned by the U.S. Fish and Wildlife Service but administered by the Wisconsin Department of Natural Resources. Sandhill, Wood County, and Meadow Valley wildlife areas constitute almost 90,000 contiguous acres.

Federal. Next to Meadow Valley is Necedah National Wildlife Refuge, 43,696 acres. Created in 1939, the Necedah area was farmed in the late 1800s when drainage ditches were dug to dry the land for agriculture. That left dry peat soils unsuitable for crops after about two years of farming. Burning the grass to generate more grass also burned the peat which further exhausted the soil, which stayed ignited until winter snow doused the flames. Farmers quit. Dams were installed in some ditches to restore the wetland.

The combined Sandhill, Wood County, and Meadow Valley wildlife areas with adjacent Necedah National Wildlife Refuge brings the total wildlife area there to almost 132,000 acres of contiguous public property. All these public properties in central Wisconsin are part of the Great Central Wisconsin Swamp, the largest wetland bog in Wisconsin, at 300,000 acres, between Wisconsin Rapids, Camp Douglas, and Black River Falls. It includes extensive forest habitat of oak, pine, and aspen with large tracts of rare oak barrens, and extensive agricultural cranberry bogs.

In addition to 1) Necedah National Wildlife Refuge is 2) Horicon National Wildlife Refuge of 22,000 acres, established in 1941 just south of Fond du Lac. Bordering it to the south is 11,000-acre Horicon State Wildlife Area, established in 1927. Together, the 33,000-acre Horicon Marsh constitutes the largest freshwater cattail marsh in the United States. Horicon National Wildlife Refuge is managed as part of a complex that includes noncontiguous 3) Green Bay National Wildlife Refuge of 1,620 acres (Plum, Pilot, and Hog islands), 4) Fox River National Wildlife Refuge of 1,054 acres near Montello, 5) Gravel Island National Wildlife Refuge of 27 acres (Spider and Gravel islands) in Lake Michigan near Washington Island, and 6) Leopold Wetland Management District of 57 waterfowl production areas of 13,000 acres located in 17 counties. Other National Wildlife Refuges in Wisconsin are 7) Hackmatack of 11,200 noncontiguous acres with 15% in southeastern Wisconsin and 85% in northeastern Illinois, 8) St. Croix Wetland Management District of 7,500 acres in 41 waterfowl production areas (WPA) in eight counties of west-central Wisconsin, and 9) Whittlesey Creek of 540 acres along the coast of Lake Superior near Ashland. 10) The Upper Mississippi River National Wildlife and Fish Refuge is 240,000 acres and 261 miles long extending along Wisconsin from Wabasha, Minnesota, to Rock Island, Illinois. 11) Trempealeau National

Wildlife Refuge, 6,226 acres in the Driftless Area along the Upper Mississippi River in Trempealeau County, is a wetland consisting of backwaters of the Mississippi and Trempealeau rivers and a tallgrass sand prairie with indiangrass, big bluestem, and 9-foot-tall switchgrass.

Wisconsin has the Chequamegon-Nicolet National Forest of 1,530,647 acres in northern Wisconsin. Established in 1933 were two national forests: Chequamegon National Forest in 3 units of a combined 865,825 acres and Nicolet National Forest of 664,822 acres. In 1993, they were combined into Chequamegon-Nicolet National Forest, with four noncontiguous sites.

Wisconsin has the Apostle Islands National Lakeshore, with 12 miles of mainland and 21 islands comprising 69,372 acres in Lake Superior near Bayfield, Wisconsin. It also has the Wisconsin Shipwreck Coast National Marine Sanctuary established in 2021, with 36 discovered and some 60 undiscovered shipwrecks from 1833 to 1918, of exceptional historic, archeological, and recreational value. Its 962 square miles are in Lake Michigan along Manitowoc, Sheboygan, and Ozaukee counties. Established in 1968, the 252-mile Saint Croix National Wild and Scenic River (including the 83-mile Namekagon River) and the 24-mile Wolf River National Wild and Scenic River were the first wild and scenic rivers in the nation.

Wisconsin has seven wilderness areas totaling 80,000 acres. 1) Blackjack Springs Wilderness is 5,800 acres northeast of Eagle River in the Nicolet unit of Chequamegon-Nicolet National Forest. 2) Headwaters Wilderness, the largest wilderness area on Wisconsin's mainland, is 22,033 acres within the Nicolet unit of the Chequamegon-Nicolet National Forest. 3) Porcupine Lake Wilderness is a 4,074-acre area in the Chequamegon unit of Chequamegon-Nicolet National Forest. 4) Rainbow Lake Wilderness is a 7,135-acre area in the Chequamegon unit of the Chequamegon-Nicolet National Forest. 5) Whisker Lake Wilderness is a 7,270-acre area in the northeast corner of the Nicolet unit of the Chequamegon-Nicolet National Forest bordering the Upper Peninsula of Michigan. 6) Gaylord Nelson Wilderness is 35,000 acres on 18 of the 21 islands of Apostle Islands

National Lakeshore in Lake Superior off the Bayfield Peninsula of northern Wisconsin. 7) The Wisconsin Islands Wilderness, one of the smallest wilderness areas in the United States, is a 29-acre area consisting of three islands (Spider, Hog, and Gravel) in Door County.

The North Country National Scenic Trail is 4,000 miles long and passes through seven states from New York to North Dakota. In Wisconsin, the trail runs from Minnesota through Douglas, Bayfield, Ashland, and Iron counties for 200 miles in Wisconsin, and then through the Upper Peninsula of Michigan. The Ice Age National Scenic Trail occurs only in Wisconsin, one of only 11 National Scenic Trails in the nation. Nearly 1,200 miles long, it follows the terminus of Wisconsin's most recent glacier of 11,000 years ago, which gouged out the landscape but did not cover the relatively flat Driftless Area in southwestern Wisconsin, with its coulees, i.e., valleys with relatively high, steep slopes extending to the Mississippi River. The Ice Age National Scenic Trail travels through 30 counties on state, federal, county, and private lands. About 675 miles have been completed. It is administered by a partnership of the National Park Service, the Wisconsin Department of Natural Resources, and the nonprofit Ice Age Trail Alliance of volunteers.

Wisconsin has 18 National Natural Landmarks between 44 and 53,531 acres of geological, biological, and historical importance that includes dunes, swales, ridges, bogs, swamps, prairies, and virgin forests. The National Park Service administers these landmarks.

The nation's largest public landowner, the U.S. Bureau of Land Management (BLM), is represented in the state, but not much. The BLM owns almost 500 small islands in the Wisconsin River. Other islands are state-owned or privately-owned in reservoirs that flooded private land.

Between Tomah and Sparta in Marion Co., Wisconsin, is a U.S. Army base, Fort McCoy, of 60,000 acres, with its own civilian wildlife biologist and wildlife management program. Near Camp Douglas in Juneau Co. is Volk Field Air National Guard Base of 800 acres. The largest ammunition factory in the world during World War II was the Badger Army Ammunition Plant of 7,354 acres in Sauk Co. Much of it (3,400 acres) became the Sauk Prairie State Recreation area in 2002.

PRIVATE LAND

Wisconsin is diverse ecologically, but most of that diversity is on private land. Although wildlife is a public resource, because of the abundance of private land in Wisconsin and elsewhere, most public wildlife is on private land. Wisconsin is 82% private land. The land practices of the private landowner thus affect the public's wildlife resource, and therefore the public. No law exists compelling private landowners to plant winter cover crops for wildlife on harvested fields or protective windbreaks, to prevent or reduce wind or water erosion of soil, or to prevent cattle from grazing woodlots, etc., all of which harm the public's wildlife resource.[198] The private landowner owns the private trees but not the public wildlife that the private trees support. Wildlife is owned by the taxpayer; anything the private landowner does to the private habitat on private landowner property affects the public taxpayer's wildlife supported by that private habitat. If private wildlife habitat is eliminated via housing development or agriculture, for example, so is the public's wildlife resource. (In states such as Texas, with almost no public land, private landowners of large private land areas sometimes hire their own wildlife biologists to manage the public wildlife resource—but on their private land for their private use.)

In 1985, the U.S. Conservation Reserve Program (CRP) provided more than 500,000 acres of wildlife habitat on private lands in Wisconsin, but in 10- to 15-year contracts; acreage has shrunk considerably since then (see Chapter 5). In 1989, the North American Wetlands Conservation Act (NAWCA) protected and improved more than 72,000 acres of wetlands in Wisconsin. This Act authorizes grants to public-private partnerships in the United States, Canada, and Mexico to protect, improve, restore, and manage habitat for waterfowl, other migratory birds, other wildlife, and fish, consistent with the North American Waterfowl Management Plan. Its success results from partnerships involving federal, state, and local governments, and nonprofit organizations such as Ducks Unlimited and community groups.

Private lands leased for hunting are called Voluntary Public Access (VPA) lands, and are managed by the DNR. Utility properties and industrial forests also exist. The private industrial timberland company, Plum Creek Timber Co., of Chapel Hill, NC, owns some 400,000 acres in northern Wisconsin. Most forested land in Wisconsin—57%—is owned by individual landowners, 32% by federal, state, county or tribal governments, and 11% by forest industry or private corporations.

Private natural areas are owned and managed by agencies such as The Nature Conservancy which owns 236,100 acres in Wisconsin. Some 70 nature centers of a few acres to over a thousand acres, owned privately and publicly, occur throughout the state, many in urban areas.

All Wisconsin's diversity in geology and habitat—and climate—produces a fascinating array of wildlife species in diverse abundance and distribution.

7.

WILDLIFE HABITAT ALTERATION AND ECONOMIC GROWTH

L arge-scale habitat alteration for economic growth has affected wildlife big time in Wisconsin and throughout the world. It has occurred throughout Wisconsin mostly since the mid-1800s. Most of it takes the form of mining, lumbering, agriculture, hydropower, and urbanization. All such activities disturb wildlife habitat and thus affect wildlife, mostly negatively.

MINING

Bucky Badger is the name of the mascot for the University of Wisconsin–Madison; its students and sports teams are known as Badgers. Wisconsin became the Badger State. But it isn't because of the badgers in Wisconsin, although this animal occurs here. It is because of lead mining.

After the War of 1812 (1812–1815), the lead region of southwestern Wisconsin attracted settlers to mine lead for paint and gunshot, particularly during the 1820s.[64] The mascot "Wisconsin badger" became known not so much because of the burrowing animal in Wisconsin but rather because of the burrowing lead miners in Wisconsin. The nickname referred originally to the lead miners of the 1830s, who worked at the Galena lead mines in

157

Illinois. The Wisconsin miners lived in temporary caves cut into the hillsides rather than in regular houses. Described as badger dens, the caves housed "badgers," that is, the miners who lived in them. Nowadays, the nickname Wisconsin Badger for Wisconsinites refers to the badger, the feisty animal in the weasel family (badger, otter, marten, fisher, mink, wolverine, skunk, weasel).

Wisconsin's two oldest settlements—Green Bay (1634) and Prairie du Chien (1685)—developed from French Canadian voyageurs along waterways during the fur trade. In the 1820s, European settlers began arriving in large numbers from the east to the Milwaukee area. In 1848, Wisconsin became the 30th state, its capital of Madison a compromise between the two population centers around Milwaukee and Prairie du Chien. By this time, Indigenous peoples had ceded all land in Wisconsin to the U.S. government. By then, the lead mining era was all but over.

Some copper and zinc mining occur in Wisconsin. But the extensive mining in Wisconsin is for non-metallic and non-gem products. Sand and gravel mining is extensive. Land reclamation after mining operations has been a problem.

Iron mining has spanned 150 years in Wisconsin beginning in the mid-1800s in Sauk and Dodge counties. Although currently no active iron mining exists in Wisconsin, potential exists in the Gogebic Iron Range, an 80-mile long belt along the northern Wisconsin-Upper Peninsula border.

Wisconsin is the nation's largest producer of frac sand. The relatively recent technological breakthrough of hydraulic fracturing and horizontal drilling has transformed uneconomic oil and gas deposits into profitable drilling operations, although that is likely to decline with its evident triggering of local earthquakes and with the world's declining use of fossil fuels. Known as hydraulic fracturing, high pressure water breaks open underground geologic formations of shale mostly. Frackers use a lot of frac sand—up to 10,000 tons of sand per well—to prop open the fractures so that the oil and gas can be extracted.

Industrial silica sand mining has experienced dramatic growth. Between 2005 and 2014, silica sand production in Wisconsin more than doubled, increasing from 31 million metric tons in

2005 to more than 75 million in 2014, in the Driftless Area where surface sand is readily available. More than 2,500 sand and gravel pits occur in Wisconsin. Among the key areas of environmental concern are air quality (especially relative to the lung disease silicosis), contamination of surface waters and groundwater aquifers, groundwater depletion, and any potential long-term land damage, especially land previously used for agriculture. Associated wildlife also suffers, of course.

Wisconsin state law requires all nonmetallic mines be reclaimed in accordance with NR 135 Wisconsin Administrative Code, which is implemented and administered by Wisconsin counties. This program is intended to ensure that mining sites are reclaimed to a post-mining land use, which can be wildlife habitat, prairie, agriculture, cranberry bog, or another use agreed by the property owner and mining company. Reclamation involves replacing topsoil.

LUMBER

The lumber barons of the late 1800s and early 1900s changed the landscape. The white pines of northern Wisconsin built houses in Ohio and elsewhere. This tree harvest began in the 1840s along the Wisconsin, Wolf, and Chippewa rivers, which were used for transporting the lumber.[45, 49] Commercial logging quickly overtook the fur trade as the Wisconsin territory's main source of income.[212]

The so-called pine woods occurred north of a line from Manitowoc to Stevens Point to the falls of the Chippewa and St. Croix rivers. The rivers were the most important factor in Wisconsin's lumber industry because they were the prime movers of logs until railroads competed in the 1890s.[212]

The white pines were 300-400 years old, up to a magnificent 200 feet tall, and 4 to 7 feet in diameter. The ruthless elimination of mature white pine and other such trees resulted in the elimination of a critical stage of forest succession—old growth—and associated wildlife. Only scattered small pockets of remnant old growth remain in Wisconsin. The old-growth stage of forest succession—and its associated wildlife component—is now essentially missing from the ecosystem. Old growth can be considered a nonrenewable resource because of the extensive time required for it to develop (see Chapter 6).

The slash left from voracious tree harvest was fuel for many hot fires which burned with such intensity that they degraded the soil, unlike normal fires. Overshadowed by the infamous Chicago Fire on the same day, the Great Peshtigo Fire of 8 October 1871, the worst fire in the nation's history, began with a slash fire and burned 1.25 million acres in eight counties including Brown County where unburned Green Bay is located,[212] thus altering wildlife habitat extensively to either the benefit or detriment of various wildlife species. The intense heat created a tornado of fire called a fire storm, not understood until World War II, killing an estimated 1,500–2,500 people and destroying all but one of the buildings of Peshtigo, population 1,700. The Chicago Fire killed 300 people but had more property loss ($4.6 billion today) and got all the press. Indirectly, the Chicago Fire expedited the extinction of the passenger pigeon, when trees were cut throughout the Lake States to rebuild Chicago; tree nesting habitat declined, and, along with human over-exploitation, so did the pigeon population. It seems little knowledge exists of this extraordinary, calamitous natural event, the Great Peshtigo Fire. (In 1915, just 12 years after the Wright brothers invented the airplane, Wisconsin became the first state to use airplanes to detect forest fires.)

By statehood in 1848, more than 75% of Wisconsin was forested.[191] Some 70 years later, virtually all of northern Wisconsin's forest had been decimated by axe or by fire burning the debris left behind. The heavily forested region in northern Wisconsin was hardly touched by the Civil War,[64] which ended in 1865. Thereafter, the rich pineries were exploited. Already by 1867, the lumber barons were recognized as damaging the landscape with reckless tree harvest.[123] During the last half of the 1800s, lumbering, full of hardship and peril, became the biggest business of the region. The peak year for the lumber industry was 1892 when an estimated four billion feet were cut—without chainsaws; in 1900 Wisconsin still led all states in production of white pine lumber. Between 1899 and 1904, Wisconsin led the U.S. in lumber production, after which production decreased rapidly as supplies dwindled.[39] It was all over by the early 1900s. The greed of the enriched lumber barons succeeded in removing a vast white pine resource in an unsustainable manner, to the detriment of the state and to Wisconsin's future human and wildlife populations. Only puny remnant stands remain now.

In the forested areas, through plant succession, huge areas formerly in northern pines (white pine, red pine) or pine/hardwoods became covered with early successional tree species such as aspen, white birch, pin cherry, and northern hardwoods especially basswood and maple. That resulted in a change of game and nongame species of wildlife; game species such as ruffed grouse and deer proliferated except in northern hardwoods. More forest land exists now than at any time in the last century, even after years of brutal deforestation by European settlers, but not old growth (see Chapter 6).

Today, forestry is the number one employer in seven counties of Wisconsin; each forestry job supports 1.7 other jobs in Wisconsin. Wisconsin's 17,000,000 acres of forest ecosystems provide wildlife habitat, scenery, recreation, $24.3 billion in forest products, and 63,000 jobs.

PULPWOOD AND HYDROPOWER

Because of the presence of the paper industry in Green Bay, home of the famed Green Bay Packers professional football team, in addition to being nicknamed "Title Town" for the team's success, Green Bay's sobriquet has sometimes been "Toilet Paper Capital of the World." There, in the 1930s, Northern Paper Company offered the world's first splinter-free toilet paper still in vogue today, thus eliminating awkward splinter removal by close friends. The city's largest industry—paper—affected the deer population; trees cut for toilet paper and other paper products left fast-growing aspen quickly regenerating, a favorite deer and beaver food in winter. Aspen also is heavily used by songbirds,[225] ruffed grouse, and other wildlife. But replacement of newspapers and letters by the internet and email is causing pulp and paper mills to close worldwide, with reduced pulp-cutting, aspen regeneration, and alteration of the densities of various wildlife species too.

Wisconsin ranks first nationwide in producing paper products. In the 1870s, Wisconsin began manufacturing paper from wood pulp from various species of smaller trees, and paper mills developed in the Fox River region—in 1882, the world's first hydroelectric plant was built in Appleton—and later along the upper Wisconsin River. The 39 miles of the Fox River from Green Bay to Lake Winnebago have 24 paper mills. Wisconsin's largest river by far, the Wisconsin River has only one dam in the lower section but 26 dams in its northern and central sections, mostly for paper production from pulpwood, the oldest (1905) in Rhinelander, and 21 storage reservoirs which add 330 miles of shoreline—more than any other stretch of river in the U.S. For that reason, the Wisconsin River is said to be "the hardest-working river in the world,"[45, 49] with its many dams for papermaking and hydroelectric power production.

Of these dams, 14 are exclusively for hydroelectric production and 11 are for paper-making and hydroelectric production. Operation of the dams and reservoirs has been coordinated by the Wisconsin Valley Improvement Company since 1907.[68] The member companies of the WVIC own and operate the dams. Located in Wausau, the WVIC is a private company responsible for coordinating the flow of the Wisconsin River and most tributaries of the upper Wisconsin River. This action affects the ecosystem of the entire river for better or worse. The dams also reduce flooding by the river. Despite all these dams, hydropower produces just 3% of the electricity in Wisconsin (see Chapter 6).

Not only have other forms of energy production eclipsed hydropower, but also awareness has been increasing about how hydro projects alter natural waterways. Upstream, high-water levels of reservoirs behind dams can erode riverbanks, causing silty, cloudy, and warmer water that contributes to inferior conditions for fish and other aquatic organisms, and can flood riparian areas. Downstream, water levels can drop daily, leaving fish and other aquatic organisms stranded, piers, rocks, and logs exposed—leading to boating hazards. Wastewater dischargers rely on river flow to dilute treated wastewater, a major problem when water levels fluctuate. The dams can block fish migrations and other movements, inhibit spawning, and disrupt the life cycle of native mussels that rely on fish as hosts. The dam, turbines, and other equipment can trap, kill, or harm fish and other aquatic organisms when they pass through.

Reservoir flooding behind dams destroys one of the most valuable wildlife habitats— riparian vegetation.[197] Reservoirs also flood wetlands and associated uplands, thus reducing associated wildlife populations by eliminating their habitat. About 150 hydroelectric dams were built in Wisconsin before the 1960s. Some 3,900 dams (about 300 owned by the Wisconsin Department of Natural Resources) occur in Wisconsin, many for sawmills. The reservoirs behind these dams create recreational opportunities such as boating, bird watching, fishing, hunting, and trapping.[45, 49]

Walleyes caught in the Wisconsin River were said to taste like the sports page from the *Milwaukee Journal* newspaper. Dumped into the river were the chemicals used in paper making, and the raw sewage from 64 cities along the Wisconsin River and other rivers. In time, the chemicals and sewage were treated before entering the river. The rivers were cleaned up to enhance quality of life and tourist potential. In 1983, Wisconsin became the first state to meet fishable and swimmable water quality standards.

After they had outlived their useful purpose, more than 650 dams constructed in the 1800s to early 1900s in Wisconsin were removed. Since 1960, over 150 dams were removed from Wisconsin streams. Dam removals over the last 50 years produced substantial improvements in water quality, habitat, and biodiversity.

AGRICULTURE

While the lumber industry transformed northern Wisconsin, the agriculture industry, mainly wheat at first, transformed southern Wisconsin. By the 1870s, dairy farming began to replace wheat; refrigerated railroad cars to transport butter and cheese required blocks of ice, opening an ice-cutting industry that shipped to

Chicago one million tons of ice a year.[212] The human population of Wisconsin was 3,245 in 1830; 305,391 in 1850; and 1,315,497 in 1880.[39] Wisconsin experienced a corresponding increase in agricultural crop production and dairy farming of about 400,000 acres in 1830; 2,900,000 acres in 1850; and 15,300,000 acres in 1880, leveling off in 1910 to about 21,000,000 acres, which has remained relatively constant since then. Almost 45% of the state's land area is in farms. Wisconsin is first in cheese and cranberry production, second to California in milk production, and third to Idaho and Washington in potato production.

Farming was Wisconsin's main economic activity, employing 80% of the population,[64] mainly in southern Wisconsin which had more prairie and savanna that lent itself to agriculture. Land was converted from wildlife habitat to agricultural production.[4] With that, trade and industry—including railroads—developed so that farmers could market their products. Nonetheless, by 1850, only about 8% of Wisconsin's land was in farms and less than half of that in cultivation.[189] (For heating and cooking, every farm had a woodlot as fuel, which, especially if ungrazed, would benefit wildlife). By 1860, 20% of the land was in farms. Wheat was king until dairy farming surged ahead in the 1870s, and never looked back. By 1900, 90% of Wisconsin farms had dairy cattle.

In 1933, the oldest Soil and Water Conservation District in the nation, and the nation's first watershed project, were developed in Coon Valley in Vernon County of west-central Wisconsin. Cash crops affected the landscape and groundwater, starting in the mid-1900s. Circular irrigation units pumped groundwater mainly for potatoes, corn, and green beans, mainly in the Driftless Area (unglaciated flatland) of central Wisconsin. Fields are huge. No legal requirements exist to control irresponsible private land use such as the huge fields left barren over winter and the woodlots with browse lines from overgrazing cattle. Wind and water erosion occurred, polluting streams. Wildlife suffered from loss of habitat. Crops were engulfed with fertilizers and pesticides spread by crop-dusting airplanes. Groundwater became contaminated with nitrates from nitrate fertilizers filtering through the porous sandy soil, which affected private and public wells (e.g., Whiting).

Some streams dried up (e.g., Little Plover River); some lakes and ponds shrunk, despite Wisconsin, in 1984, being among the first states to have groundwater protection laws.

On the one hand, Wisconsin has destroyed almost half (47%) of its original 10 million acres of wetlands (24% of the state) through draining and filling for agricultural production (corn, potatoes, hay), accompanied by heavy pesticide loads. On the other hand, Wisconsin has produced wetlands for cranberry production, but accompanied by heavy pesticide loads. Wisconsin cranberries are produced from 21,000 acres of wetlands on about 250 farms supported by huge networks of ditches, dikes, dams, and reservoirs.

Wisconsin produces 60% of the nation's cranberry crop and over half the world's supply, twice as much as second place Massachusetts. Commercial production began in Wisconsin in the early 1850s, near Berlin in Green Lake County. Later, the center of the industry moved to the marshes in central Wisconsin around Wisconsin Rapids, Warrens, and Tomah. Advances in technology and agricultural research investigating drainage methods, water control, insects, and diseases helped Wisconsin become the nation's leading cranberry producer.

But heavy use of chemical pesticides and fertilizers in cranberry bogs has caused problems with wildlife and water contamination. Construction of bogs for cranberries eliminates natural wetlands for a host of wildlife. Water quality and the overall health of these man-made ecosystems—and the natural ecosystems they impact—remain a concern.

URBANIZATION AND ROADS

The impacts of urban sprawl and roads have caused loss of wildlife habitat. Much of the forests, meadows, and wetlands have been replaced by buildings, pavement, and sterile urban landscaping, leaving smaller, degraded, and more fragmented wildlife habitat. Such habitat reduces survival of some wildlife species for lack of such things as unfragmented large home ranges, feeding areas, nesting sites, breeding ponds, and hibernation sites. Just since the 1960s, 67% of the larger lakes in northern Wisconsin have been developed for housing, with the loss of one of the most productive wildlife habitats—riparian habitat—near and along the shoreline.

In 1850, two years after Wisconsin became a state, its human population was 305,000, with 36% foreign-born, mostly from the British Isles. In 1900, 2,000,000 people lived in Wisconsin. In 2020, 5,900,000 people lived in Wisconsin. In 1870, 12 cities had at least 5,000 people; by 1900, 33 cities did, with 17 over 10,000. In 2020, 777 cities, populations ranging from 24 (Jump River) to 596,886 (Milwaukee), existed in Wisconsin's 72 counties, with 89 cities having more than 10,000 people. Eastern Wisconsin contains more than 50% of its human population and 75% of its industry.

In 1905, Wisconsin registered 1,492 automobiles. Ten years later, in 1915, 79,790 existed. In 1965, 50 years later, 1,517,397 existed. In 2015, another 50 years later, 5,823,555 automobiles, buses, trucks, and motorcycles existed, of which 2,229,199 were cars. By 2020, the grand total was 6,072,320 (*Wisconsin Blue Book*).

In 1917, the Wisconsin Legislature authorized, for the first time, construction of 5,000 miles of roads. By 2020, Wisconsin had 115,674 miles of federal, state, county, town, and city roads, as a road map will readily reveal. Sprawling housing and business developments have made driving mandatory in our culture, producing one-third of all greenhouse gases in the U. S., along with water pollution from oil, grit, and road salt runoff from roads, driveways, and parking lots.

These cities and these roads have reduced the quality and quantity of wildlife habitat by disturbing and eliminating much and fragmenting most. The balance of human habitat versus wildlife habitat has not been determined; carrying capacity for humans versus wildlife has not been determined. And it is too late for wildlife species extinct from human encroachment. Yet despite detrimental alteration of wildlife habitat, wildlife management has recovered many threatened wildlife species for sustained viewing and hunting (see Chapter 5).

8.

WILDLIFE VALUES AND LEGACY

ECONOMIC VALUE OF WILDLIFE

The U.S. Department of Commerce's Bureau of Economic Analysis shows that outdoor recreation for 2021 generated $862 billion in economic output and 4.5 million jobs to the U.S. economy, more than oil and gas extraction, mining, and agriculture. These data emphasize the importance of lands, waters, and recreational infrastructure and activities from coast to coast. These data show that people continue to venture into the outdoors for adventure, interest, health, and socialization, as businesses across the industry work to expand participation.[44x, 228x]

By using four measurements of wildlife values—expenditures for wildlife-related activities, conservation investments by governments and nongovernmental organizations, wildlife conservation volunteers, and amenity value of residential properties near wildlife refuges—by applying the respective economic multipliers, and by adjusting for inflation, the estimated annual economic benefit of terrestrial wildlife alone in the United States is $346 billion,[96] as reported in 2017. That figure is generally comparable to the activity generated by such economic industries as gas and oil, agriculture, mining, and others.

The Wisconsin Department of Tourism Office of Outdoor Recreation reported for 2022 that outdoor recreation contributed

$9.8 billion (2.5%) to Wisconsin's GDP and supported 94,042 jobs with $4.7 billion in employee compensation.

The largest industry in Wisconsin is manufacturing, followed by agriculture and tourism. In 2022, tourism generated $23.7 billion of Wisconsin's economy, much of which is outdoor recreation, the main reason travelers visit Wisconsin annually. Wildlife generates $2.6 billion annually in Wisconsin, of which deer hunting generates $2.2 billion (88%) annually, most of it in just nine days during the gun deer season. Wildlife viewing for deer in Wisconsin, mainly during summer, also is popular.

Conducted every five years since 1955, the National Survey of Hunting, Fishing, and Wildlife-Associated Recreation for 2022[255x] shows the total spent in the U.S. was $394.8 billion: 14.4 million hunters spent $45.2 billion, 39.9 million anglers spent $90.4 billion, $9 billion was unspecified, and 148.3 million wildlife watchers, including 96.3 million birders, spent $250.2 billion. (Of the wildlife watchers, birdwatching is the fastest-growing activity in America.)

The National Survey in 2018,[255] for 2016, ranked Wisconsin second to Texas (a much bigger state) in the number of resident hunters (763,383) and second to South Dakota in the number of non-resident hunters (131,137). Of all hunters in Wisconsin, 88% hunt deer, 26% hunt turkey, 24% hunt small game, and 12% hunt migratory birds. In the number of deer shot per square mile, Pennsylvania ranks first at about 8.1, then Michigan at about 6.5, then Wisconsin at about 6.0, then Texas at about 3.3. *Statista* reported that Wisconsin leads by far with 4.2 million hunting licenses, tags, permits, and stamps issued in 2021; the next closest state was Pennsylvania with 2.4 million.

The 894,520 hunters spent $2.5 billion on hunting in Wisconsin in 2016 (equipment and trip-related). The 1,247,000 anglers spent $1.4 billion. In addition, the 2,359,000 wildlife watchers spent $1.5 billion. The combined hunting, fishing, and wildlife watching expenditure for Wisconsin was $5.5 billion for 2016. In Wisconsin, hunting alone supports over 34,000 jobs. Hunting generates $2.6 billion in salaries and wages, and $228 million in taxes, with a "ripple effect," i.e., economic multiplier effect, of $4 billion.

These data, though indicative, are from the comprehensive national survey of 2016,[255] which shows wildlife viewing doing well at a 20% increase, fishing hanging in there at an 8% increase, and hunting declining by 14%.

For more than a century, Wisconsin's hunters, trappers, and anglers have paid 90% of the fish and wildlife management that has created world-class hunting, trapping, and fishing here. That money has benefited the non-consumptive users of Wisconsin's wildlife. Healthy habitat for fish and wildlife provides the foundation for Wisconsin's $23.7 billion tourist industry in 2022 and even Wisconsin's quality of life.[10x, 108x, 155x]

Hunters pay their way, but wildlife watchers do not, for no license is required, and the equipment they use for wildlife watching is not taxed, nor any portion of it, for wildlife work, unlike guns and ammunition. The public wildlife areas used by wildlife watchers are supported by hunters but not non-hunters. Some folks suggest that campers, canoeists, kayakers, paddle-boarders, cross-country skiers, snowmobilers, ATVers, birdwatchers, wildlife-area visitors, and other outdoor users help pay for conservation. Others have suggested a half-penny general sales tax to share the costs, and a tax on bird food, bird feeders, and bird houses. Mostly, such suggestions meet with protest from non-hunters and non-anglers. But the decline in hunting licenses, and therefore hunting equipment and the taxes on it that go into the federal Pittman-Robertson fund and then back to the states for wildlife management, has reduced budgets for the wildlife work that both consumptive and non-consumptive users want.

Since the 1980s, ecotourism has become the fastest-growing part of worldwide tourism.[215] Much if not most of the tourism in Wisconsin is ecotourism which attracts people to its many resorts on the many lakes for fishing vacations, to the Dells of the Wisconsin River, the parks and shoreline of the Door Peninsula, and other parks for camping, hunting and fishing, to federal and state wildlife areas for wildlife viewing and hunting, to the Great Lakes, the Mississippi and Wisconsin rivers, and the thousands of other lakes and streams, and to trails for hiking, snowmobiling, and hunting especially for deer (see Chapter 6). Use of wildlife requires equipment, travel, lodging, and food; thus, it is big business.

Wildlife *is* big business, but often it is not recognized, not understood, and not accepted in that capacity, and little of its value and this vast spending generated by wildlife extends to actual wildlife management.[87x]

The economic value of ecosystem biodiversity, essential to all life, is so huge and complex it is incalculable.

NON-ECONOMIC VALUES OF WILDLIFE

In his essay on "Wildlife in American Culture,"[142] Aldo Leopold wrote that a person cannot measure culture, but that most folks think cultural traits exist in the customs, sports, and experiences of interacting with wild things. He listed three such values: 1) the value that stimulates awareness in history, i.e., national origins and evolution; 2) the value that reminds us of our interdependence with the soil-plant-animal food chain and its organization; and 3) the value in experiences exercising ethical restraints collectively known as "sportsmanship."

The values that wildlife provides society[52x, 109] are 1) commercial; 2) recreational; 3) biological, i.e., the contribution of wild animals to productive ecosystems; 4) scientific and educational; 5) aesthetic, i.e., wildlife and their habitats as objects of beauty or historical importance, and as they become part of literature, poetry, art, and music; 6) social, i.e., the community benefits economically, physically, and mentally, resulting in increased facilities (e.g., a medical doctor who accepts a lower salary because of wildlife and fish opportunities) and a happier and healthier community; and 7) negative, i.e., such things as personal injury, disease transmission, and property damage that affect society.

The relationship between humans and wildlife is complex, including the values wildlife provides humans.[52x] Humans use and value wildlife in the following ways:[97]

Direct user = a consumptive or non-consumptive user of wildlife; *Primary beneficiary* = a business benefiting directly from the direct user's expenditures; *Secondary beneficiary* = a business benefiting from expenditures of a primary beneficiary; *Option holder* = one who is willing to pay a premium for some future use of a wildlife commodity; *Vicarious user* = one who benefits indirectly just by knowing wildlife is present in an area; *Altruistic user* = one who sees value in wildlife for the enjoyment of present and future generations; *Environmentalist* = one who considers wildlife an integral part of the overall concern for the natural environment; *Alternative resource user* = one who sees wildlife as negative values in terms of wildlife incompatibility with other resources.

Mental health, i.e., human happiness, increases with more bird and plant species in a region.[260x] Esthetic values of wildlife in North American culture include art, photography, film, television, literature, popular magazines, and festivals. Moreover, major wildlife conservation initiatives, e.g., the Endangered Species Act, demonstrate the extent that society values wildlife, i.e., society is concerned enough to act. But society placed wildlife in that precarious position in the first place.

CONSUMPTIVE VS. NON-CONSUMPTIVE USE OF WILDLIFE

Consumptive use of wildlife applies only to game animals; it means removing the animal from the wild usually by killing it via hunting or trapping. Non-consumptive use applies to both game and nongame species of wildlife by hearing it (birdsongs, calls, snorts, bugles [elk], howls, growls, fights, tail slaps [beaver], drumming [ruffed grouse], etc.), or observing it (trail cams, photography, binoculars, spotting scopes, drones) or its sign (tracks, scats, trails, food remains, feathers and hair, cuttings, dens, nests, lodges, dustings, rubs, scrapes, dams, browse piles [beaver], etc.). Non-consumptive users tend to be highly selective in focusing on charismatic wildlife with strong visual appeal (e.g., Prairie Chicken, in Chapter 5), many of which are game species. Non-consumptive use can be consumptive if it disturbs wildlife too much, stressing it to disperse elsewhere, neglect offspring, or not reproduce. Some wildlifers say no such thing exists as non-consumptive use, for trails are made and wildlife is disturbed as their stress increases with the approach of non-consumptive users.

Unlike revenue for wildlife management from consumptive use (hunting licenses, Pittman-Robertson funds), little revenue is generated from non-consumptive use for wildlife management. Unfortunately, no such tax exists on binoculars, bird books, bird seed, or photographic equipment for non-consumptive use of wildlife such as bird watching and wildlife photography. Wildlife watchers and other non-consumptive users continue to pursue their activity on public wildlife areas acquired and managed with funds generated by consumptive users, i.e., hunters, although a small fee is sometimes charged for visitors. For conservation, state lawmakers make the DNR depend more heavily on license sales and federal funding than do most other states, according to the Wisconsin Policy Forum, a nonpartisan research group. Such funding is influenced by heavy reliance on deer hunting license-sales in Wisconsin, which are declining due to chronic wasting disease in deer.

Park systems and wildlife refuges establish un-manipulated natural settings as remnant wilderness, attracting non-consumptive wildlife users who often oppose sporting interests. Non-consumptive use of wildlife now greatly exceeds consumptive use of wildlife.

SOCIAL VALUE OF WILDLIFE

Take birdwatching. Wisconsin is ranked second nationally in birdwatching participation. But studies indicate that deer are the most popular type of wildlife among non-hunters (as well as hunters), even more so than songbirds and eagles, long thought to be the favorites.[265]

Hunting in general has strong social tradition, as any enthusiastic duck hunter will readily admit.[156, 157, 158] Deer hunting in Wisconsin is a strong social event (see Chapter 5). Studies from the University of Wisconsin-Madison and elsewhere show deer hunters to be a highly committed group. Over 60% of Wisconsin's deer hunters say they would miss deer hunting more than all or most of their other interests including Thanksgiving, which falls within the annual 9-day gun deer hunt. Hunting, especially deer hunting, provides outdoor and social satisfaction other activities do not provide. In Wisconsin, the annual 9-day gun deer season surrounding Thanksgiving is traditional—so much so that wildlife biologists are unable to alter it to an earlier time in northern Wisconsin when bucks are in the rut sooner and more active than those in southern Wisconsin. The split season makes sense biologically but is socially unacceptable. The DNR tried it in 1976; 88% of hunters shot it down—and slammed the DNR in the process. "The effort to change the deer season was a bloody lesson for wildlife managers of the power behind tradition" (p. 183).[67] Many Wisconsin deer hunters view the fall gun season as the biggest social event of the year. Vacation plans are made, some schools close, northern Wisconsin industries slow down or close, southern Wisconsin businesses adjust work schedules to reduce absenteeism. No tradition is more instilled in Wisconsin, or the entire American public, than the sight of this graceful, attractive, large, majestic animal or the sport of hunting it. This tradition has been passed on to succeeding generations. It's a cultural thing.

Now the tradition of deer hunting in Wisconsin is being challenged by chronic wasting disease (CWD) in its deer population. It is a progressive, fatal, transmissible nervous system disease that affects animals in the deer family. CWD is threatening deer hunting, as the declining sale of deer hunting licenses reveals. Nobody wants a deer with CWD, and that is affecting the vast monetary value of deer hunting and the income to the Wildlife Division's budget to manage wildlife.

NUISANCE WILDLIFE

A nuisance animal is one that is interacting with a human in a negative way, by human standards. Personal injury, disease transmission, or property damage might be involved. Sometimes—usually—a human moves into an area occupied by an animal that then becomes a nuisance to the human rather than the other way around. For example, setting up a farm in wolf country will result in the taxpayer paying for loss of livestock by wolves. In either case, the nuisance animal must be controlled (if the human cannot be encouraged to leave). Sometimes a wildlife restoration program is too successful, e.g., sandhill crane recovery in Wisconsin, with accompanying crop depredation, and Canada geese recovery in Wisconsin with their defecation in city parks.

The U.S. Department of Agriculture Wildlife Services has district offices in Rhinelander and Waupun that deal with nuisance birds, bears, and wolves. WDNR Service Centers handle other types of nuisance wildlife problems. Service Centers are listed by city, county, and DNR region, with the central office in Madison. Nuisance Wildlife Guidelines are available from the DNR and elsewhere.[103] The Wisconsin Trappers Association provides a Nuisance Wild Animal Removal Referral List of names and phone numbers of trappers that can help. Help also can be obtained from Pest Control Services.

LEGACY IN WILDLIFE MANAGEMENT

Wildlife is historically, culturally, and economically important to people worldwide. All 50 states of the United States and ten provinces of Canada have a huge investment in wildlife management, with a government wildlife agency that employs wildlife biologists. Various departments in federal governments of the United States and Canada also employ wildlife biologists who work in the states and provinces (see Chapter 2). Other countries have a wildlife agency, but protection and enforcement, research and management, and information and education are not nearly as developed as in the United States and Canada.

Hunting and fishing are so popular and such big business in Wisconsin partly because of its top ranking in the trophy record books of Boone and Crockett[124] and Pope and Young[211] for white-tailed deer, black bear, and turkey, and world records for musky, bass, and brown trout, and the globally unique spear fishing for lake sturgeon.[269] Wisconsin residents hunt and fish at nearly twice the national average. Nationally, Wisconsin is second in the number of nonresidents hunting here, third in the number of anglers fishing here, and second in birdwatching participation.

The various values of wildlife provide various and substantial social, economic, and ecological values to humans. Considering the indispensable value of Earth's ecosystem biodiversity—and how we humans fit in with the other biota—conserving the world's wildlife and wildlands is an absolutely essential, critical investment in the future of humans and other animals.

EPILOGUE

The wildlife ecology and biodiversity of Wisconsin, the nation, and the world is extremely complex, for it is influenced by economic systems, human population growth and associated "development," inequitable wealth and resource use worldwide, rampant environmental problems and ignorance—and life-threatening climate change. People need space and resources (such as heat and electricity), which have serious accompanying problems to the ecosystem and its wildlife and human inhabitants. To accept responsibility and make decisions, some leaders like to say that the buck stops here. But without environmental awareness by the general public and especially by politicians, the buck trumps protection of wildlife habitat, wildlife, biodiversity of the ecosystem, and thus the environmental and ecological health of society. The almighty dollar, especially from so-called Big Business, traditionally speaks loudest—a huge societal problem.[45x] Now, with the complexity of ecosystem biodiversity and societal disregard through environmental ignorance, the wildlife, biodiversity, and ecological health affecting all living things, including humans, is suffering from human encroachment and accompanying environmental problems in air, water, and land—and from ecological systems being altered and even trashed by climate change. Society is now—surprisingly and shockingly—experiencing these effects, despite warnings for decades from scientists.

177

WEALTH, POPULATION, AND NATURAL RESOURCES

The life, liberty, and pursuit of happiness mentioned in 1776 in the *Declaration of Independence* have been taken to an extreme, leading to excessive, unbalanced capitalism that now threatens our very life support system—our natural resources, the biodiversity of our ecosystems—and the pursuit of happiness. Capitalism is a good system, but when taken to an extreme, it causes the serious, even deadly, environmental problems the world is experiencing with global warming and ecosystem destruction.[45x, 190x]

Leopold wrote that "The combined evidence of history and ecology…runs counter to our current philosophy, which assumes [erroneously] that because a small increase in density enriched human life, an indefinite increase will enrich it indefinitely" (p. 235-236).[142] When he wrote that, in 1945, the U.S. had 140,000,000 people. The U.S. had 333,287,557 people in 2020. In 2000, it had 281,421,906 people. In 1900, it had 76,212,168 people. In 1800, it had 5,308,483 people (In 2022, Wisconsin had 5,893,718 people). This population growth was accompanied by housing and economic "development," i.e., expansion. "We need more jobs" is a common expression; but we'll always need more jobs if we add more people. The slogan on the Statue of Liberty, "Give me your tired, your poor, your huddled masses yearning to breathe free, the wretched refuse of your teeming shore," is now obsolete because with over 340 million people in 2024, the United States now seems to be pretty full, as ecosystems deteriorate and population problems increase.[45x] It isn't discrimination against immigrants; it's excess humans approaching the carrying capacity of ecosystems to support humans (as with the carrying capacity for all other living things, as taught in basic wildlife courses, as a farmer knows the number of cows a pasture can support). It's also excess humans spreading into and destroying ecosystems so essential to survival, global warming now a major concern. But even the attitude of that slogan on the Statue of Liberty gets complicated; with about 5% of the world's population, the U.S. uses about 25% of its resources.

The United States is a wealthy country, some of its wealth coming from the natural resources of other less-wealthy countries.

Understandably, perhaps to get their share, but certainly to improve their life, people want to emigrate to the U.S. and other wealthy nations. Such nations need to help improve the economy of these poor countries. Such issues require attention and adjustment worldwide; it doesn't seem like it should be complicated, but it seems like it is.

Perhaps the U.S. has an obligation to look after Earth's people to a lesser or greater extent by helping restrict its population growth, by admitting them into the U.S. to share its wealth (even though mostly in the hands of a few ultra-wealthy), and/or by providing the world's people with more foreign aid in the form of economic assistance via U.S taxpayers. For example, we could contribute by aiding in the maintenance of the Amazon rainforest, at least for North America's wintering neotropical birds and for world carbon dioxide reduction. (U.S. foreign aid is just 0.7% to 1.4% of the U.S. budget.) To some degree, these means are currently used, with varying success. Wildlife, especially migratory wildlife, extends beyond political borders; international economic coordination and management of wildlife and its habitat are required for its survival and wellbeing, as well as that of humanity.

The U.S. has the greatest income inequality of the G7 nations (wealthiest advanced countries of the world). The unequal distribution of wealth is far worse in the U.S., where 10% of the population owns 75% of the wealth, than it is elsewhere (57% in Canada). The extremely wealthy folks in this capitalistic unbalance[214x] have even been given a name, the Ultra High Net Worth Individual (UHNWI), worth at least $30 million. They are the 1% of the world population that has 24% of its wealth, and therefore, unbalanced clout. (In 2018, the U.S. had 70,540 UHNWI; China was second with 16,510, and Canada ninth with 3,010). This excessive wealth controlled by so few has resulted in excessive land "development," industrial production, exploitation of fossil fuels, accompanying pollution (with associated disease) of land, water, and air, global warming, encroachment of and severe reduction of wildlife habitat, and business as usual—all of which seriously threaten wildlife, biodiversity, and even our human descendants.[45x,] [190x] Moreover, a few excessively wealthy individuals contribute excessive monies to certain politicians and thus have exceptional and disproportional political clout. Perhaps a limit should be placed on annual income of people with excessive ("obscene") wealth. (The entertainment industry, including sports, is one of the wealthiest industries in the world, especially relative to its contribution to society).

The relatively recent (1933) profession of wildlife management, which began in Wisconsin, has sought to preserve and sustain the natural resource ecosystem, especially habitat that supports not only wildlife but also humanity. But it has been a losing effort. Stupid as it seems and is, the almighty dollar that disrupts the ecosystem speaks louder than the information and education about the ecosystem that supports humanity and other life forms. As much as folks want a better and brighter future for their kids and grandkids, their conduct falls miserably short here.

Wildlifers use the term "carrying capacity," taught in wild-life courses everywhere, to explain the limits any system has, whether it's a pasture for cows, a woodland for deer and blue jays, the vehicles on a road, the seats in an airplane, the visitors to Disney's Magic Kingdom—or economics. Knowledge exists of how many cows a certain size pasture can support or how many deer a certain size woods can support. In fact, for animals like bears, wildlifers use "biological carrying capacity," the number of bears the habitat can tolerate, and "social carrying capacity," the number of bears people can tolerate. For potentially nui-sance species in human-inhabited areas, social carrying capacity is used, for it is lower than biological carrying capacity, resulting in fewer human-wildlife nuisance problems. But it's as though the term carrying capacity does not apply to people, as though the number of people that can be placed in a given area is endless. At 340 million, the population of the United States continues to increase, as though the number of animals a given area can support applies only to wildlife but not to people, despite all evidence to the contrary, such as social problems, gridlocked highways, residential and business "development" (with reduced wildlife habitat and biodiversity), climate change, ad infinitum, with a declining quality of life.

Society tends to evaluate most things economically, which is why wildlifers must compete their resource aggressively that way; data indicate such wildlife economics is favorably competitive (see Chapter 8). But as Leopold[142] put it long ago in 1949:

"a system of conservation based solely on economic self-interest is hopelessly lopsided. It tends to ignore, and thus eventually to eliminate, many elements in the land community that lack commercial value, but that are (as far as we know) essential to its healthy functioning. It assumes, falsely, I think, that the economic parts of the biotic clock will function without the uneconomic parts." (p. 229–230)

Extinctions and global climate change reinforce that. The economy should be linked with land management of natural resources and climate. Economists, and society, must be more enlightened—and careful.

Here in America, we have our reproduction under control now. Human population increase in the United States is now being driven more by immigration than reproduction (the U.S. birth rate = 1.64/woman, below the 2.1 considered replacement); 227,000 people are added to our planet every day. The U.S. immigration policy is one of the most lenient in the world, along with that of Canada and Australia. The world population of humans is 8 billion. (Bordering the U.S., Canada is the 2nd largest country in the world geographically and has 41 million people). With the U.S. human population at 340 million, now we must heed the advice of people like Richard D. Taber,[234] who, a half century ago, wrote, "Finally, and most important, none of these recommendations will be practical if we continue to pack more and more of mankind and his works into the landscape of North America. The control of human populations is the first necessity if the multitude of populations of other forms of life is to survive" (p. 151). That is already apparent in some countries on Earth. If the human population limit in the U.S. is not placed at 340 million where it is now (2024), then where? Twice as many, 680,000,000? Fewer? It's time to figure it out. With Leopold's warning in 1945[140] (U.S. population 140 million), and his former graduate student Taber's warning 20 years later in 1970[234] (203 million) about population excess (333 million in 2020), the catastrophic impact of global warming is beginning to be felt along with the severe damage humans are causing to the biodiversity of ecosystems on which all life depends.[45x] It is presumptuous and naïve to think that, unlike other animals, the human population can grow infinitely with its "economic growth" in a finite world. Sadly and dangerously, the public is mostly unaware and uninformed.

The Sierra Club reports that nearly half the people in the U.S. breathe dirty air, and oceans are laced with plastic, even seven miles deep in the Mariana Trench. Human population increase[45x] is destroying the biodiversity complexity of ecosystems and compromising their carrying capacity to support humans as well as wildlife, exemplified by extinct and endangered species, global warming, and pollution, leaving this dangerously unhealthy situation for later generations of humans to resolve, *if they can.*

The knowledge of a wildlife biologist is unmatched in society, for society generally is environmentally uninformed, despite attempts at environmental education in the school system. Such lack of knowledge really slows down sophisticated, essential protection of the natural environment. The ecotourism industry and hunting notwithstanding, the value of wildlife and the ecosystem (see Chapter 8) is not readily apparent and thus not readily competitive against the almighty dollar of other human endeavor, usually for short-term gain. Even if the wildlife value is apparent, without federal or state regulation, the almighty dollar for short-term gain speaks louder for some industrialists and "developers," notwithstanding the future of their kids and grandkids and those of other people—the beneficiaries of a healthy, essential, and enjoyable natural environment.

Just how much natural wildlife habitat of various types must be protected sustainably is uncertain for a balanced, healthy world of ecosystems, sustainable healthy populations of wildlife and humans, and balanced human endeavor. And climate change, which affects every living thing, further complicates our ability to determine the required extent of wildlife habitat necessary for the survival and well-being of all living things, including humans.

The recent books on sustainable development and on climate change should be informative.

The vast importance of the wildlife profession in preserving wildlife habitat and a healthy ecosystem—our basic life support system—for a sustainable future is overshadowed by its lack of profound political and even personal recognition and support commensurate with its vast responsibility and its importance to society. On the eve of what appears to be an environmental crisis, with global warming increasing in intensity, the higher frequency of hurricanes and wildifires, and rising sea levels, etc., maybe wildlifers need to play tougher and rougher politically somehow to maximize protection of critical biodiversity for society and wildlife. To appreciate and accept the complexity and the benefit of wildlife and the ecosystem, an uninformed public, especially its leaders, absolutely needs substantial environmental education in schools and universities.

ENVIRONMENTAL AWARENESS AND IGNORANCE

"In the wildlife profession, habitat means everything; without it, nothing else matters. Wildlife habitat is the very basis for wildlife management. Intensive land use from a growing human population is reducing wildlife habitat at an alarming rate. The highest priority in the wildlife profession is habitat protection and the improvement of reduced amounts of habitat coupled with improving environmental literacy of society. A healthy ecosystem is the foundation of society. Wildlife managers are ecologists and recreationists with increasingly important roles in society. The demand for a healthy ecosystem and the recreational uses of wildlife and its habitat are influencing legislation and helping boost tourism as one of the top industries of many states and provinces of the United States and Canada. Habitat improvement will help maintain a healthy ecosystem in our stressed environment."

Thirty years have passed since I began a book with that.[197]

Always go with your best science. Unfortunately, environmental illiteracy (ignorance) far exceeds environmental literacy (awareness). I expressed such concerns 30 years ago.[197, 203] Despite much societal and political denial of scientific proof of global warming, The Nature Conservancy and other nongovernmental wildlife organizations (NGOs) refer to climate change as the biggest environmental threat in history. This is because the ecosystem suffers from society's lack of environmental awareness and environmental education, despite contributions of authorities since the early 1900s[222, 254, 261x] and despite improved environmental laws and increased environmental activism by some folks.[101, 215] For example, although wildlife is a public resource, on private land it often is ignored by environmentally uneducated landowners who cause habitat destruction by poor land management. Examples include plowed fields left over winter without a cover crop to hold soil and benefit wildlife, cows left to graze woodlots and forming browse lines that destroy ground and shrub layers and associated wildlife, and pesticides and fertilizers that seep into ground water, streams, and private wells. (Almost half of Wisconsin is farmland; see Chapter 7.) Few public laws safeguard private land.

Never before has humanity had such an awareness of what we are doing to our planet, nor the power to do something about it. Although scientists are deeply knowledgeable about environmental impacts, to their ultimate consternation, bewilderment, and frustration, their knowledge often is not applied to policy, as though the electorate and politicians know more than scientists. In 1988, *TIME* magazine's annual "Man of the Year" was "Planet of the Year: Endangered Earth;" 33 years later, in 2021, after release of the report "Intergovernmental Panel on Climate Change," which found a rapidly narrowing opportunity to limit the impact of climate change, the U.N. Secretary-General dubbed it "a code red for humanity." *TIME*'s cover story of 1988 went unheeded. To its profound detriment, society has been careless about limiting and adapting its culture to restrict its impacts on the surrounding and sustaining biotic systems.[69]

In 1935, the Wisconsin Conservation Education Statute was passed. Wisconsin is the first state in the U.S. to have such a requirement. The legislature requires teachers to have "adequate instruction in the conservation of natural resources" in order to be certified to teach science or social studies. The legislature also requires conservation of natural resources to be taught in public elementary and high schools. The Wisconsin Department of Public Instruction (1949),[270x] Chapter PI 8, legislative mandate states: "Environmental education objectives and activities shall be integrated into the kindergarten through grade 12 sequential curriculum plans, with the greatest emphasis in art, health, science and social studies education." I remember receiving no such environmental education in my 12 years of elementary and high school in Sheboygan Falls, WI (1944–57). No doubt other schools were and are like that, in Wisconsin and elsewhere.

The environmental ignorance in society—in the 21st century—is appalling and threatening. Everyone in high school and college should be required to take at least two courses with titles like "Natural Resources, Global Warming, and Economic Sustainability." Rarely is something like that a required course as it should be. Most universities have "general degree requirements" that all students must take, but they seldom include natural resources, a critically important subject because a healthy ecosystem is our life support system, and everyone should know it and have a feel for it! That might help produce future environmentally-informed politicians as well as citizens, so that a properly informed and enlightened electorate will make decisions for the good of Earth and society.

The book *The Failure of Environmental Education (and How We Can Fix It)* (2011)[215] presented a dire picture of our critical environmental problems. Environmental education to fix things includes an understanding of sustainable economic growth instead of infinite economic growth from a finite Earth; unbridled population, infrastructure, and building growth; unbridled industry, special interests, and lobbying against regulation (product defense); fossil fuels; unbridled advertising, consumption, and planned obsolescence; political maneuvering; meat consumption, and associated methane production; excessive carbon dioxide and methane production from deforestation and melting of permafrost, for example; chemical and other pollution; animal and plant extinction and endangerment; and the impact of wealth and poverty. That book offers a comprehensive description on how we can fix things with appropriate environmental education to develop an environmentally literate and active society. All these things affect Earth, which can support only so much life, and in a balanced scheme called *biodiversity* that includes only so much wildlife and so many humans and other biota.

Because of the profound impact humans have had on the environment and the extreme problems created especially since about 1950, we are living in what some have described as the *anthropocentric epoch*, i.e., the *Anthropocene*, in which humans substantially alter Earth's surface, atmosphere, and systems of nutrient cycling. Earth is only so big, and during this anthropocentric epoch of just 70 years, humans have stressed it severely and dangerously, ignoring all scientific warnings about the dangers that would ensue from decades of extraction and over-consumption, the accumulation of great wealth in small pockets of society, and general disregard for our role as guardians of the global commons for ourselves and future generations. This disregard has altered Earth's atmosphere, land, and water so substantially that we are living ourselves out of our life-providing environment—rendering this the most perilous moment in human history. Eleventh-hour technological solutions to fix things, especially global warming, is unlikely, and certainly not dependable and worth the risk. After all, it was technology that got us into this fix in the first place.[215]

The folks one meets on the street in Wisconsin and elsewhere are good people who are going about their lives and just don't know this stuff. For example, most folks are unaware that any animals are in danger of extinction, apparently never having been adequately exposed to "this stuff" in school despite Wisconsin's legislation in 1935 to teach environmental education there.

Teaching environmental education in a university to natural resource students touches only a tiny percentage of the population, like preaching to the choir. Clearly, elementary schools, middle schools, high schools, and universities nationwide and worldwide need to improve environmental education, a critical subject far more important than most other courses taught. Universities are not handling environmental education properly in educating society's leaders. That needs to change in this historic era of critical environmental problems, for as deadly as climate change is, it is not a highly regarded political entity in society (see Climate Change and Unprecedented Dangerous Problems).

Since 1972, the North American Association for Environmental Education (NAAEE), has been in existence for a half century now, with its 56 state, provincial, and regional affiliate organizations in the United States, Canada, and Mexico. NAAEE has some 20,000 members across government, business, early childhood education, formal and informal education, higher education, science education, and other sectors of society. Its guidelines combine knowledge of biological systems, physical sciences, social science, and political science into an integrated set of objectives.[215]

Founded in 1974, the Wisconsin Association for Environmental Education (WAEE) consists of about 400 professional organizations and individuals with diverse backgrounds who acknowledge the need for excellence in environmental education, foster responsible environmental action, and seek environmental justice.

In 1990, the Wisconsin Environmental Education Board (WEEB) became law. The board is comprised of 17 members consisting of administrators, politicians (two Republicans and two Democrats), educators, and representatives from agriculture, forestry, business and industry, labor, conservation and environmental groups, and museums, zoos, and nature centers. "The WEEB's mission is to provide leadership in the development of learning opportunities that empower Wisconsin citizens with the knowledge and skills needed to make wise environmental decisions and take responsible actions in their personal lives, workplaces and communities." With such a mixture of so many committee members, that's a tall order.

To improve environmental literacy in Wisconsin, the Wisconsin Center for Environmental Education was legislated in 1990. Housed within the College of Natural Resources at the University of Wisconsin–Stevens Point, the WCEE assists in developing, disseminating, implementing, and evaluating teachers and students in the K–12 environmental education programs in

Wisconsin. The Wisconsin Association of Environmental Education supports state-wide efforts in environmental education by identifying environmental education priorities, creating avenues for networking and professional development, sharing research and expertise, and disseminating exemplary environmental education activities of members and member organizations—a tall order for statewide impact.

To promote environmental education, the U.S. Congress passed the National Environmental Education Act of 1990 to improve environmental education. Congress acknowledged that "threats to human health and environmental quality are increasingly complex, involving a wide range of conventional and toxic contaminants in the air and water and on the land" and that "there is growing evidence of international environmental problems, such as global warming, ocean pollution and overfishing, and declines in species diversity, and that these problems pose serious threats to human health and the environment on a global scale." The Office of Environmental Education is within the U.S. Environmental Protection Agency (EPA).

In my high school, no one knew about advising me into the wildlife or related natural resource profession, despite the wildlife profession having started in Wisconsin in 1933, and despite the existence of the Wisconsin Conservation Department since 1927. I discovered the wildlife profession my senior year (1960–61) at the University of Wisconsin—where the profession began in 1933. True, I'm a bit naïve; but no doubt others were like me, and still are. In an informal survey published in 2017 of nearly 75 high school career counselors, not one knew what a wildlife biologist was and that becoming a wildlife biologist was a career option.[90] This is outrageous and unacceptable in this day and age of animal extinctions, climate warming, environmental pollution that affects people's lives, pocketbooks, even survival, and other damage to the biodiversity of ecosystems—when a wildlife agency exists in federal governments and in all 50 state and ten provincial governments in the United States and Canada, which hire wildlife biologists.

Despite all these efforts, and although Wisconsin has one of the nation's strongest recycling programs—97% of state households participate—environmental unawareness is widespread in Wisconsin and society in general, including its leaders, as explained in the book *The Failure of Environmental Education (and How We Can Fix It)*.[215] Those citizens who are environmentally aware must understand how political decisions are made and that those with money make policy, often if not usually with lobbyists (routinely former governmental officials with connections) who represent industry and other special interest groups rather than the people; this is a big reason that mass environmental education is needed. The environment belongs to all the people.

Founded in 2004, the Center for the Advancement of the Steady State Economy (CASSE) in Arlington, Virginia (headed by a wildlife graduate from the University of Wisconsin–Madison), surveyed university economics departments and found few ecologically-minded courses dealing with the limits to economic growth. If an environmental economics course is taught, it focuses on traditional cost-benefit to resolve natural resource problems; the students thus continue to make the same economic mistakes that created the current set of environmental crises such as global warming, pollution, and species extinction. CASSE promotes the relationship between economic growth and biodiversity conservation by education to resolve the conflict of economic growth with ecological protection/sustainability and economic sustainability.

Although economic dynamism has been driving society's social, political, and civic life, ecologically-minded university economics courses should reveal the limits to economic growth, rather than foster the false notion that economic growth is infinite in a finite world. Maybe the term "sustained economics" or "economic sustainability" is preferable and ultimately more practical and realistic than "economic growth" or "economic development."[224x] "Economic sustainability" would require much thought, adjustment, and compromise. It's the unsustainable but traditional "growth" part of the term that's the problem. Society's acceptance and resolution of economic sustainability rather than economic growth is the challenge.

It is high time for economists to compromise and collaborate with wildlife scientists to influence world leaders for a sustainable ecosystem, with appropriate monetary remuneration from society. This vast, unique, and critical responsibility that wildlifers, and teachers of environmental education and other education, provide society's leaders and everyone else, should be among the highest paid in society for this incomparable responsibility and service. Instead, their salaries are pathetically low.

The Gross Domestic Product (GDP) of economic measurement was developed in the 1930s and 1940s. It takes no account of environmental contributions by nature and the ecosystem to society and economics. Studies are revealing that the vast contribution of biodiversity and the ecosystem to the economic, physical, mental, and emotional health of society needs to be included into the GDP.

The environmental problems this generation is experiencing—for the first time in history—reveal society's limitations and its environmental illiteracy and that society is now approaching and exceeding its limit to economic growth and to population growth. Society must respond. Environmental illiteracy is no longer profitable or harmless, but still normal, unfortunately. It is no longer acceptable. The world has reached this point.

The weak "clout" of environmental education has contributed strongly to our present-day dilemma of climate change and its impact on life-sustaining biodiversity, among other things. The rampant, dangerous environmental illiteracy in society has led us to it. In 1949—75 yeara ago—Leopold wrote in *A Sand County Almanac*,[142] "much of the damage inflicted on land is quite invisible to laymen." After 75 years, that shouldn't be so. Environmental education including ecology must be taught to everyone; it is the best hope for solving our environmental problems. "Blindly following a model of infinite economic growth, when we all dwell on a planet with a finite capacity to support life, is obviously reckless" (p. 195).[215]

CLIMATE CHANGE AND UNPRECEDENTED DANGEROUS PROBLEMS

No good way exists to separate policies for the economy, trade, energy, and security from those affecting land use, soils, water, climate, and biodiversity of ecosystems, some already irreparably damaged from extinctions of biota requiring eons to evolve, rendering the ecosystems more simplistic than they ought to be. Our work in the wildlife profession has helped alert the world to climate change and its impact on the biodiversity complex supporting us all, and the ecosystem upon which biodiversity and all biota depend. For decades, wildlifers have been concerned about preserving biodiversity. Despite some early legislation to protect select wildlife species, the rate of extinction continued to weaken biodiversity and the ecosystem; to preserve it, wildlifers finally succeeded in getting the federal government to pass the Endangered Species Preservation Act in 1966, and a more comprehensive and powerful Endangered Species Act in 1973—50 years ago.[7x, 7y] No Endangered Habitat Act exists, despite the problems.

The year 2023 was the hottest on Earth since records began in pre-industrial 1850. According to scientists with the National Oceanic and Atmospheric Administration (NOAA) and the National Aeronautics and Space Administration (NASA), the world is facing a climate crisis driven by fossil fuel emissions. Unless nations transition away from polluting fuels and transform their economies, experts warn that this level of warming in oceans and atmosphere will unravel ecological webs and cause human-built systems to collapse.

With global warming presently occurring,[25] Wisconsin's well-documented Tension Zone[39] (see Chapter 6) is likely to move northward; the locations, behavior, and timing of various birds, other animals, and plants in Wisconsin and elsewhere are changing. In 2021, the Wisconsin Initiative on Climate Change released its report "Wisconsin's Changing Climate: Impacts and Solutions for a Warmer Climate," which reported increases of 17% in precipitation and 3°F in temperature since 1950, and an expected increase of 3–9°F in 40 years. The Wildlife Society reported in 2022 that in central Wisconsin, snowshoe hares are extirpated from Sandhill Wildlife Area because global warming has caused snow to melt earlier, eliminating camouflage for these winter-white hares, thus facilitating predation. Their predators have had to switch to other prey, reducing populations of ruffed grouse and juvenile porcupines. Things are interconnected.

Species become rare or extinct for several reasons including habitat loss, habitat degradation, highly specialized habitat needs, disturbance sensitivity, exploitation, persecution, predation, genetics, parasitism, disease, pollution, and competition. Climate change and invasive species are expected to become even bigger influences in the future and are affecting rare species now. Thus, the complex biodiversity of ecosystems, on which human society absolutely depends, is affected as temperatures and sea levels rise alongside abnormal and intense weather patterns. Even condominium dwellers in large cities are affected because of ecosystem disruptions that occur from these influences.

Human destruction of nature is contributing directly to climate change.[45x] The world now has so many people that we have to protect ecosystems from us. Since 1900, the number of people on the planet has risen fivefold while the average lifespan has doubled. More people living longer are producing and consuming more, including energy. Aggressive and excessive advertising is persuading folks to accumulate excessive and unneeded material possessions (as the proliferation of roadside storage units attests), to be replaced through planned obsolescence, all rendering our highways more dangerous as more huge, powerful semis compete with sedans and SUVs for road space while delivering product to stores and warehouses. People are inhabiting larger spaces and generating more waste and greenhouse gas. In the past few decades, the pace has accelerated dramatically. The continued economic and scientific advancement of humans is the greatest threat to every other plant and animal species as they are crowded out in the human quest for living room.[274]

The quality of nature, i.e., the health of ecosystems on which we and all other species depend—our very life support system—is declining globally at rates unprecedented in human history, and the rate of species extinctions is accelerating, with grave impacts now likely on people around the world as the ecosystem's biodiversity weakens. Worldwide, we are eroding the very foundations of our health and quality of life, food security, livelihoods, and economies.[190x] Earth is limited in its ability to support life, but that seems readily dismissed.

The World Wildlife Fund has kept track of almost 21,000 populations of more than 4,400 vertebrate species in the world from 1970. *The World Wildlife Fund Living Planet Report 2022* described a catastrophic decline of two-thirds (69%) of the world's animal populations, putting at risk the myriad ecosystem services that people depend on, and increasing the risk of zoonotic diseases like Covid. Humans, too, are exacerbating climate change. *The Living Planet Index* is one of the most comprehensive measures of global biodiversity.

The overwhelming evidence from a wide range of knowledge from over 450 researchers in 50 countries, using some 15,000 scientific and government reports, paints an ominous picture. So says the United Nations report issued in 2019, *Global Assessment Report on Biodiversity and Ecosystem Services*, by the United Nations Intergovernmental Science-Policy Platform on Biodiversity and Ecosystem Services (IPBES) and approved by all 109 nations involved. It highlighted five ways humans are reducing Earth's biodiversity: 1) Eliminating or damaging habitat (75% of land, 85% of wetlands, and 67% of oceans); 2) Overfishing oceans (33% of fish stocks overfished); 3) Climate change from burning fossil fuels (50% of mammals and 25% of birds already affected); 4) Pollution; and 5) Invasive species. The report stated that 1,000,000 species are threatened with extinction. But what about business as usual? According to the report, business as usual is a disaster for the world.

The wealthy countries must do more; polluters and their supporters must pay to repair what they damaged. Yet corrective action by lawmakers, oil producers, and others is pitifully, dangerously slow. Electorate beware. Delaying is a lousy gamble, especially for our kids and grandkids.

Humans should be part of the healthy biodiversity of an ecosystem, not competitors of it. Unlike with most animal populations, the number of humans that will unbalance the biodiversity of an ecosystem seems unclear, but that it has been excessive in some ecosystems is clear. Its control is politically awkward and untenable presently, resulting in, incredibly, worldwide climate change affecting all biodiversity of all ecosystems. Humans can't (won't) control themselves, despite knowledge available from wildlifers and other scientists. It looks like nature will have to control things, however ruthless that might be and probably will be if things, especially politics, do not change.

Today's leaders and citizens are the first generation to realize that we are living in the era of human-caused global climate change, and could be the last to slow and reverse the process.[3x] If our generation does not begin to change climate change forthwith, our descendants, however skilled, will likely be unable to cope with the outcome. The legacy we leave our grandkids will be a planet uninhabitable or grossly less habitable, which technology probably cannot change. How proud our grandkids will be of us. People express concern for their grandchildren, but the immediate almighty dollar trumps environmental concern and the natural environment their grandchildren will inherit. That can be seen currently with animal and plant extinctions, ecosystem destruction, global warming, pollution (such as PFAS, nitrates, and many others in water, air in cities, chemicals and plastics in oceans, noise pollution in oceans and elsewhere, light pollution, etc.), and similar natural environmental degradation and catastrophes.[45x] An example is the Great Pacific Garbage Patch, about twice the size of Texas, a debris field of a soup of plastic brought together in the North Pacific Ocean by a swirl of currents known as a gyre, affecting all kinds of ocean wildlife through ingestion and ensnaring.

Over half a century ago, in 1968, Garret Hardin[86] published "Tragedy of the Commons." The issues Hardin brought up continue today, as greedy people decimate public resources by exploiting them unmercifully and selfishly in the commons before others can. For a gross example, in 1992, Canada placed a moratorium on cod fishing, i.e., no commercial fishing for northern cod, because after centuries of fishing the once vastly abundant and apparently endless populations of northern cod in international waters, stocks had collapsed as nations competed to get "theirs," in unfettered and unregulated harvesting, destroying stocks and habitat. Stocks have not recovered these many years later. In 2004, Myron Arms[6] made poignant comments applicable today.

Writing about the cod collapse, he said (p. 145–146):

"Ours is the generation, it seems, that has finally been forced up against the limits. Our burgeoning population, recently risen past 6 billion [over 8 billion in 2023], coupled with centuries of industrialization and rising standards of living, have combined to stress the Earth's natural systems on a planetary scale. Once-massive reserves of essential commodities have been decimated. Thousands of species have become extinct. Entire regions have been stripped of their natural cover. Ground water has been contaminated. Water tables have dropped. Topsoil has eroded into the rivers. Large areas of the oceans have been fished to exhaustion. For other generations in other settings, such occurrences have taken place on local scales. For ours, they have finally started to take place on global scales.

"Maybe the miners and foresters and fishermen of earlier generations just didn't know any better. Maybe they really were 'honest and intelligent' people who were simply never required to face up to the long-term impacts of their actions. But what about now—when the impacts of our extractive industries extend to every corner of the planet and when the long-term effects are increasingly apparent for everyone to see? Are we…doomed to follow those who came before us to the same inevitable ends? Or might we somehow learn to [transform] the way we act, to curb our appetites, to treat the Earth and the oceans with a different kind of caring?"

Add to that global climate change from melting ice caps and glaciers, rising sea levels, extreme temperatures, drought and wildfires, rain and floods, hurricanes and tornadoes, blizzards and hail—with increasing frequency and intensity, with the deterioration and elimination of ecosystems, with displacement, reduction, extirpation and extinction of wildlife populations, with spread of wildlife diseases. All this has serious implications for our health and economy. Action from environmentally uninformed political leaders and the electorate is not comforting.

The Nov. 7/Nov. 14, 2022, issue of *TIME* magazine reported that "wealthy countries have spent more than a century emitting carbon dioxide unchecked, and they owe it to the rest of the world to pay for the damage they have caused…In any typical conception of fairness, the parties most responsible for causing the problem should be responsible for cleaning it up." That would include the people who have become extraordinarily and obscenely rich from oil extraction and sale (e.g., Shell, ExxonMobil, Chevron, BP), enabled by society buying the stuff. Even though containing just a fraction of the global population of humans, the developed nations of the United States and Europe are mostly responsible for historic emissions. According to the Intergovernmental Panel on Climate Change, we will be witnessing "the inundation of small island states and tens of millions of climate migrants in sub-Saharan Africa." Unfortunately, the main news outlets in the U.S. have a long history of diminishing or misrepresenting the climate story (1% of coverage in 2021 by ABC, NBC, CBS, and Fox News). "Only 39% of Americans know that most scientists agree that climate change is happening today."[102x]

In August 2021, the U.N.'s Intergovernmental Panel on Climate Change (IPCC) produced a report stating that irrefutable evidence reveals human influence has warmed the atmosphere, ocean, and land with irreversible results for centuries to millennia, and action preventing further decline must be taken immediately. The report was written by more than 230 leading scientists from countries around the world citing more than 14,000 research articles. Moreover, in September 2021, some 250 health and medical journals worldwide simultaneously published the same editorial: "Call for Emergency Action to Limit Global Temperature Increases, Restore Biodiversity, and Protect Health." The editorial stated that "the greatest threat to global public health is the continued failure of world leaders to keep the global temperature rise below 1.5°C (2.7°F) and to restore nature." And this hearkens back to the profound environmental illiteracy among our leaders and society from the lack of environmental education, now critical, as the world is belatedly experiencing.

Due to the destruction it causes, global climate change, from the expanding human population supporting nonrenewable resource extraction and use, is beginning to catch attention. Substituting renewable energy is essential but must be accomplished with no or minimal wildlife habitat loss, or society will still have a problem with biodiversity. In November 2021, negotiators from nearly 200 countries met in Glasgow, Scotland, for the COP26, i.e., the 26th Conference of the Parties to the United Nations Framework Convention on Climate Change—a conference to determine what to do and how to do it regarding controlling climate change. Scientists have estimated that the world must keep from exceeding 1.5°C (2.7°F) globally above the pre-industrial level.

We must make two things happen this decade:[57x] 1) Global carbon and methane emissions must be reduced 50% by 2030, focusing on the G20 countries (world's biggest economies), which are responsible for 85% of global GDP and 80% of global greenhouse gases. 2) All remaining healthy ecosystems must be safeguarded, and depleted ones regenerated; that's where wildlifers play a substantial role.

Two types of an international United Nations Conference of the Parties (COP) occur: climate and biodiversity. The first climate COP occurred in 1995. In November 2022, several oil-producing nations of nearly 200 countries meeting at the COP27 UN climate summit in Egypt failed to agree to phase out fossil fuels—a gross miscalculation. They did agree to set up a fund to help vulnerable, low greenhouse gas-contributing countries cope with climate disasters.

The United Nations Biodiversity Conference (COP15) of nearly 200 nations met in Montreal, Quebec, in December 2022. The UN agreed to protect, by 2030, 30% of land and water considered important for biodiversity. Currently, 10% of marine and 17% of terrestrial areas are protected. The UN also committed to raising $200 billion by 2030 for biodiversity.

In 2023, Dubai, United Arab Emirates hosted COP28 with nearly 200 nations and a goal of curtailing fossil fuel production and use. The results of the conference were frustrating. Fossil fuels—coal (the dirtiest), oil, gas—contribute the most to some national economies and to greenhouse gases and global climate change, but reduction was not required. Agriculture, from farm to fork to dump, also contributes substantially, including to biodiversity loss.

Society's scientists recognize the urgency of protecting bio-diversity and reducing greenhouse gases and climate change. Nonetheless, society's politicians and economists foolishly assume their intellect and knowledge somehow exceed that of scientists, thus failing to protect society by recognizing the urgency of the problem, and messing around with a potentially irreversible deadly situation for their grandkids and even soon enough for themselves.

As the world's only superpower, the United States has the world's largest economy and is the world's second largest emit-ter of greenhouse gases after China. The passage in 2022 of the ambiguously-named U.S. Inflation Reduction Act is import-ant, even though it barely passed and climate change, instead of standing alone, was included in a bill with healthcare costs and tax enforcement. The law signals that the energy transition in the U.S. has begun, although climate change will get worse before it gets better.

Climate change also is connected to sustainable investing. We must divest from companies that threaten the future of the planet, for climate change presents a risk to every industry and the traditional capitalist ethic of increasing money in a free market system, what some call environmental, social, and governance (ESG) investing.[1x] But many folks, including political leaders, are anti-ESG—a major problem—despite research showing that socially diverse companies are more profitable and resilient.

To replace the polluting fossil fuels of oil, gas, and coal, soci-ety is pushing for non-polluting renewable energy. But some clean-energy companies around the world are damaging biodi-versity, for example, with windmills that kill migrating birds and bats, solar panels that completely cover formerly diverse fields, tidal (river) generators that kill marine organisms, and hydro dams that flood biodiverse-rich riparian habitat. Perhaps geothermal energy and nuclear fusion are the answers, although nuclear errors are devastating. Wildlifers are investigating wildlife conservation relative to renewable energy.[180x] Choices presently aren't easy.

If expeditious enough, resolution of global climate change should involve awareness and better management of related issues such as reducing consumption of nonrenewable energy along with size limits of human populations—and its accompanying encroachment of wildlife habitat, with reduced or eliminated biodiversity. Seems like society should be able to handle these environmental problems, just as society has handled other major problems in the past.[88] But society has no experience or expertise with so threatening a problem as the magnitude of climate change and its worldwide power over the ecosystems that support humanity and the biodiversity critical to the survival of all biota. Politicians uninformed of and/or insensitive to global climate change, especially coupled with unstable, ignorant and irresponsible juvenile-behaving leaders unleashing nuclear weapons, could cause such a destructed world mess that evolution might very well have to start over. To benefit future generations of humans—and wildlife—worldwide cooperation and coordination will be difficult but necessary although seemingly impossible. The stakes of climate change are too high. If humans cannot limit their encroachment, resource exploitation, and accompanying ecosystem degradation, nature itself will provide the limits, and humanity will suffer the consequences with the rest of the biota.

Extremism of anything is generally unsound. Although the almighty dollar trumps everything in an extreme capitalistic society, there is reason for hope. Young voters are viewing unfettered capitalism as punishing desirable qualities like fairness, and rewarding undesirable qualities like greed, selfishness, and lack of empathy. A study at Harvard University in 2016, and a Gallup poll in 2018, showed that most young voters believe that capitalism as it exists today does more harm than good in the world, and that nature is alive and with value that cannot be accounted for in a capitalist market system. Climate change is motivating them. They are investing in socially and environmentally responsible stocks—and voting—for it will be their world, good or bad.

Countries need to recognize and legally protect nature's right to exist and thrive. (Ecuador made history in 2008, when it became the first country to do so). In that wildlife profession that had its origin less than 100 years ago in Wisconsin, wildlifers can provide their knowledge of biodiversity in ecosystems to guide and help control the climate change and biodiversity loss that now threaten the world—and to educate the public to it.

For the good of our descendants, the sustainable size of human populations must be identified to control its already evident over-use and harm of life-sustaining wildlife habitat and biodiversity. Human expansion and infrastructure, things like housing and strip malls and vehicles and agriculture and oil wells, are causing present and future life-threatening impact on climate and nat-ural resources, things extremely difficult and maybe ultimately impossible to correct. It has come to that.

In 1994, I began a book[203] with four statements. I'll end this book with them; they need repeating these 30 years later.

Finally, and most important, none of these recommendations will be practical if we continue to pack more and more of mankind and his works into the landscape of North America. The control of human populations is the first necessity if the multitude of populations of other forms of life is to survive.

—Richard D. Taber[234]

The law locks up both man and woman
Who steals the goose from off the common,
But lets the greater felon loose
Who steals the common from the goose.

—Medieval English Quatrain

We do not inherit the land from our ancestors.
We borrow it from our children.

—Chief Seattle

A thing is right when it tends to preserve the integrity, stability, and beauty of the biotic community. It is wrong when it tends otherwise.... To keep every cog and wheel is the first prerequisite of intelligent tinkering.

—Aldo Leopold[142]

APPENDICES

APPENDIX 1: EARLY WILDLIFE BOOKS

Early wildlife books up to the 1920s include the 9-volume *American Ornithology; or the Natural History of the Birds of the United States*[263x] by ornithologist Alexander Wilson in 1808–1814; *The Birds of America*[6x] by naturalist John J. Audubon in 1838; *On the Origin of Species*[43] by naturalist Charles Darwin in 1859; *Man and Nature: or Physical Geography as Modified by Human Action*[163] by environmentalist George P. Marsh in 1864; *The American Beaver and His Works*[180y] by anthropologist Lewis H. Morgan in 1868; and *Economic Relations of Wisconsin Birds*[108y] by agricultural scientist Franklin H. King in 1882.

Other important wildlife books from the time include *The Birds of Wisconsin*[117] by ornithologists Ludwig Kumlien and Ned Hollister in 1903; the 4-volume set *Lives of Game Animals*[223] by Canadian biologist Ernest Thompson Seton in 1909–1928; *The Extermination of the American Bison*[97x] in 1889, *Our Vanishing Wild Life*[98] in 1913, and *Wild Life Conservation in Theory and Practice*[99] in 1914 by American preservationist William Hornaday; *Bird Guide: Land Birds East of the Rockies*[211x] in 1909, and *The Canadian Bird Book*[211z] in 1914 by naturalist Chester Reed; *Western Bird Guide: Birds of the Rockies and West to the Pacific*[211y] by naturalists Chester Reed, Harry Harvey, and Rex Brasher in 1913; *Birds of America*[208] by editor Gilbert Pearson in 1917.

Early wildlife books published in the 1920s include the 21-volume *Life Histories of North American Birds*[14] by ornithologist

Arthur Cleveland Bent, with 19 of them in 1919-1953; *The Conservation of the Wild Life of Canada*[91] by Canadian entomologist Gordon Hewitt in 1921; *Bird Companions*[160] by naturalist Angelia Main in 1925; *Animal Ecology*[52] by British biologist Charles Elton in 1927.

Early wildlife books in the 1930s include *The Bobwhite Quail: Its Habits, Preservation, and Increase*[226] by conservationist Herbert Stoddard in 1931; and *Game Management*[133] by wildlife professor Aldo Leopold in 1933.

Early wildlife books in the 1940s include *American Wild Life, Illustrated*[271x] by the Writers Program of New York City in 1940; *The California Sea Otter Trade: 1784-1848*[189z] by historian Adele Ogden in 1941; *Wildlife Conservation*[61] in 1941, *Wildlife Refuges*[62] in 1943, and *Wildlife Management*[63] in 1951 by wildlife biologist and director of the U.S. Fish and Wildlife Service Ira Gabrielson; *Ducks, Geese, and Swans of North America*[115] by naturalist Francis Kortright in 1942; *The Wild Turkey in Virginia: Its Status, Life History and Management*[184] by wildlife professor Henry S. Mosby and zoologist C. O. Handley in 1943; *A Guide to Bird Watching*[92] by zoologist Joseph J. Hickey in 1944; *The Life of the Robin*[119] in 1943, *Darwin's Finches*[120] in 1947, and *The Natural Regulation of Animal Numbers*[121] in 1954 by British ornithologist David Lack; *The Ruffed Grouse: Life History, Propagation, Management*[30] by wildlife biologist Gardiner Bump and others in 1947; *The Land and Wildlife*[70] by ecologist Edward H. Graham in 1947; *A Field Guide to the Birds*[209x] by ornithologist Roger Tory Peterson in 1947; *Birds of the West*[21x] by biology professor Ernest Booth in 1948; *Wildlife Management: Upland Game and General Principles*[251] in 1948, and *Wildlife Management: Fur Bearers, Waterfowl, and Fish*[252] in 1953 by wildlife professor Reuben Trippensee; *The Way to Game Abundance*[71] by Wallace B. Grange in 1949; *King Solomon's Ring*[154] by Austrian ethologist Konrad Lorenz in 1949; *A Sand County Almanac and Sketches Here and There*[140] by Aldo Leopold in 1949.

Early wildlife books in the 1950s include *American Wildlife and Plants: A Guide to Wildlife Food Habits*[165x] by naturalists Alexander C. Martin, Herbert S. Zim, and Arnold L. Nelson in 1951; *Practice of Wildlife Conservation*[264] by wildlife professor Leonard Wing in 1951; *The North American Buffalo*[212y] by naturalist Frank G. Roe in 1951; *Our Wildlife Legacy*[2] by wildlife professor Durward Allen in 1954; *The Passenger Pigeon* by wildlife writer Arlie Schorger in 1955; *The Great Buffalo Hunt*[64x] by historian Wayne Gard in 1959; and *Wildlife of Mexico: The Game Birds and Mammals*[146] by Aldo Leopold's son and wildlife professor Starker Leopold in 1959.

APPENDIX 2: WILDLIFE EDUCATION IN WISCONSIN

Of the 13 four-year campuses in the Universities of Wisconsin, 11 are mainly teaching campuses with some research. Only Madison and Milwaukee are research campuses with authorized PhD programs, conducting research with both MS and PhD candidates. When time and inclination permit, faculty members at the other 11 campuses in the UW system may conduct research, but with MS candidates only, resulting in short-term research projects. Their heavier teaching loads reduce time and inclination to write proposals for grants to conduct faculty research and publication (and corresponding career development).

The University of Wisconsin–Madison offers bachelor's, master's, and doctoral degrees in wildlife ecology. The University of Wisconsin–Stevens Point offers bachelor's and master's degrees in wildlife ecology (which, on the diploma for the MS degree, reads "Natural Resources"). Northland College in Ashland offers a bachelor's degree in natural resources with an emphasis in fisheries and wildlife ecology.

UNIVERSITY OF WISCONSIN–MADISON

The University of Wisconsin–Madison is a large university (50,000 students) within the capital city of Madison (270,000 people) located on an isthmus and lands surrounding four lakes—Lake Mendota, Lake Monona, Lake Kegonsa, and Lake Waubesa.

"Professional training in wildlife management has been offered at the University of Michigan since 1927, when the Department of Forestry was reorganized as the School of Forestry and Conservation" (p. iii).[261] But the first university wildlife program in the world began in 1933, when the University of Wisconsin, in southcentral Wisconsin, authorized for Aldo Leopold the position of Chair of Game Management, within the Department of Agricultural Economics. Leopold's appointment would have state, national, and even international significance. Here was a guy without a PhD, and a degree in forestry, presuming to be a professor of wildlife. But he couldn't have had a degree in wildlife because none existed until he came along. He is no doubt one of the few, if not the only wildlife professor with such non-qualifications. But he nonetheless had what it takes to start a new profession of wildlife because he was a self-taught wildlifer, with on-the-job training, curiosity, inclination, intensity, aptitude, intellect, assertiveness, dedication, energy, ability—and genius.

Beginnings. Leopold's first office was in the soils building. There he taught the first wildlife class in the nation every spring semester from 1934 to 1937, in addition to occasional short courses for farmers and other interested people. It was called Survey of Game Management. Offered for the first time in March 1934, it began as a half-semester course to orient all levels of students, often a turning point in their careers. It emphasized principles of game management and field techniques. That spring he took on his first graduate student, Franklin Schmidt, who studied prairie chickens (see Chapter 1). He also supervised the work of Wallace Grange, of the Wisconsin Conservation Department, on cyclic phenomena in wildlife, until funding fell through. Leopold took on his second graduate student in fall 1934, Leonard Wing, who continued work on cycles.[264]

In 1937, the wildlife program moved into an old house at 424 University Farm Place, once the residence of Dean Harry L. Russell and his family, on the agriculture campus. It was Russell who was most influential in hiring Leopold. In 1939, Leopold changed the name and content of the introductory course in wildlife from Game Management 118 to Wildlife Ecology 118,[174] an indication that the new profession was expanding ecologically. He never used his book *Game Management*[133] as a required text, instead having students read directly from the published literature.

The wildlife program at the University of Wisconsin in Madison was the world's first wildlife graduate program, i.e., a program to provide students with a Master of Science (MS) or Doctor of Philosophy (PhD) in wildlife science. No undergraduate wildlife degree was authorized, i.e., a student could not obtain a Bachelor of Science (BS) degree in wildlife science, then. In 1972, the first students graduated with a BS in wildlife ecology. Eventually the BS would include coursework that The Wildlife Society would accept to certify a student as an Associate Wildlife Biologist (AWB). Leopold focused on his graduate students and on the wildlife course for them and any biology or other undergraduate student who enrolled in it.

In spring 1937, three of Leopold's first four wildlife graduate students received their degrees: Leonard Wing (PhD), Art Hawkins (MS), Ellwood Moore (MS) (see Chapter 1.) This was a landmark. These three men were the first formally educated, (university-trained) wildlife professionals in the world, the world's first wildlifers, although their degree probably was in zoology because the wildlife degree had not yet been approved. They essentially constituted the origin of the new profession of wildlife science. His students Fred Hamerstrom (PhD, 1941) and Fran Hamerstrom (MS, 1940) became the first university-trained wildlife biologists in the world to work as wildlife researchers. They worked for the Wisconsin Conservation Department.

From the UW's Department of Wildlife, under Aldo Leopold, Leonard Wing (at University of Michigan), Irv Buss (at Washington State University), Bob McCabe, and Joe Hickey were the first university-trained wildlife professors in the world in the wildlife profession. Wing had a PhD in zoology (probably) but with wildlife courses. Buss and McCabe had an MS and a PhD in wildlife. Hickey had an MS in wildlife and a PhD in zoology. Others, such as Paul Errington (PhD, 1932 U. Wisconsin) of Iowa State University and Reuben Trippensee (PhD, 1934 U. Michigan) of the University of Massachusetts had PhDs in zoology and became early wildlife professors, productive in teaching and writing. Like Aldo Leopold, they had no university training or degree in wildlife ecology, for none existed when they were in college.

Wildlife Ecology Major. Leopold developed Survey of Game Management, first taught in 1934, into a new 3-credit course in wildlife. Wildlife Ecology 118 was approved in 1938, and taught for the first time in 1939. Open to any UW student, 45 enrolled, ten more than ever in the survey course. Upon Leopold's death in 1948, his former graduate student and recent colleague Joe Hickey taught the course and continued doing so until his retirement in 1976. Then the course, now called Wildlife Ecology 318, Principles of Wildlife Ecology, for upper-level undergraduate (and graduate) students, was taught by Dr. Stanley Temple.

In spring 1942, just 31 students enrolled in Wildlife Ecology 118, the third consecutive year of decline since a high of 45 in 1939, a reflection of students enlisting and being drafted into the military for World War II. In spring 1944, only 11 students enrolled in Wildlife Ecology 118, and only 12 in the farmer's short course. Wildlife Ecology 118 reached its all-time low in spring 1945, when just eight students enrolled; the farmer's short course had just 15 students. In 1946, Leopold offered a new class: Advanced Game Management 179. It was designed to give wildlife graduate students instruction in wildlife research; Leopold's 12 grad students enrolled. In 1947, Leopold's last time teaching Wildlife Ecology 118, 66 students enrolled in it—too many for effective field trips.

In 1939, Leopold advanced from a Chair of Game Management within the Department of Agricultural Economics to form the one-man Department of Wildlife Management in the College of Agriculture, the first academic wildlife department in the world dedicated to the formal development, through education and training, of future wildlife professionals entering the emerging vocation of wildlife management. In addition to Leopold's biweekly seminars with his graduate students, he taught three courses: Game Management, Survey of Game Management (changed to Wildlife Ecology about 1945), and Wildlife Techniques.[167] From 1933 to 1946, the wildlife program was just

Leopold until he hired two of his former graduate students. In 1945, Bob McCabe (MS 1943, PhD 1949) became an instructor under Leopold and then Leopold's teaching assistant in 1946, teaching the Wildlife Techniques course, and in 1949, an assistant professor in the UW's Department of Wildlife. Joe Hickey (MS 1943) joined the faculty in late 1947[174] as an assistant professor, just a few months before Leopold died in spring 1948. Although McCabe and Hickey did not yet have their PhDs, almost no other wildlife PhDs except Leopold's students were available for a wildlife faculty appointment in those days because professional education in the wildlife profession had just begun.

As it turned out, McCabe and Hickey were outstanding. After Leopold's death in April 1948, Hickey and McCabe took over the wildlife department for the next 3.5 decades.[174] Hickey was department chair from 1948 to 1952. In 1951, McCabe officially joined the one-man faculty of Joe Hickey. McCabe was chair for 27 years, from 1952 to 1979. In 1956, Leopold's last graduate student (1947), Robert Ellarson, became the third member to join the wildlife faculty, as wildlife extension biologist. Both Hickey and McCabe have been so accomplished in the wildlife profession that they have received the highest award in the wildlife profession, the Aldo Leopold Memorial Award. Hickey, McCabe, and Ellarson were inducted into the Wisconsin Conservation Hall of Fame at the University of Wisconsin–Stevens Point, along with their mentor, Leopold, and the third person in the original Leopold position (after Hickey), Stan Temple; so, too, were wildlife extension biologist Scott Craven and wildlife documentary writer Arlie Schorger.

In 1959, the Department of Forestry and Wildlife Management was formed to organize wildlife and forestry research into one department. In 1962, the disciplines separated into the Department of Wildlife Management and the Department of Forestry. In 1964, the wildlife department was moved into a new building named appropriately enough Harry L. Russell Laboratories, or Russell Labs, along with three other departments also in the School of Agriculture and Life Sciences. A few days after the move, Building 424, Harry Russell's old house, the genesis of formal wildlife education (where I once sat for my wildlife class in 1961), was torn down.

In 1967, the Department of Wildlife Management was renamed the Department of Wildlife Ecology, which better described the department's emphasis on the interrelationship of wildlife with its environment. To the chagrin of the wildlife department, in 2007, the two departments of wildlife and of forestry were combined into the Department of Forest and Wildlife Ecology within the College of Agricultural and Life Sciences. Its stated mission is "to provide science-based research, instruction, and extension that supports forest and wildlife conservation and management in an ecologically, economically, and socially sustainable fashion." Wildlife support to the academic program is readily available from the Wisconsin Department of Natural Resources, with its nearby headquarters in Madison. Through the late 1970s, the wildlife faculty that continued the legacy of Aldo Leopold involved Robert A. McCabe, Joseph J. Hickey, Arlie W. Schorger, Robert S. Ellarson, Lloyd B. Keith, Orin J. Rongstad, Robert L. Ruff, Stanley A. Temple, Scott R. Craven, and Donald H. Rusch—all with PhDs.

The wildlife program has come a long way since Aldo Leopold's time. Wildlife 118 (Wildlife Ecology) has had two name alterations and has been elevated to Wildlife 318 (Principles of Wildlife Ecology), an upper-level (junior and senior) course. More wildlife courses have been added to the curriculum, now taught by ten wildlife faculty members. For a BS or BA in wildlife ecology, six courses of 20 credits in wildlife and six courses of 26 credits in biology are required. That and other coursework fulfill the requirements of The Wildlife Society for qualification as an Associate Wildlife Biologist.

Wildlife students may join the Student Chapter of The Wildlife Society. Members will associate with fellow wildlife ecology students as well as with wildlife graduate students and with faculty and other wildlife professionals. Members become more aware of local, national, and international resource issues, and gain valuable experience and friendships. Internships are available.

The Nelson Institute. The Nelson Institute for Environmental Studies is an environmental studies major that augments the wildlife major and is often taken with it as a double major. Within the Nelson Institute are the Center for Climatic Research, Land Tenure Center, Center for Sustainability and the Global Environment, and Center for Culture, History and the Environment. In 2007, the Nelson Institute and the Wisconsin Department of Natural Resources began a partnership called the Wisconsin Initiative on Climate Change Impacts, which determines the climatic effects on forests, fisheries, agriculture, human health, and more, and how human communities can respond. Mainly for graduate students, all centers provide training, e.g., in climate change, that complements the wildlife major.

The Institute began in 1970, when Wisconsin's Gaylord Nelson began Earth Day (see Chapter 1). Nelson's name was added to the institute in 2002. It has equal status with the UW's 11 constituent schools and colleges. An oddity on a college campus, the Nelson Institute contains mostly faculty who are cross listed in other departments. The institute offers undergraduate degrees, but only as a double major to some other major. It has been housed in Science Hall.

Wildlife Research: MS and PhD. The venerable wildlife graduate program of the University of Wisconsin–Madison is generally ranked as one of the top five in the nation.

In addition to his teaching, Aldo Leopold began using research projects to train students in the new profession of wildlife ecology. The first students were MS or PhD candidates who had to have a research project, selected by the major professor, and thus received training in planning and setting up the project, collecting data, analyzing the data collected, and writing the thesis (MS) or dissertation (PhD). All this took planning discipline, field discipline, analytical discipline, and writing discipline—features useful in professional wildlife work of any type.

Faculty teaching loads are relatively light, allowing time to write proposals, obtain grants, and conduct the research program at the University of Wisconsin–Madison. That research program involves all aspects of wildlife ecology, such as ecosystem and biodiversity; habitat use, alteration, and restoration; species biology; pest, invasive, and over-abundant species; physiology; toxicology; epidemiology; climatology; human dimensions; management assessment; law enforcement; and policy implications. The research program is enhanced by the vast library holdings on campus and a comprehensive reprint file collection on wildlife within the wildlife program (see Chapter 3). Number, type, and length of research projects for graduate students depends upon availability of funding and faculty time. The wildlife faculty has a reputation for productive publishing of wildlife research results. With their major professor (advisor), PhD and MS wildlife students at UW–Madison have studied and published on aspects of game and nongame species of wildlife throughout Wisconsin, North America, and the world. With society's high interest in wildlife, these types of projects have resulted in high media attention, which has enhanced the identity and reputation of the wildlife program and its ability to attract funding, to attract and educate students, to conduct high quality research, and to help society.

Wisconsin Cooperative Wildlife Research Unit. In collaboration with the University of Wisconsin–Madison's wildlife program, the Wisconsin Cooperative Wildlife Research Unit began there in 1972, with Dr. Donald J. Rusch the first Unit Leader. Responsibilities are to provide education to and conduct wildlife research with wildlife graduate students on projects in Wisconsin and elsewhere and to furnish technical advice to society about managing wildlife resources. With its graduate students, the Wildlife Unit collaborates with the Wisconsin Bureau of Wildlife, the U.S. Fish and Wildlife Service on the national wildlife refuges in Wisconsin and elsewhere, and other wildlife organizations on research projects. The Wildlife Unit at UW–Madison has been exemplary in conducting research projects and producing high-caliber wildlifers (see Chapter 3).

Arboretum. To augment the wildlife program, a three-mile trip from the UW campus in Madison takes students to the 1,260-acre University of Wisconsin–Madison Arboretum—the Arb—along the south side of 320-acre Lake Wingra, with nearby 28-acre Henry Vilas Zoo and 45-acre Vilas Park along the north side of Lake Wingra. In 2021, the National Park Service designated the Arboretum a National Historic Landmark for its role as a pioneer in ecological restoration.[37] In an urban environment, the Arboretum, with its visitor center, is a magnificent outdoor classroom and laboratory for teaching and research, connected to an extensive system of bike trails and parks; Madison has the most parks and playgrounds of the 100 largest cities in the U.S.

In the early 1930s, the Arboretum was pasture and cultivated field that had been neglected. In 1933, the university bought 246 acres, designating the land as an arboretum. As part of his initial faculty appointment, Aldo Leopold served as the Arboretum's first research director. The Arboretum has evolved into the 1,260-acre, widely recognized site of historic research in ecological restoration and includes the oldest collection of restored ecological communities in the world: prairie, savanna, deciduous woods, coniferous woods, wetlands—and associated wildlife, all within the city limits of Madison.

Named after famed plant ecologist John Curtis, Curtis Prairie is 71 acres of the Arboretum, and the world's oldest ecologically restored prairie, including big bluestem and Indian grasses that tower 7 to 8 feet tall. First cultivated in 1836, it became a horse pasture that was returned to native vegetation, thus setting the stage for restoration ecology to emerge as a science.[100] Curtis Prairie is the first restored prairie in the world. It is where restoration ecology began. Next to the Curtis Prairie, in a 21-acre area known as the Leopold Pines (named for Aldo Leopold), are the largest trees, consisting mainly of red pines and white pines and some red maple and white birch planted by the Civilian Conservation Corps in 1933–1937.

Public use of the Arboretum is a balance of education, research, and recreation.

Kemp Natural Resources Station. A University of Wisconsin Agricultural Research Station, Kemp Natural Resources Station contains 231 acres with some of the last remnants of old-growth forest in the Lake States, as well as other distinct ecosystems. Located near Woodruff in northern Wisconsin, on the shore of Lake Tomahawk, Kemp Station is a teaching and research facility operated by the College of Agriculture and Life Sciences.

A two-week, 2-credit wildlife ecology summer camp at Kemp Natural Resource Station, taught every other summer, is an optional but excellent learning experience for wildlife students, with transportation and room and board.

University of Wisconsin-Extension. Wisconsin residents have access to the Universities of Wisconsin's resources and research through the University of Wisconsin–Extension. UW–Extension has four divisions: Cooperative Extension, Continuing and Online Education, Business and Entrepreneurship, and Public Broadcasting. In 1907, UW–Extension was created as a division of the University of Wisconsin–Madison, and reorganized in 1965. In 1956, Bob Ellarson joined the wildlife faculty as the first extension wildlife biologist, with his 23-year radio program "Wonderful World of Nature," until 1978, when he retired. Scott Craven was Ellarson's successor in 1979, until his retirement in 2011.

Specialists in the University of Wisconsin-Madison's Department of Forest and Wildlife Ecology conduct statewide natural resource programs including wildlife extension programs that advise and serve Wisconsin citizens on matters relating to wildlife. A wildlife extension biologist provides information and programs on-site or through publications, distance education technologies, off-site programs, and other media. Programs include Wisconsin Coverts Project (woodland wildlife management programs for private landowners), backyard wildlife habitat enhancement and nuisance wildlife abatement, pesticide applicator training, Farm Technology Days for information about farm wildlife management for income, recreation and pest control, and wildlife biology to school and youth groups.[198]

Wisconsin Sea Grant. In 1972, the U.S. Department of Commerce designated the University of Wisconsin–Madison a Sea Grant College. It is a statewide program of research and education dedicated to the stewardship and sustainable use of the nation's Great Lakes and ocean resources. The program has emphasized research on estuarine systems, fisheries, ecosystem dynamics, water quality, and micro-contaminants. Headquartered at the University of Wisconsin–Madison, under the Graduate School, in the Office of the Vice Chancellor for Research and Graduate Education's Aquatic Sciences Center, it includes offices on campuses in the coastal cities of Superior, Green Bay, Manitowoc, and Milwaukee. It is funded by the National Sea Grant College Program, National Oceanic and Atmospheric Administration, U.S. Department of Commerce, and matching contributions from the state and private sector.

UNIVERSITY OF WISCONSIN–STEVENS POINT

The University of Wisconsin–Stevens Point (8,000 students) is located in Stevens Point (26,000 people), which is along the Wisconsin River in central Wisconsin, with branch campuses in Marshfield and Wausau. It is a teaching university. Semester teaching loads are heavy ($\geq$12 credits/semester), with little extra time to write proposals for research grants or to conduct research and publish results.

The largest undergraduate wildlife program in the world is located at the University of Wisconsin–Stevens Point within its College of Natural Resources, the largest in the nation and widely recognized as the nation's leading undergraduate natural resource program. Its national award-winning Student Chapter of The Wildlife Society (est. 1971) is one of the best in the nation, having received The Wildlife Society Student Chapter of the Year Award eight times.

From Conservation Education to Wildlife Major. In 1937–1938, the wildlife program had its humble, simplistic origin as part of a conservation course when the bulletin (course catalog) for Central State Teachers College at Stevens Point listed Conservation 107 (no title) for the first time. Also listed in the 1937–1938 bulletin was Conservation 207 (Conservation of the Natural Resources of the United States), taught by Charles Watson, hired in 1913 to teach geography. Until 1946, these were the only two conservation courses taught.

The teacher for Conservation 107 was Fred Schmeeckle (1893–1967) from Nebraska, hired in 1923 with no PhD (MS from U. Minnesota) to teach agriculture when the university's name remained as it was at its inception in 1894, Wisconsin State Normal School at Stevens Point, a two-year normal school for teachers, one of nine in Wisconsin. Schmeeckle thought the curriculum lacked an important conservation focus. In 1926, Wisconsin State Normal School changed its name to Central State Teachers College at Stevens Point, now a four-year teacher education program.

Schmeeckle began the wildlife program as part of a conservation course he started teaching in 1937–38. In 1946, Schmeeckle created the one-person Department of Conservation Education, the first program of its kind in the nation, housed within the College of Applied Arts and Science.

In 1946, Central State Teachers College at Stevens Point became the first college in Wisconsin to establish a conservation education major for the teacher preparation program. That major appeared for the first time in the course catalog of 1946–47, expanding to nine conservation courses, among them the only wildlife course, Conservation 204, Problems in Wild Life Management and Recreation (three credits), taught on a "to be arranged" basis. (*Wildlife* was first spelled as one word in the 1954–55 catalog). Conservation 107 was finally given a title, Survey Course in Conservation, for three credits, but it was not required for the major. Thus, the Department of Conservation was born in 1946. In 1948, the first students—eight men—graduated with a BS degree in conservation.

In 1947, Walter Sylvester (1918–1957) was hired; he obtained a PhD in conservation from the University of Michigan in 1952. In 1951, State Teachers College at Stevens Point changed its name to Wisconsin State College at Stevens Point, offering a four-year liberal arts curriculum. In 1955, Sylvester began a two-week summer camp session that eventually became the comprehensive six-week requirement for all the natural resource students. In the 1958–59 course catalog, the course "Technics of Fish and Wildlife Conservation" first appeared.

Schmeeckle headed the department and continued to teach conservation education until retirement in 1959, often taking students to study natural resources in a convenient outdoor area attached to the campus, now the 280-acre Schmeeckle Reserve.

In 1964, the college again changed its name: State University at Stevens Point. In 1965, Dr. Fred Baumgartner (1910–1996) was hired. In 1966, Dr. Raymond K. (Andy) Anderson (1928–2000) was hired, having studied prairie chickens with Fred and Fran Hamerstrom and receiving a PhD in wildlife from UW–Madison. Anderson, a top wildlife ecologist, was instrumental in aggressively developing and directing the wildlife major. (After retirement in 1990, Anderson continued his wildlife work by coordinating the Wisconsin Department of Natural Resources' successful reintroduction of elk into the Clam Lake area). In 1971, Dr. Lyle Nauman, a wildlifer, was hired. Then, three full-time wildlife faculty members existed, all with PhDs.

In 1968, the Department of Conservation Education changed its name to the Department of Natural Resources. Also in 1968, the major in wildlife was approved. The program had the same five courses in wildlife and two courses in fisheries as taught in 1967.

From 1968 to 1977, fisheries was contained in the wildlife major. Thus, two options existed: fisheries management and game management. In 1977, fisheries was placed in the water major, and the term "game management" was replaced by the more comprehensive term "wildlife management."

By 1971, the Department of Natural Resources had grown large enough to be elevated to the status of College of Natural Resources (CNR), even as the university's name changed to the University of Wisconsin–Stevens Point. In 1973, the wildlife program, along with the entire College of Natural Resources, moved from its location in Old Main, once the only building on campus, into its own building, the new College of Natural

Resources Building, or simply, the CNR Building, expanded in 1997. It was shared with the College of Letters and Science's Department of Biology until 2018, when Biology moved into the new Chemistry Biology Building.

In 1975, the first retirement on the wildlife faculty occurred with Dr. Fred Baumgartner. The first wildlifer hired for the new CNR Building then was Dr. Neil Payne, future author of two wildlife habitat books while there.[197,203] In 1978, Dr. Jim Hardin was hired, and in 1979, Dr. Kirk Beattie. By 1979, the number of wildlife faculty members was five, all with PhDs.

In 1982, an outside wall of the CNR Building received a unique mosaic mural, the largest of its kind in the nation, 50 x 150 feet consisting of 286,200 ceramic tiles, each a two-inch square, each with a white-tailed deer, beaver, prairie chicken, mallard, bison, trout, or bluegill among 28 different pictures. These are arranged to depict an enlargement of Leonardo da Vinci's Vitruvian Man in the center, surrounded by a large white-tailed deer, badger, robin, musky, the Wisconsin River, and Sauk chief Black Hawk, among other things.

Dr. Daniel O. Trainer (1926–2007), a specialist in wildlife diseases, was hired in 1971 to become the first dean of the new College of Natural Resources, and led it with accomplishment and distinction until retiring in 1988. In 2007, the CNR Building became the Daniel O. Trainer Natural Resources Building (TNR for short), named after its long-time, charismatic dean, and author of two books on wildlife diseases.[44,250] As dean from 1971 to 1988, Trainer is recognized for managing the college to become a premier undergraduate natural resource institution in the nation. His protégé Christine Thomas served as dean of the CNR from 2005–2020 and now writes a biweekly outdoors column for *Wisconsin Outdoors News*. Like Leopold, Trainer and Thomas were on the Natural Resources Board of the WDNR and inducted into the Wisconsin Conservation Hall of Fame, joining UWSP's Fred Schmeeckle and George Becker.[12] Thomas began the international Becoming an Outdoors Woman (BOW) program in 1991. As dean, Thomas was involved with obtaining

$7,000,000 in endowment funds in perpetuity to support the activity of the wildlife faculty and students.

Dr. Byron Shaw, water (1943–2016) and Dr. Michael Dombeck, forestry, of the College of Natural Resources at the University of Wisconsin–Stevens Point, were inducted into the Wisconsin Conservation Hall of Fame. Shaw pioneered work on agricultural pesticide contamination of groundwater. Dombeck was the only leader of both the U.S. Forest Service and the U.S. Bureau of Land Management, the nation's largest land-management agencies.

Until 1985, the five majors within the CNR—Wildlife Ecology and Management, Forestry, Fisheries and Water Resources, Soil and Waste Resources, Resource Management—had no formal department chairs because the CNR did not want to departmentalize and segregate each major when the CNR philosophy was intended to be comprehensive and integrated. (The separate Department of Paper Science, in a separate building, was attached to the CNR). Such divisions also would be costly with administrative support. Instead, in 1985, the five college divisions were officially called disciplines rather than departments, with administgrative support only in the dean's office.

Thus, although the wildlife major existed since 1968, in 1985, the Wildlife Discipline was officially born, along with the other four CNR disciplines. Henceforth, each discipline would appoint a "discipline coordinator" to coordinate administrative details, to hold weekly meetings within the discipline, and to meet weekly with the dean, these positions to be rotated within each discipline every three years. For years, the discipline coordinators received no monetary remuneration for functioning essentially as department chairs. The first discipline coordinator of the Wildlife Discipline was Dr. Lyle Nauman.

From 1993 to 1999, Dr. Mark Boyce,[23] a wildlifer, held the endowed Vallier Chair of Ecology in the CNR, and with his wife, Dr. Evelyn Merrill, a wildlifer, increased the wildlife faculty to seven.

Over the years some faculty members from the Biology Department have had a joint appointment with wildlife. Several university associates have served as adjunct professors of wildlife, including Fred Hamerstrom, Fran Hamerstrom, and Dick Hunt from the Wisconsin Department of Natural Resources Wildlife Bureau, contributing their credentials and academic services to the wildlife program and the CNR. (On sabbatical in 1986, I loaned my office to Dick Hunt while he taught a waterfowl course). Fred and Fran Hamerstrom and Dick Hunt were inducted into the Wisconsin Conservation Hall of Fame.

The philosophy of UWSP's College of Natural Resources is to train each student in a specific natural resource major, but with a background of related natural resources for perspective. Since 1971–72, in order to give students a more comprehensive background in natural resources, each discipline had its own introductory course required of all CNR students regardless of major selected. In 1998, a stronger integrated approach was developed, with four different introductory courses required of each student in the CNR. Almost all of the natural resource courses tend to be heavily field oriented, with so many outdoor laboratories that each faculty member must hold a bus driver's license to drive a bus full of students, adding additional responsibility to an already responsible position. The bus size dictates the size of the laboratory classes (about 24).

In 1983, course requirements for the bachelor's degree in wildlife were adjusted to satisfy the coursework certification requirements of The Wildlife Society for Associate Wildlife Biologist. By 2020, 14 wildlife courses of some 43 credits were listed in the course catalog, with seven wildlife courses of 21 credits and eight biology courses of 27 credits required for the BS in Wildlife Ecology and Management. Internships are available.

Treehaven and Europe. Between the sophomore and junior years, CNR students must take all the field courses in the seven-credit, six-week summer camp: wildlife, forestry, soils, water and fisheries, and plant identification. The wildlife professor teaches the wildlife course and the required field identification of 200 plants labeled in the field.

Before 1962, an abbreviated summer camp was conducted at various outdoor locations such as Peninsula State Park and

Devil's Lake State Park. In 1962, the six-week summer camp was required, at the Clam Lake Field Station, a former Civilian Conservation Corps camp on Chippewa Lake, near the village of Clam Lake, in Chequamegon National Forest.

In 1985, a new site, called Treehaven, began to be used for summer camp on land given by Dorothy and Jacques Valliers to the UWSP College of Natural Resources. Located near Tomahawk, Wisconsin, 75 miles north of the campus in Stevens Point, Treehaven is 1,400 acres of wildlands where habitat types have been identified and a land use plan developed.[205] Treehaven contains dormitories, a cafeteria, classrooms, and faculty quarters. Conferences are held here, but its primary function is education. Almost all students in UWSP's College of Natural Resources must attend six weeks of summer camp here, usually between sophomore and junior years. Two sessions are conducted each summer, and a third, if needed, is held at the Central Wisconsin Environmental Station.

An alternative to summer camp is the more expensive 6-week European natural resource program, during which a restricted class size of about 40 students studies natural resources in Krakow, Poland at Jagiellonian University, one of the oldest universities in the world (est. 1364), and in the Black Forest of Germany. (I led trips there in 1983 and 1998.) There the instruction is handled by the Polish and German natural resource professionals. In addition, a two-week abbreviated summer camp, held at the Central Wisconsin Environmental Station (CWES) near campus, is given to those students going to Europe.

Options and Minors. Students majoring in wildlife may elect any minor offered by the other natural resource majors, e.g., forestry, fisheries and water, soils, law enforcement.

Dean Dan Trainer's father had been a game warden (conservation officer) for the Wisconsin Department of Natural Resources (WDNR). With that enticement and his interests, in 1972, Trainer began a needed environmental law enforcement minor to augment the wildlife program in the CNR and train potential conservation officers—the only such program in

Wisconsin. Most Wisconsin conservation officers (game wardens) with the WDNR have taken that option. Other minors developed and administered by the wildlife discipline have been the wildlife minor, the captive wildlife management minor, and the conservation biology minor.

Master of Science. Although the job placement rate for graduates with a Bachelor of Science or Bachelor of Arts in wildlife from UWSP has been above the national average, much of the employment has been limited-term employment (temporary, no benefits), the employee referred to as an LTE. The Master of Science (MS) in wildlife is considered the terminal degree for career wildlife employment.

In 1970, the Master of Science in natural resources was authorized. Despite heavy undergraduate teaching loads (12–15 credits/semester), the wildlife faculty began writing proposals for grants to support graduate students and research. Thus, the wildlife research era at UWSP began, although not as aggressively as possible if more time from teaching were available for writing proposals for research grants, directing research, and publishing results.

In keeping with the integrated comprehensive approach in natural resources, graduate students in each discipline (wildlife, forestry, soils, fisheries and water, environmental education) must take at least one course in at least two disciplines besides their own. The degree simply reads generally as "Master of Science in Natural Resources," with no specific natural resource focus mentioned, unfortunately (e.g., "Master of Science in Natural Resources—Wildlife," Master of Science in Natural Resources—Forestry," etc.).

Over the years, the wildlife faculty and their graduate students, with occasional help from undergraduate wildlife students in the Student Chapter of The Wildlife Society, have studied various species of wildlife mostly in Wisconsin, often in collaboration with the WDNR's Wildlife Division, the U.S. Fish and Wildlife Service, the National Park Service, and the U.S. Forest Service. With society's high interest in wildlife, these types of projects have resulted in high media attention, which has enhanced the identity of the CNR and its ability to attract and educate students, attract funding, and help society.

Wisconsin Cooperative Fishery Research Unit. The Wisconsin Cooperative Wildlife Research Unit is at UW-Madison but the Wisconsin Cooperative Fishery Research Unit is at UW-Stevens Point, established in 1971. Dr. Dan Coble was the first Unit Leader. Rarely, a wildlife research project funded by the Fishery Unit would support a wildlife graduate student, with the wildlife major professor, in collaboration with the Unit Leader, directing the research (as I did in 1984).

Other Programs. With little time to write grant proposals by this heavily engaged teaching faculty, the wildlife discipline reached a milestone when endowment research money became available, in a business that relies so much on research for producing professional wildlifers. The Wisconsin Center for Wildlife (WCW), located in the wildlife program, brings wildlifers, students, and landowners together for instruction about sustainable wildlife management and how to resolve wildlife problems. Within the WCW are the Douglas R. Stephens Endowed Chair in Wildlife (in 2013), the Kennedy-Grohne Endowed Chair in Waterfowl and Wetlands (in 2016), the Gerald and Helen Stephens Professor of Wildlife (in 2017), the Doug and Carol Federighi Graduate Fellowship in Waterfowl and Wetlands (in 2018), and the Black Bear Research Endowment Fund (in 2020).

The Museum of Natural History, the largest natural history museum in the Universities of Wisconsin, is housed at UWSP. The museum contains natural resource collections reflecting the diversity in nature and human cultures, with over 400,000 specimens from 11 scientific disciplines.

Since 1950, the Wisconsin Conservation Department, later renamed the Department of Natural Resources, has established blinds to observe the courtship behavior of prairie chickens on nearby Buena Vista Marsh within the Town of Plover in Portage Co. where the famed Fred and Fran Hamerstrom,[36, 253] former graduate students of Aldo Leopold, conducted their lifelong studies for the DNR (see Appendix 5; see Chapter 5). Every April since 1966, for study of this grouse and for entertainment, the CNR's wildlife discipline has coordinated the placement of blinds on the traditional courtship display areas, called "booming grounds," and arranged reservations and instruction for people to enter and observe the dramatic display and eerie "booming" sound of male prairie chickens, count them, and record information. An annual event, it is an excellent learning experience for students and others, and has developed into a tourist attraction for people from as far as Chicago and Minneapolis.

Every two years or so between semesters, a wildlife faculty member has conducted a two-week wildlife field trip to various locations for interested wildlife students: Crab Orchard National Wildlife Refuge in southern Illinois, White River National Wildlife Refuge in Arkansas, Rockefeller Wildlife Area on the Louisiana coast, Welder Wildlife Foundation in Texas, Aransas National Wildlife Refuge on the Texas coast, Santa Ana National Wildlife Refuge on the Rio Grande in Texas, Kerr Wildlife Area on the Edwards Plateau in Texas, YO Ranch private hunting preserve in Texas, and the headquarters of the Missouri Conservation Department in Jefferson City. (I led a group of 15 there in 1977–78, 1981–82, and 1988–89.)

Every two years or so two faculty members from the College of Natural Resources lead 14 students on a three-week field trip between semesters to Costa Rica to study ecosystems in various natural areas, ecotourism being the number 1 industry in Costa Rica. (I led a student group there in 1996–97.)

The University of Wisconsin–Stevens Point has been designated a Bee Campus in Wisconsin, one of a growing number of them in the U.S. By providing pollinating insects and birds with healthy habitats, Bee Campus USA is a campus program that promotes education and awareness of pollinators. Some 400 species of bees inhabit Wisconsin.

Schmeeckle Reserve. "Someday this area will serve as an island of green in the City of Stevens Point." So said Fred Schmeeckle when he took his students into it. Named after him (see *From Conservation Education to Wildlife Major*), Schmeeckle Reserve is a 280-acre natural land area within the Tension Zone (see Chapter 6) and attached to the campus of the University of Wisconsin–Stevens Point—a short walk north from the classroom. In 1956, the university began acquiring the mostly farmland, proposing to use it as a natural area. Schmeeckle Reserve was officially established in 1976. In 1977, Ron Zimmerman became its first director. He immediately managed to acquire an adjacent 20 acres of farmland including a house that was converted into the visitor center by 1979. To facilitate the initial development of Schmeeckle Reserve, shortly after the land was acquired and administered by the CNR, a comprehensive seasonal wildlife inventory was conducted by habitat in 1977 and 1978 and recorded in the MS thesis by my wildlife graduate student Tom Engel.[54] It is now used in Schmeeckle Reserve for comparative historical baseline data.

The Reserve contains upland and wetland habitats, a stream (Moses Creek), a 23-acre artificial groundwater lake (Lake Joanis), deer and other wildlife, five miles of boardwalk and other trails, and a visitor center. In an urban environment, the Reserve was created to serve as an outdoor classroom for students and teachers, to protect and restore native ecological communities, and to provide recreational opportunities for society. The 27-mile Green Circle Trail around the Stevens Point and Plover area passes through Schmeeckle Reserve and is headquartered in the visitor center.

Wisconsin Conservation Hall of Fame. Within Schmeeckle Reserve's visitor center at UWSP is the Wisconsin Conservation Hall of Fame wherein natural resource conservationists throughout Wisconsin are inducted to honor them for their outstanding contribution to Wisconsin's natural resource legacy. Created in 1984, its first inductees were Aldo Leopold and John Muir.

Central Wisconsin Environmental Station (CWES). Since 1975, the UWSP College of Natural Resources has operated a 200-acre field station and environmental learning center, the Central

Wisconsin Environmental Station (CWES), with Dr. Rick Wilke as the first director. It is located near Amherst, 17 miles east of Stevens Point, on glacial Sunset Lake surrounded by towering white pines. The mission is to foster in youth and adults the understanding, appreciation, motivation, and skill development to help them acquire an understanding of a sustainable balance between the economy, the environment, and the community. It has a swim area on Sunset Lake, pontoon boats, canoes, kayaks, paddle boats, equipment for water study and fishing, ponds and beaver sloughs for aquatic ecology study, terrestrial wildlife study (deer, songbirds, waterbirds, etc.), mixed forest and pine plantation for forestry study, orienteering courses and map and compass study, archery, volleyball, hiking and cross-country skiing, and an amphitheater.

CWES has a 22-person lodge and log cabins. The station hosts summer camps, group meetings, school programs, and has building rentals and food service.

APPENDIX 3: WISCONSIN'S OFFICIAL DOG: AMERICAN WATER SPANIEL.

Wisconsin has its own dog. Of only five dog breeds developed in the U.S., the American water spaniel is the only dog breed developed in Wisconsin. The strong tradition of hunting the abundant wildlife in Wisconsin for subsistence resulted in the development through selective breeding here of a versatile hunting dog. The American water spaniel, Wisconsin's state dog, originated in the Wolf River and Fox River valleys of Wisconsin more than 100 years ago. With its size of 30–45 pounds and shoulder height of 15–18 inches, the dog fits nicely into canoe, skiff, or duck blind for aggressively retrieving ducks and geese in frigid water withstood by its brown, tightly curled to wavy double coat.

Easily trained, with its versatility, intelligence, and hunting instinct, this tough dog also can be used proficiently to find and flush upland game birds, and for rabbit and squirrel hunting. At its one end are long, lobular, and thickly furred ears; at the other end is a fully haired, moderately long, tapered tail that serves as a rudder in swift water. The American water spaniel developed a reputation as a rugged, hard-working, dependable, versatile hunting dog.

Recognized as a distinct breed in 1940 by the American Kennel Club, the Wisconsin-developed American water spaniel adapts to urban and rural environments and serves as both hunting dog and family companion.

APPENDIX 4: GUNS

Guns and hunting. They go together. Hunters don't use weapons. They use rifles and shotguns; nobody calls them weapons. Weapons are for war, not for hunting.

Because of the interest by some folks, many if not most being non-hunters, in military assault weapons and high-capacity ammunition magazines, their increased purchase in recent years has increased monies to state wildlife agencies via PR (Pittman-Robertson Act) monies. That's the good news. The bad news is that the increased manufacture and availability of these types of firearms has resulted in more mass killings of humans in America. Our crooks now out-gun our cops!

When the Second Amendment was written 230 years ago (1791), only single-shot, muzzle-loading guns were available then for hunting or otherwise. Of 27 constitutional amendments, the Second Amendment is the only amendment involving technology, which evidently and naively was not expected to change over time. By being unable to anticipate the technological change in single-shot muzzleloaders 200 years later, our Founding Fathers, brilliant though they were, made a gross mistake; more precisely, James Madison did, the main author of the first ten amendments, known as the Bill of Rights, all ratified on 15 December 1791. (Madison's last name graces Wisconsin's capital city.)

Madison, our fourth president (1809–1817), and preeminent author of the U.S. Constitution, did a good job on nine of those first ten amendments to it, but a lousy job on the Second Amendment, causing confusion and grief today. Poorly written without foresight, the Second Amendment is subject to misinterpretation. A strict interpretation of it, intended when ratified, applies only to the single-shot muzzle-loading guns available then, which means that only those types of guns should be used today if the Second Amendment is strictly adhered to and thoroughly believed in as it is by so many. Instead, some people foolishly think the Second Amendment applies to military assault weapons for society as well as for the military, a type of gun inconceivable in the 1700s.

"A well-regulated Militia being necessary to the security of a free State the right of the people to keep and bear Arms shall not be infringed." So says the Second Amendment. But we have no militia, which is a citizen organization. So that part is wrong. At least machine guns, RPGs (rocket-propelled grenades), rifle grenades, and flamethrowers are still illegal in society even if "the right of the people to keep and bear Arms shall not be infringed."

Repeal the Second Amendment? Only one constitutional amendment has been repealed; the Twenty-First Amendment repealed the Eighteenth Amendment, prohibiting the making or selling of liquor. But the Second Amendment should be re-written with today's perspective.

Now, military assault weapons (defined by the name ASSAULT)—with high-capacity ammo magazines—are authorized for use in society as well as in the military, much to the chagrin of the out-gunned police and the families of mass shootings, and to the delight and wealth (and shamelessness) of gun stores and gun shows, and of extremist organizations and gun manufacturers which lobby and finance some politicians.[215] For ten years, 1994 to 2004, the ban on assault weapons in the U.S. was law. The experiment worked. Mass shootings declined substantially. Nonetheless, despite the evidence, politicians allowed the law to expire, and mass shootings tripled thereafter, to the grief and disgust of society. In the United States, 393.3 million civilian guns exist, or 120.5 guns/100 people, far more than in any other country. (Next-door neighbor Canada has 12.7 million, or 34.7 guns/100 people.) The result is more gun violence and mass public shootings of people in the United States than in any other "developed" country—a shameful, sick distinction for the most "developed" nation in the world.

In 2023, an outrageous 604 mass shootings occurred in the U.S. (four or more folks shot in one location at the same time), with

754 deaths and 2,443 injuries—virtually all done by males. The number (percentage) of deaths by the profusion of easily acquired guns, including military assault rifles, in American society exceeds that in other nations including our culturally-similar next door neighbor Canada; such nations view the U.S. with disapproval and contempt in this regard, even warning their citizens to avoid the U.S., thus affecting tourism in the U.S. The NRA (National Rifle Association), the gun industry, and their lobbyists are, in a sense, culpable, along with the politicians they influence. Guns are now the primary killer of children in America. And yet some folks in society are both pro-guns and pro-life (anti-abortion), silly and contradictory as that is!

When I was in Vietnam with the Marines in combat, we used military assault weapons. Such rifles are not needed or used or sometimes even legal for hunting when an abundance of various types of hunting rifles are readily available and have been for years, such as the bolt-action .30-06 I've used for hunting deer, caribou, and moose. The newer rifles should be configured to limit shell capacity in the same way as older, traditional hunting rifles. And like all shotguns, my pump 12-gauge shotgun must have a plug in it so that only three shotgun shells can be inserted for legally hunting ducks; thus, no more than three ducks per hunter can be killed at a time. Seems like society is reverting to the old Wild West days when every man wore a six-gun, except that those guns were six-shooters; they shot six bullets before reloading, when society didn't have high-capacity ammo magazines. And once again, society in the U.S. has a proliferation of handguns (seldom used for hunting) like the old days, like the "Wild West."

Mass shooting has become a national public health crisis. Mortality by guns is a health issue. It should be treated like any other serious health issue in society by figuring out how to reduce it, as with measles, Covid, polio, etc. The mortality rate of automobiles has been reduced by some control, e.g., seatbelts, speed limits, rearview mirrors, etc., but vehicles have not been taken away. The same should hold for guns. Clearly, as with automobiles, some control is essential for public safety. With guns, we are asking for trouble, and we are getting it.

Other methods also must be addressed to reduce gun violence, such as mental health treatment, but nothing compares to assault guns. The evidence is clear; military assault weapons are much too dangerous for society. Abolishing military assault weapons and high-capacity ammo magazines in society, as the public prefers, would not interfere with hunting but would be a huge help to society and should be easy to do, with political will. Folks want to hunt, in the hunting tradition of North America, but no one wants to get shot in a grocery store or a church or a school or a parade or a concert or any other place.

APPENDIX 5: A 60-YEAR MEMORY

My lifelong best friend Sam Lev and I graduated from Sheboygan Falls (WI) High School in 1957. (In 1966, we met in the Philippines when both our ships were there, he a Navy pilot returning from combat in the Vietnam War, me a Marine Corps combat engineer heading for combat in the Vietnam War). In 1959, I was working on a BA in zoology when Sam and I were sophomores and roommates at the University of Wisconsin–Madison. We took an ornithology class normally taught by famed ornithologist John T. Emlen, Jr.,[53] but he was on leave for research in Africa, I think; we had a visiting German professor as our teacher. The course required an overnight field trip to observe the unusual courtship behavior of prairie chickens. I passed the professor's excuse note to my army ROTC instructor, a Captain Miller, who was amused by the wording. To my embarrassment, with a wry smile he read it to the entire class, to wit: "Please excuse Neil Payne so that he can watch the dancing of the prairie chicken."

Sam and I left Madison with the class of maybe 15 or 20 of us and drove to an old farmhouse in Plainfield, Wisconsin, where legendary wildlife biologists Fred and Fran Hamerstrom lived. I had never heard of them. Their yard had a red-tailed hawk attached to a stump with a dead male pheasant on it, apparently for food. Inside on the back of the couch was a dead starling for the ferret in a cage, and stuck headfirst in coffee cans were two or three raptors to be processed and released. Fred briefed us that evening about how to collect prairie chicken data from the blind the next morning. It was the busy season for the Hamerstroms, with little housekeeping. We slept in our sleeping bags upstairs in the "ballroom" unfinished from before Civil War days, we were told. I had an upper bunk and could hear mice run around in the ceiling a few inches above my head.

After a breakfast of sloppy scrambled eggs prepared hurriedly by Fran (pronounced "Frahn" with an "ah") who would publish the book, *Wild Food Cookbook*,[82] Fred (called "Hammy" by friends) drove us to the Buena Vista Marsh and dropped us off separately to individual blinds. I was dropped off alone somewhere in the dark, a little intimidating, and was told the blind was on the other side of the field. I had no idea what a blind looked like and was too embarrassed to ask. Was it a pit in the ground or something standing upright made of logs, or what?

I tore my raincoat while going through a barbed-wire fence. I couldn't see the blind, and I worried that I would be late getting to it and flush away the prairie chickens. I got down low to the ground hoping to see an upright blind that might be silhouetted against the faint light of sunrise on that flat land. There it was, much to my relief, in the distance! I walked to it, unhooked one guy line, tipped up one end, bent low and got inside to sit on the low stool so that my head wouldn't brush the ceiling. It was made of canvas stretched over a wooden frame, 4 feet high by 4 feet wide and 5 or 6 feet long. The two-person blind had a viewing flap on each side. No coffee was allowed because you couldn't leave the blind to pee and startle the prairie chickens. What prairie chickens, I wondered! What was I doing here, alone in the dark? I had no idea where I was.

Then, as I sat in that dark blind—I heard one! I had never heard or seen one before in my life, but I just knew it was a prairie chicken "booming." Turns out there were 11 of them assembled there. Ten of them had their own small territory on this booming ground. The eleventh one just wandered around the edge of the booming ground, chased from territory to territory, apparently too weak to defend his own. The weakest cocks had their territories on the edge of the booming ground where they wouldn't have to defend the outside part from other cocks. These outside cocks were more susceptible to predators. All were quiet and hunkered down when a short-eared owl flew over. After that, the booming erupted again. I also heard and saw several sandhill cranes nearby. But no hens appeared that morning. I drew the ten territories and recorded my periodic counts.

A blind is placed at the edge of a booming ground but often within a prairie chicken's territory. In fact, one chicken was so used to my blind that at times even flew to the roof and displayed. I put my hand against the canvas roof of the blind and could feel his feet dance during his display. By 8 o'clock, things had quieted down. As instructed, I tipped the blind so I could emerge. With that, I made my final count as the prairie chickens flew away. I attached the guy line to the stake to secure the blind, walked to the road, and waited for my ride. At the Hamerstrom house we submitted our information and were debriefed. One student didn't take things seriously and failed to collect data; in his gentle way, Fred expressed dismay with him. A cup of coffee, and back to Madison we went, sleeping most of the way. Altogether a wonderful, memorable experience. I was officially a "boomer," i.e., a guest and prairie chicken observer of the Hamerstroms (one of an estimated 7,000 over the years). I had seen 11 cock prairie chickens. My friend Sam saw 15 cocks, one hen, and one hawk, he still recalls.

A lek is a courtship display area for some species of grouse: ptarmigan, sage grouse, sharp-tailed grouse—and prairie chickens. In the Buena Vista Marsh of central Wisconsin, 21 or so of these traditional sites occur, to which the prairie chickens return annually, an area of short grass and forbs that will facilitate courtship display, and no surrounding shrubs or trees for predator concealment. These leks are known as booming grounds. Every April morning at sunrise, the males arrive in flight at the booming ground to stake out small territories side by side, display, and receive the hens that visit them later. About 8 o'clock a.m. or so, the prairie chickens leave the lek in flight.

The cock with the best display, as perceived by the hens, does 90% of the breeding, lucky guy, thus passing on the best survival genes of the males. A lek might be 200 feet in diameter, roughly circular, with maybe 10–20 territorial cocks, each territory roughly circular about 30 feet in diameter. In early April, much fighting ensues between cocks, with feather pulling and spurring as they establish their territorial borders. Once established, territorial borders not obvious to the human eye are pretty much honored, with many stare-off matches but little actual fighting then. By the end of April, activity decreases, because breeding is complete.

During a male's display, his back is parallel to the ground, his tail is up and spread, his pinnae are angled up and forward (looking a bit like rabbit ears), his eyebrow patches expose orange skin beneath, his orange air sacs are exposed and inflated—and he does indeed do a little dance! At its conclusion, he clicks his tail feathers together (inaudible unless close) and emits about three strange-sounding humming sorts of "boom" from the air sacs for a few seconds—a sound that can be heard by the human ear for a half mile or so on a quiet morning, even though the penetrating sound isn't so loud. It's wonderful. When the hens appear, the males go nuts with their displays. It is quite the sight and sound to behold.

Here it is, some 65 years later; I can remember the details of that experience almost like it was yesterday, with no idea, of course, that someday I would live nearby. Quite an impression. For the past 45 years I have lived just a few miles from that blind on the Buena Vista Marsh, with no idea which booming ground my blind was on back then. But over the years while working as a professor of wildlife ecology at the nearby University of Wisconsin–Stevens Point (UWSP), I have sat in a blind variously with my wife, kids, and friends—just down County Trunk F from my house on the shore of the Wisconsin River. In fact, our wildlife program at UWSP is responsible for setting out the blinds, taking reservations, and collecting the blinds every April and storing them. And to think I didn't even know what a blind looked like when I used it for the first time—once upon a time! What a pleasant and fascinating experience and memory for an inexperienced, naïve young man (and future wildlife biologist and professor, still somewhat naïve, as is my wont) these many years later. I was 20 then; I am 85 now, enjoying that vivid memory.

That vivid memory is embellished with an addendum 30 years later. In January 1989, my wife Jan and I were staying at Welder Wildlife Refuge in Sinton, TX, with our son Mark and 14 university wildlife students on a two-week field trip I was leading. It was our wedding anniversary, and the students bought us a cake. Joining my wife and me, and son and my wildlife students for the celebratory cake, was a wildlife couple staying at Welder too, but en route from Wisconsin to Mexico to study raptors. There I was, their naïve former student guest of 30 years earlier who couldn't find the prairie chicken blind, now a professor and author, with Fred and Fran my colleagues as university associates at the University of Wisconsin–Stevens Point where I worked. I was honored by the presence of internationally renowned Fred and Fran Hamerstrom, joining us to mix with my students and to celebrate the wedding anniversary of their boomer and his wife.

APPENDIX 6: A FUNNY THING HAPPENED ON MY WAY TO THE OFFICE

In the College of Natural Resources (CNR) Building where our wildlife program was housed at the University of Wisconsin-Stevens Point, we did not have a decent classroom in which to dissect animals. In 1987, Dean Dan Trainer sent me to Madison to get some ideas for such a classroom from the new vet science program at the University of Wisconsin–Madison and from the U.S. Fish and Wildlife Service's disease lab in the National Wildlife Health Center. Armed with that knowledge, I designed a new classroom to be included in the CNR building addition planned for completion in 1997, the classroom to be used for wildlife population dynamics, wildlife techniques, and wildlife diseases. Unfortunately, such a classroom, although multi-use, ultimately was deemed too expensive, and was cut from the plan and CNR building addition, leaving the largest wildlife program in the nation, and the College of Natural Resources, once again with a glaring omission in teaching capability, as a golden opportunity to rectify it passed.

In a class called Wildlife Population Dynamics, I taught 24 students how to determine reproductive rates. I had collected about 20 skinned beaver carcasses from trappers and stored them in our walk-in freezer in the CNR Building. My lab was on Thursday, so on Tuesday I instructed the stockroom guys to spread out the frozen beaver to thaw for two days on the basement floor, which had a floor drain, and to discard the carcasses late Thursday after my class. On Thursday I took my class down into that hot basement, adjusted the lone floor lamp, bent down, and showed the students how to cut open the female beaver lying on the floor, then remove and cut open the uterus to count placental scars, and then remove and slice the ovaries to count corpora lutea. About half the beaver on the floor were males, difficult to sex for they have no external genitalia, but once the carcass thawed, the baculum could be felt. (It is much smaller than my black bear baculum swizzle stick).

Four days later, on my way to the office the following Monday, I walked into the CNR Building to a powerful "hum," as they say in Newfoundland where I used to work as a wildlife biologist. The entire first floor stunk! I thought that over the weekend the electricity had gone off again to the big freezer as it had in the past, and that everything therein had thawed and rotted again. I walked to my office, 306, on the third floor. Just as I reached for my office door, I thought, "Uh-oh." I made a beeline down to the basement—and sure enough. There they lay, just where they were placed for thawing the previous Tuesday, cooking for six days in that hot basement—20 dissected beaver, rotting away! The odor was overpowering. The stockroom guys finally managed to clean up the place. Still, the odor lingered in the four-story building for several days. We wildlifers were always suspect, of course, what with the animals we handled. Several of my colleagues asked me what the annoying stench was. Embarrassed to confess, I said, "Maybe the big freezer went out again and everything thawed and rotted."

And maybe it didn't.

APPENDIX 7: WISCONSIN WILDLIFE CONNECTIONS

9/11 AND NEWFOUNDLAND AND LABRADOR

My wife Jan and I couldn't get out. So we helped out. We had just driven the five hours from our home in Campbellton, which is near Gander in northcentral Newfoundland, to the provincial capital city of St. John's in southeastern Newfoundland in order to fly from St. John's to Chicago and then drive to our home in Wisconsin. That was 9/11, in 2001. We were due to fly out on 13 September. Instead, we stayed in St. John's with friends and former wildlife colleague Jim Inder and wife June. For several days we all helped to prepare and donate food for the unexpected, stranded guests, and delivered it to Mile One Stadium, the hockey stadium where all the plane people landing in St. John's were taken.

For the first time in history, the U.S. Federal Aviation Administration closed its airspace to arriving flights and grounded all flights over the United States. Before reaching the halfway point between Ireland and Newfoundland, dozens of flights turned around to head back to Europe. Of 132 aircraft approaching from Europe and diverted to Atlantic Canada, most (75) were diverted to Newfoundland: 38 to Gander, 21 to St. John's, eight to Stephenville, seven to Happy Valley-Goose Bay in Labrador, and one to Deer Lake. Dozens of other flights enroute across the Pacific landed in western Canada. Few of the almost 14,000 people on the planes knew where Newfoundland was; some had never heard of it. And that's where they were stranded for four days.

It all has to do with geography. It so happens that because Newfoundland juts out so far into the North Atlantic, as Canada's easternmost province, it sits near the Great Circle Route for airplanes and ships traveling between North America and Europe—the shortest distance following the curvature of Earth. (Check the globe). Enter 9/11 in 2001. (Enter the *Titanic* too, in 1912, Newfoundland the closest land.[201])

The popular Broadway musical, "Come From Away"[214y] (shown in Milwaukee, Madison, Appleton, and across North America) is about the "plane people" flying from Europe who were diverted to Gander, Newfoundland, during the 9/11 crisis.[44y]

(Our house is less than an hour away). The mayor, city council, airport authorities, police, and citizens of Gander were stunned by the spontaneity of the startling and massive event almost doubling the size of their community in an instant. In northcentral Newfoundland, the 6,122 dazed and anxious passengers and 473 crew, from 95 countries and different cultures, exited 33 passenger planes, four U.S. Air Force planes, and one private plane. The 17 airlines (not Air Canada but ten U.S. airlines) came from Ireland, England, Italy, Germany, France, Holland, Belgium, and Hungary. One was destined for Canada (Gander), the rest for the United States. (Gander has a huge airport from World War II days).

The community of Gander responded beautifully, with compassion, organization, and performance. But the passengers were too many for Gander, so nearby communities were contacted to help house passengers in private houses, schools, and churches. Schools were cancelled; students helped care for the stranded passengers using the schools' cafeterias, shower facilities, and other rooms. Residents bought, prepared, and served food to the passengers, who were not allowed to remove luggage from the planes due to security, and also provided things such as toothbrushes, other comforts, and local entertainment. Finally realizing that the local people were donating everything personally, the passengers arranged donations from among themselves for scholarships, computers, lighting, carpeting, etc.

After a few days in St. John's of being stranded ourselves because no planes were flying, Jan and I returned to our home in northcentral Newfoundland for a while longer, driving through Gander enroute. Touchingly, our next-door neighbors expressed their sorrow over what happened to America. A week later, we drove through a vacant Gander back to St. John's in our rental car and flew to Chicago to return to Wisconsin. In my book, *The Newfoundland Mystique*,[201] is a section in Chapter 1 labeled, "9/11—The Newfoundland Connection."

In Wisconsin I grew up, raised my family, and still live. But I have a strong connection to Newfoundland where I still live in summer and which hired me for my first wildlife job as their first bear and fur biologist (1967–71)—straight out of the U.S. Marine

Corps and Vietnam from where I first contacted Newfoundland. That job in Canada required a long haul from Fallbrook, California, next to the USMC's Camp Pendleton, 4,100 miles to St. John's, Newfoundland and Labrador (plus a 100-mile ferry ocean-ride from Nova Scotia). I drove there with wife, baby, and collie in a 1965 Volkswagen bug that I had bought in North Carolina while stationed there at Camp Lejeune (now the target of numerous lawsuits promoted in TV ads because of contaminated water used by my wife and Marines like me stationed there from 1953 to 1987).

I gained experience fast there because I started at the top. Four of us ran the entire wildlife show for the Canadian province of Newfoundland and Labrador: Director of Wildlife Dave Pike, Chief Biologist and Big Game Biologist Frank Manuel (my boss and one of the three most influential professionals in my life), Small Game Biologist Jim Inder, and Bear and Fur Biologist Neil Payne.[200] Coincidentally, Frank, Jim, and I had studied at the University of Wisconsin–Madison, although not simultaneously. My biggest hangup in Newfoundland? The grocery stores didn't carry my Wheaties.

After I had been in the deadly Vietnam War with the Marine Corps, a deadly event in Newfoundland occurred while Frank and I were traveling in a car on the Trans-Canada Highway (TCH) in summer 1970, right behind a car involved in a head-on collision. Of ten people, two died and the rest were injured. We watched it unfold. What a mess. Just the two of us were present at first. Our wildlife uniforms provided us some authority to control things until help arrived.

The Canadian province of Newfoundland and Labrador has scenery, icebergs, whales, puffins, shipwrecks, fossils, fogbanks, Inuit, Viking settlement, African genesis, the *Titanic* nearby, 9/11 plane people, etc. Newfoundland (42,000 mi^2) is somewhat smaller than Wisconsin (65,000 mi^2). It is an island (with one road across it—the Trans-Canada Highway), the furthest point east in North America; it juts northeast into the cold North Atlantic Ocean. Labrador, 2.5 times larger and further north, is on the mainland between Quebec and the Atlantic Ocean. Due to its isolation, visiting some communities is like stepping back in time. In virtually no other place of Canada and the United States did electricity, telephones, indoor plumbing, and roads arrive so late in remote areas, not until the 1960s or 1970s, and even later in some places.[201] The province has half a million people; Wisconsin has 5.9 million. Wisconsin has 75 indigenous species of mammals. In its simple ecosystem, Newfoundland has 15 indigenous species of land mammals, mostly distinct races including caribou, but not the introduced moose (now with the highest density in North America). I hunted caribou and moose in Newfoundland and deer in Virginia, Washington state, and Wisconsin.

During the four years (1967–71) in my new wildlife job, I gained much experience: initiated research live-trapping black bears, river otter, pine marten, and the introduced red squirrel; conducted aerial census and research on Newfoundland beaver, which is a distinct race, with the lowest reproductive rate in North America; established a beaver trapline management system with legislative support throughout Newfoundland; coordinated the lynx-snaring program around caribou calving grounds; legally maneuvered to close the polar bear hunting season in Labrador; helped introduce arctic hare to a remote island devoid of the competitive snowshoe hare; designed the iconic caribou arm patch for the Newfoundland and Labrador Wildlife Division; obtained from a donor the trophy caribou head hanging in the Wildlife Division office; developed a small reference library; and wrote my first publication[194y] which became "Occasional Paper No. 1," a 75-page booklet for the trappers. In a way, that was an inauspicious writing start for me.

Inauspicious writing start because of the biopolitics involved. I called the publication "Newfoundland and Labrador Fur Guide," a good but provocative publication, as it turned out, because I naively did not put on it the name of the minister heading our department, who wanted political credit. Even the premier, Joey Smallwood, got into the act. For my "infraction," I'm in the records of the House of Assembly in the Confederation Building (capital building), where the premier said I should be reprimanded! (Perhaps that also meant the director of wildlife and the chief biologist who supported me and approved the publication). The premier's silliness made the newspaper; practically a local celebrity for a day or so, I was interviewed by the newspaper. This was my first experience with biopolitics. That popular publication of 1969 had to be reprinted twice, in 1973 and 1980—with the department minister's name.

As a wildlife biologist with the Newfoundland and Labrador Wildlife Service (1967–1971), I would meet Stan Temple in Newfoundland in 1969, and with Super 8 camera, film a bit of his field work when he was studying merlins for a graduate degree at Cornell University. Dr. Stanley Temple[241, 242, 243, 244] became the Beers-Bascom Professor in Conservation at the University of Wisconsin–Madison (1976–2008), filling the faculty position once held by Aldo Leopold (1933–1948) and Joe Hickey (1948–1976). After retiring, Stan became a Senior Fellow at the Aldo Leopold Foundation in Baraboo, Wisconsin, and in 2021 was inducted into the Wisconsin Conservation Hall of Fame.

In 1906, 20 caribou from Newfoundland were placed on wealthy Henry Clay Pierce's estate at Cedar Island Lodge, on the Brule River near Brule, Douglas County, WI.[104, 218] All were believed to have died in one year. Newfoundland caribou are a distinct race with record antlers.

In 1956, 169 ruffed grouse were taken from central Wisconsin's Sandhill Wildlife Area (where two of my former graduate students, Ned Norton [black bears[189y, 205x]] and Mike Zeckmeister [beaver[275, 276]] later were the wildlife managers) and introduced to Newfoundland. Willow ptarmigan and rock ptarmigan were the only native upland game birds there, and they occurred in open areas on the barrens; the forested area contained no game bird. Now thousands of ruffed grouse are shot and snared annually in Newfoundland's forests for subsistence and recreation. In the Canadian province of Newfoundland and Labrador, the main method of harvesting snowshoe hares—rabbits, as they are called there—is by snaring. Ruffed grouse are underharvested in Newfoundland because the people are used to hunting in open areas for ptarmigan. And ruffed grouse occur in brushy rabbit habitat and use rabbit trails, often ending up in rabbit snares. As a wildlife biologist there in 1969, I suggested having a snaring season on ruffed grouse. Grouse have been snared legally there since 1970.

Few dog breeds have developed in North America. Of five developed in the United States and five in Canada, two were developed in the Canadian province of Newfoundland and Labrador—the Newfoundland dog and the Labrador retriever—and one in Wisconsin—the American water spaniel.

One of the most intellectually stimulating events of Aldo Leopold's life occurred in 1931. It was a conference mainly about cyclic phenomena in wildlife of Labrador,[102,174] documented for years in annual fur returns from Labrador trappers (and years later pursued by Lloyd Keith[108] of the University of Wisconsin). The conference was held on the Matamek River in Quebec just south of Labrador, when Newfoundland and Labrador was a colony of England before it became the tenth province of Canada in 1949.

Four wildlife biologists there with whom I worked, and another before me, obtained some of their graduate education in wildlife at the University of Wisconsin–Madison where I got my bachelor's degree. Dr. Lloyd Keith has had graduate students who studied snowshoe hare, arctic hare, and caribou in Newfoundland and published their results. Two Newfoundlanders were my graduate students at the University of Wisconsin–Stevens Point, taking classes there. One did her research on introduced mink and Newfoundland muskrats.[225x] The other did his research on prescribed burning and Newfoundland willow ptarmigan.[225y]

While working in Wisconsin, I published twenty articles in technical journals of my wildlife research conducted in Newfoundland, as well as my wildlife research in Wisconsin. During retirement in Wisconsin I wrote two books about Newfoundland,[200,201] maintained friendships with former co-workers of the Newfoundland and Labrador Wildlife Division, and return with my wife from Wisconsin to Newfoundland every summer to live.

In Wisconsin, Aldo Leopold began *A Sand County Almanac*[142] with, "There are some who can live without wild things, and some who cannot. These essays are the delights and dilemmas of one who cannot." I used part of that statement in 2011 for my book title, *Wildlife Delights and Dilemmas: Newfoundland*

and Labrador.[200] A history, it also contains 123 short stories of wildlife adventures from us early wildlife workers there. On its cover is the Newfoundland caribou crest of the Newfoundland and Labrador Wildlife Division. Although a Wisconsinite, I designed it in 1969 while working there. Worn as an arm patch and cap patch, the previous logo excluded "Labrador," which is part of the provincial name, and it featured three conifer trees

Logo and arm patch of the Newfoundland and Labrador Wildlife Division (*left*: 3 conifers, replaced by *right*: caribou, designed by Neil F. Payne).

instead of the iconic Newfoundland caribou that would make the logo more unique in North America. Proud of it, I have one on a sweatshirt, a t-shirt, a polo shirt, a windbreaker—and a 50-year-old work shirt and winter coat still around. And on the Christmas tree.

WASHINGTON STATE

From the Pacific Ocean to the Atlantic Ocean, the distance is 4,533 miles across the continent between Seattle, Washington on the west coast of North America and St. John's, Newfoundland on the east coast (with a 113-mile ocean ferry ride); Stevens Point, Wisconsin, is about equidistant in between. This guy from Sheboygan Falls spent his entire wildlife career at those three locations: Newfoundland and Labrador, 1967–71; Washington, 1973–75; Wisconsin, 1975–98.

Richard D. Taber, Estella Leopold, and I received university degrees at the University of Wisconsin–Madison, and we all worked at the University of Washington in Seattle.

Aldo Leopold's daughter Estella Leopold and I grew up in Wisconsin. At the University of Wisconsin she received her

BS degree in botany and I received my BA degree in zoology. Aldo Leopold's graduate student at the University of Wisconsin, Richard D. Taber, received his MS degree in wildlife working on pheasants in Wisconsin.

At the University of Washington, Estella was a professor of biology in the Biology Department; Dick Taber and I were professors of wildlife in the College of Forest Resources. Dick was my boss while I conducted research on the upper Columbia River[207] and the areas of Snoqualmie National Forest and Mount Rainier National Park.[206] I was in Wisconsin when Dick and I co-authored a book.[235] Although not simultaneous colleagues, Estella, in Washington, and I, in Wisconsin, became email pen pals (see End of an Era).

UTAH

I completed my PhD at Utah State University in Logan the same year, 1975, that I returned from Washington to Wisconsin to begin work at the University of Wisconsin-Stevens Point. Thus, my PhD dissertation[195] completed at Utah State connects Wisconsin to Utah and to Newfoundland and Labrador where the research was done. (I took a class at Utah State from Aldo Leopold's former graduate student Dr. Al Stokes.)

VIETNAM

Neil F. Payne, 090220, Captain, USMC. Combat engineer. Home of Record: Sheboygan Falls, Wisconsin.

I have the dubious distinction of being the only direct family member in a war since the Civil War. The Marine Corps assigned me the MOS (military occupational specialty) of "combat engineer," or 1300. I was a 1302, i.e., a combat engineer officer. As most folks know, the Vietnam War was justifiably controversial and extremely contentious in the United States. In 1967, a few months after I got out of the Vietnam War, when I was already in Newfoundland, that controversial war caused severe demonstrations on the UW campus in Madison against recruiting company

DOW Chemical, maker of napalm and agent orange, between college students and campus police in the Commerce Building where I had attended class.[162x] In 1970, college students on campus exploded a bomb in Sterling Hall, killing a researcher.

In May 2023, my son Mark arranged for me to attend the Honor Flight of Vietnam veterans to view the war memorials in Washington, D.C.—a big deal, more emotional than I anticipated after more than a half century had passed since my being in Vietnam. Our flight took 110, only eight of us Marines. (How many of us 110 Vietnam Era veterans actually served in Vietnam I do not know). Mark, former big game guide in Montana and Idaho before college at UWSP, accompanied me as my "Guardian."

Chuck McGinnes, Vietnam War; son of my major professor. Panel 4W, Line 129. Charles D. McGinnes, PFC, U.S. Army. Only child. From Blacksburg, Virginia. Pregnant wife. Forever 20, he'd be 72 (now in 2023), his contribution to society never realized.

That's where his name is on the Vietnam War Memorial, "The Wall," in Washington, D.C., along with 58,000 others: Panel 4W, Line 129. His father told me that Chuck was shot from ambush as he walked "point" on patrol, and that he bled to death when no one retrieved him, 16 April 1971.

In 1961, I met Chuck in Blacksburg, Virginia, after I arrived from Wisconsin for graduate work in wildlife as Burd McGinnes's MS graduate student. Chuck was 11 years old and a cocky kid. I liked him, and we interacted a bit because I was the youngest and only single wildlife graduate student. He was 13 when Burd brought him to southeastern Virginia on Hog Island State Wildlife Area in the James River, where Burd had assigned me my MS research project on cottontail rabbits. We fished together and spent the night together.

Chuck's father, Dr. Burd S. McGinnes (1921–1998), Unit Leader, Virginia Cooperative Wildlife Research Unit, had been my advisor for my MS in wildlife at Virginia Tech. Burd had been in the Marine Corps, partly the reason I joined the Marine Corps during my indecision about a wildlife career. In my first wildlife job after Vietnam and the Marine Corps, I was working as a wildlife biologist in Newfoundland and Labrador when Burd wrote me and requested that I write Chuck in Vietnam, since I had been in Vietnam too. I received a letter from Chuck in response. A week or so later I heard he was dead. I wrote his parents and forwarded Chuck's letter.

Burd told me that when he saw the military vehicle stop in front of the house, he moaned, "Oh, no. Oh, no. Oh, no." He'd had a premonition; he knew.

* * *

In 1961, Burd had accepted me as an MS graduate student to become a wildlifer; in 1998, I retired as a wildlifer, and Burd died that year. In 1992, while a wildlife professor at the University of Wisconsin–Stevens Point, I published a wildlife book[197] that I dedicated "to Burd S. McGinnes, my mentor."

Bucky Egan, Vietnam War; Adam Payne, my son. Panel 15E, Line 20. Donald J. Egan, Jr., 1st Lt., USMC. Named after his dad, from Troy, New York. A wife and two daughters. Forever 24, he'd be 81 (now in 2023), his contribution to society never realized.

That's where his name is on the Vietnam War Memorial, "The Wall," in Washington, D.C., along with 58,000 others: Panel 15E, Line 20. On my PRC-10 ("Prick-10") radio I heard the explosion, heard him die, not knowing what it was or who it was. My friend. In his ontos. Blown apart by a 250-pound dud American bomb boobytrapped by the Viet Cong near Phu Bai. *12 February 1967.*

At mail call later that same day, I received a letter from him, thanking me for the book I had sent to him about resumes and job locations for when he would leave the USMC in a few months. *I received a letter from him the day he died!* He said he was getting almost "too short" to read the book. (His tour of duty in the Marine Corps was to end a month after mine would end in May). That same day—12 February 1967—I would learn from the Red Cross that *my son Adam Neil Payne had been born two days earlier,* on 10 February 1967. An ocean apart. A world apart. But still a connection. It was a day of mixed emotions—a unique memory in life, unexperienced by most folks! *Three months later, in May, after leaving Vietnam and the USMC, I would finally meet my son.*

I didn't know Bucky well. We were in different parts of the same unit, had different jobs, and didn't live together. We had trained together at Camp Pendleton, California, and shipped out together from San Diego, California, to Subic Bay, Philippines, then to Dong Ha, South Vietnam (six miles from the DMZ, the Demilitarized Zone separating South Vietnam and North Vietnam).[194x, 196x]

While still in Vietnam, I had written to the Newfoundland and Labrador Wildlife Service for a job as a wildlife biologist, for I was leaving Vietnam and the Marine Corps in May 1967. I got the job, and that's where we went when Adam was six months old and I left the Marine Corps, stopping enroute at my home of record in Sheboygan Falls, Wisconsin, to visit my parents. Adam lived his first six months in Fallbrook, California, in a house trailer I bought because base housing in Camp Pendleton was full with families from Marines in Vietnam; then four years in St. John's, Newfoundland, where I worked as a wildlife biologist and his brother Mark was born; 1.5 years in Logan, Utah in student housing while I worked on a PhD in wildlife; 2.5 years in Seattle, Washington, where his sister Erin was born while I worked in wildlife at the University of Washington. Then he grew up on the Wisconsin River in Plover, Wisconsin, while I worked as a wildlife professor for 23 years at the University of Wisconsin–Stevens Point. Adam would graduate from the University of Wisconsin–Madison, where I did.

Adam knows the story well. On 12 February, two days after his birthday, I play the song "Land of 1000 Dances" because that's the day I learned of Adam's birth, that's the day Bucky Egan died, and part of that song Bucky would sing at times (the "na-a na na na na" part). A few years ago I gave Adam a glass beer mug for his birthday—except instead of saying "10 February 1967" (his birthday), it says "Vietnam 12 February 1967."

A UNIQUE WISCONSIN WILDLIFE CONNECTION

Unlike my wife Jan's ancestor (Francis Cooke), mine didn't make the Mayflower in 1620. But ten years later, in 1630, my ninth great-grandfather, William Phelps, arrived at the Massachusetts

Bay Colony from England on the ship *Mary and John*. Born in 1639, exactly 300 years before me, my 8th great-grandmother, Martha (Kitcherel) Wright, was killed and scalped there by Indians in 1708.

I am a sixth generation Wisconsinite. I have known seven generations of my family, all in Wisconsin; the genes of my revered great-grandma Bilgo now occur in my own great-grandchildren.

My great-grandmother, Susan (Griggs) Payne, was born in Ontario in 1848. She was in Ontario because we had ancestors in New York on both sides of the Revolutionary War and the losers were evicted to Canada. After her birth, her parents moved from Ontario with their three children to the Town of Mitchell, Sheboygan County, Wisconsin, to farm, where members of the Payne family had settled from New York in 1857, and where they are buried in Mount Pleasant Cemetery. Susan Griggs married Stephen Payne and probably gave the middle name of John Alexander Griggs, her brother killed in the Civil War, to her son Charles Alexander Payne, my admired and beloved grandfather and a farmer, who influenced me to pursue a career with animals.

I knew someone personally who was born during slavery, before the Civil War, before Abraham Lincoln became president—my great-grandma Alvina Bilgo of Cascade, Wisconsin, who died at 96 when I was 17. She was born in 1859. (Her granddaughter, my mother, 150 years later in 2009, would live to witness the first Black person become President of the United States, and the first women to vote in 1920.) To this day I regret never having asked her about her childhood, her parents, her grandparents. In the two wars to develop and to preserve the nation, 13 of my ancestors were in the Revolutionary War—both sides—and at least 12 for the North in the Civil War, including two of my great-grandfathers, Stephen Payne and William Steinke. The latter had recently immigrated from Germany and then had an arm shot off. He is buried in the Winooski Cemetery of Sheboygan County. For three years I lived across the street with my parents and younger brother in a house without running water.

William Steinke was the father of my grandfather George who had a tavern in Cascade. My grandpa didn't make moonshine. He bought it from two moonshiners, sold it, and was arrested during Prohibition when he didn't get the stuff hidden under the lilac bushes fast enough. (As a little girl, my mom used to help hide it, which, I suppose, made her complicit). My son, Adam, spent most of his career as the County Administrator of Sheboygan County, coincidentally the very county where I grew up, and thus in charge of the county jail where his great-grandfather had been incarcerated. (Grandpa George died eight years before I was born, evidently from drinking too much of his illegal stuff; the death certificate reads "cirrhosis of the liver." He is buried in the Cascade Lutheran Cemetery with other relatives, including my parents).

In 1939, *The Wizard of Oz* and *Gone with the Wind* were filmed, the Great Depression ended, World War II began, and I was born,[199] my first memory being of our rented house without running water and a mouse in the back hall that scared stiff at age 3 this future wildlife biologist who would someday live-trap bears. Sometimes we neighborhood kids played in the nearby city dump, until Old Franz the caretaker would emerge from his shack and raise his curved pitchfork at us. The milkman delivered our milk with a horse and wagon. My grandfather let me hold the reins of Star and Flora, his impressive mother-daughter team of draft horses pulling the hay wagon. At Christmastime in Sheboygan Falls, I listened on our huge upright radio to Billie the Brownie on WTMJ from Milwaukee.

After World War II, which ended in 1945, I was in the first generation to attend school; I began kindergarten in 1944 and graduated from high school in 1957. The high school classes of 1957 have unique status in Wisconsin because they are making history in a long-term study (until death) called the Wisconsin Longitudinal Study (WLS), conducted by the Institute of Aging and Adult Life at the University of Wisconsin-Madison (wls. wisc.edu). The report includes information such as family, health, education, military, financial matters, reproductive rate, mortality rate. A random sample was selected of 10,300 men and women, involving 1/3 of all folks graduating from 400 high schools in 1957 in Wisconsin. I'm in the sample.

In 1961, I received a BA in zoology from the University of Wisconsin, the first person in my family's direct ancestral line to receive a college degree. In 1964, I received an MS in wildlife (studying rabbits)[195] from Virginia Tech, then went through OCS in the Marine Corps at Quantico, VA, got married then and lived in Fredericksburg, VA on a street (Hanover) still with bullet holes from the Civil War, and ended up in the Vietnam War. In early 1967, from Dong Ha, South Vietnam, I began looking for my first wildlife job, contacted the Newfoundland and Labrador Wildlife Service, and got a job as a wildlife biologist.

I really liked my job in Newfoundland and Labrador, but after four years I resigned in 1971 due to low salary. My next stop, with my wife and two sons, was 3,500 miles (and a ferry ride) distance in a 1970 Falcon station wagon (bought in Toronto while attending a polar bear conference) to Logan, Utah (1971–73) for a PhD in wildlife (studying Newfoundland beaver) at Utah State University, received in 1975. The assistant unit leader of the Utah Cooperative Wildlife Research Unit, Dr. J. Juan Spillett, accepted me as his PhD candidate, along with my already completed beaver work in Newfoundland as a PhD proposal, and allowed me to complete the PhD dissertation (which produced seven publications) while on my next job. After Utah I worked for Aldo Leopold's last surviving graduate student, Dr. Richard D. Taber, in the College of Forest Resources at the University of Washington in Seattle (1973–75).[206, 207] But it was a research position for 2.5 years only, studying the effect on riparian vegetation and wildlife of water released from dams along the huge upper Columbia River (in collaboration with the Washington Game Department and the U.S. Army Corps of Engineers); at the end of it I was out of work with no paycheck. I had to scramble for a wildlife job.

In 1975, by pure coincidence I returned to Wisconsin after a 14-year hiatus involving the Marine Corps, the Vietnam War, wildlife pursuits, and four single and seven family moves across the United States and Canada. Pure coincidence because so few positions and opportunities are available for someone with a PhD in wildlife, especially at a university. In 1975, when I was without a job, I knew of only two such positions, one of them at the University of Maine where I came in second.

In an unlikely event, it just so happened that the year I needed work, a university wildlife position opened in my home state of Wisconsin at the University of Wisconsin-Stevens Point. In 1975, I sought and accepted a position as assistant professor of wildlife ecology in the College of Natural Resources at UWSP, working for Dr. Dan Trainer, dean of the college. Only two locations in Wisconsin are available with a professorial wildlife program: UW-Madison and UW-Stevens Point. Many states and provinces provide no university wildlife programs; others have one or two universities with a wildlife program. Thus, few such positions are available. But I had returned to Wisconsin.[199] (Not helpful along the way were my debilitating migraines every two weeks or so since age seven, now mostly history.)

I drove a large U-Haul the 1900 miles between Seattle and Stevens Point, towing my station wagon with my canoe on top, mooned enroute from a passing car. My two young sons sat next to me in the U-Haul looking into the bags of things my wife had prepared for them, and my dog and cat were in the towed station wagon. My wife flew two weeks later with our new baby daughter.

Although I worked with willow ptarmigan, rock doves, mallards, blue-winged teal, other waterfowl, songbirds, raptors, water birds, and massasauga rattlesnakes, as a wildlifer my interest was mostly with mammals (like when I was a kid). During my career, I worked with and/or published mostly on cottontail rabbit, marsh rabbit, snowshoe hare, arctic hare, black bear, beaver, red squirrel, gray squirrel, northern and southern flying squirrels, mink, muskrat, lynx, marten, fisher, otter, opossum, raccoon, gray fox, white-tailed deer, moose, caribou, various species of big game, small game, furbearers, and small mammals along the Columbia River in Washington, and even with horses. (I joke that I know pert-near everything there is to be known about horses on account of I once took a 3-credit college course in Western Horsemanship and got an A.)[195y]

I have three kids: Adam, born on the Pacific coast in California (three months old before I saw him), Mark, born on the Atlantic coast in Newfoundland (15 minutes old before I saw him), and Erin, born on the Pacific coast in Washington (two weeks old before I saw her). I joke that my wife Eileen threw litters all over the place; it's an indication of how much we moved in a relatively short time and the difficult, stressful decisions and action involved. Eventually we lived in the North, South, East, West, and Central United States and eastern Canada.

As a wildlifer, I now go back a ways. I met Earth Day originator Gaylord Nelson. I knew three of Aldo Leopold's kids (Starker, Nina, Estella). I met Aldo's son Luna and Aldo's brother Frederic. I knew eight of Aldo Leopold's 26 graduate students: two as my teachers (Joe Hickey, Al Stokes), two as my university associate colleagues (Fred Hamerstrom, Fran Hamerstrom), one as a contemporary advisor (Bob McCabe), two as state wildlife contacts (Cy Kabat, Jim Hale), and one (Dick Taber) as my boss and book co-author[235] and author of the forewords in two of my other books.[200, 203] I was proud of my association with Dick Taber. Having worked for him 1973–1975, I think he was glad we became acquainted and friends; I don't think he would've gotten his hardcover book published otherwise.[235] It is displayed with his other achievements in his scholarship shadow box at the University of Montana.

The first edition of the *Wildlife Techniques Manual*[182] was my textbook, and its editor was my teacher and MS committee member Henry Mosby (see Chapter 3). With biodiversity and habitat critical to survival, I wrote two books on wildlife habitat improvement[197, 203] (UWSP University Scholar, 1992). I taught my graduate students and thousands of undergraduate students about wildlife ecology, published technical articles in journals, and wrote a few more books after retirement in 1998.

After retirement, my wife and I wintered a few years on Sanibel Island, Florida, regularly visiting there the Ding Darling National Wildlife Refuge, named after a college graduate from Beloit College in Wisconsin and Aldo Leopold's friend and associate. Also after retirement, I was drawn from Wisconsin back to Newfoundland, where my wife and I have a summer house on the ocean shore, visiting annually my former wildlife co-workers there. In 2001, during the disaster of 9/11, we were in Newfoundland, where the planes from Europe were diverted; we helped buy food, make sandwiches, and feed the "plane people" stuck there.[44y]

I've been lucky: 1) not getting killed or injured in the Vietnam War or crashing on the road or in a low-flying plane censusing beaver or capsizing in a 14-foot boat traveling to islands in the Atlantic Ocean and on the Columbia River for wildlife work (although capsizing once in a canoe while hunting caribou) or injured live-trapping bears and other animals; 2) traveling here and there for education and work adventure, my wife Eileen accompanying me; 3) divorcing gently and remaining friends; 4) marrying Jan in a commuter marriage for 11 years between Wisconsin and Illinois to accommodate our kids and careers (professor of nursing, professor of wildlife ecology); 5) satisfying careers; 6) enjoying our present lifestyle (Wisconsin, Florida, Newfoundland); 7) gazing at that enlarged wonderful picture on the wall of Jan and me with our six accomplished, good, adult kids (her three: Patty, Shari, Gail; my three: Adam, Mark, Erin); 8) and now, somewhat shockingly, I'm a great-grandfather. Planning was involved, certainly. But I've been lucky.

I'm still a wildlifer. But I had various wildlife and other experiences: born and growing up in Wisconsin with ancestral roots here, leaving Wisconsin for some years and doing what I did and where I did it, including in the Vietnam War at age 27–28 in 1966–67 (my son Mark at age 53 taking me at age 84 to Washington, D.C., on the Honor Flight for Vietnam War veterans in 2023), returning to Wisconsin to work in the wildlife profession at a university and teach, write books, and retire in the same state with my deep roots. I've collaborated on wildlife research with, and some of my students work with and even retired from, the Wisconsin Department of Natural Resources. (My two closest associates there were Chuck Pils and Bruce Kohn).

Since my birth, I have lived in 28 different places, including five (by age five) while growing up in Sheboygan County, Wisconsin, and nine with the USMC. A round trip. I turned 18 in Sheboygan Falls. I turned 19 in Madison. I turned 23 in Blacksburg,

Virginia. I turned 24 on Hog Island State Wildlife Area, Virginia (not talking to a single person that day). I turned 25 enroute to joining the Marine Corps in Quantico, Virginia, and was 25 in Camp Lejeune, North Carolina. I was 26 in Vieques Island, Puerto Rico. I turned 27 in Fallbrook, California. I turned 28 in Vietnam. I turned 29 in St. John's, Newfoundland. I turned 33 in Logan, Utah. I turned 34 in Lynnwood, Washington. I was 36 in Plover, Wisconsin—18 years after graduating from Sheboygan Falls High School at age 18.

I have lived in or visited some 30 countries. I have owned car license plates in Wisconsin, Virginia, North Carolina, California, Newfoundland and Labrador, Utah, Washington, Illinois, and Florida. Every move brought excitement and anticipation, apprehension and stress.

The University of Wisconsin–Madison provided my wife Jan and me our professional foundations, both of us with a bachelor's degree initially. Jan is a retired professor of nursing and I am a retired professor of wildlife ecology. Thus, in a way, she and I have been in professions with similar goals. The medical profession is concerned about the health of society in the short run. The wildlife profession is concerned about the health of society in the long run.

The University of Wisconsin–Madison provided my son Adam and me our professional foundations, both of us with a bachelor of arts degree—Adam's in communications, mine in zoology— and a master's degree there in urban and regional planning for Adam, who became Secretary of the Wisconsin Department of Natural Resources at the same time that his father was publishing a book about Wisconsin wildlife. That brief coincidence probably constitutes a somewhat distinctive father and son simultaneous contribution to Wisconsin's natural resources.

A question I would ask my graduate students during their final oral exam in defense of their thesis was, "Is there anything you would do differently?" Invariably the answer was *yes*, hindsight being 20/20. Is there anything I would do differently in my life? Hard to say exactly, circumstances often dictating or at least influencing decision over so long a time. Timing and the word *if* can enter a decision—*if* something hadn't happened then, or *if* something had. Certainly I would have modified or altered some things, including behavioral, and the failings I had as a husband and a father, and as a wildlifer, now that hindsight lends me more perspective. The round trip of locations and adventures since I left my relatively humble origins so long ago has taught and given me much, from pride to humility. Is there anything I would do differently in my life relative to my locations and adventures regarding my round trip *Return to the Falls*?[199] Except for the incidental stupid things I've done and said at times along the way, not much I guess. As I said, seems like another time, another place, another me; it was.

All of this stuff seems to yield a strong, perhaps somewhat unique, connection to Wisconsin and its wildlife. And now I am a weathered old guy, a retired, aging wildlifer. But with age comes wisdom—if only I could remember it.

It has been quite a trip.

REFERENCES

1. Addis, J., et al. 1995. Wisconsin's biodiversity as a management issue: A report to Department of Natural Resources managers. Wisconsin Department of Natural Resources, Madison. 240pp.

1x. Aguirre, J.C. 2023. $Drill, baby, $Drill. Sierra 108(3):30-37

2. Allen, D.L. 1954. Our wildlife legacy. Funk and Wagnalls, New York. 422pp.

3. *Andrews, C.G. 2013. Travel wild Wisconsin: A seasonal guide to wildlife encounters in natural places. University of Wisconsin Press, Madison. 246pp.

3x. Antholis, W., and S. Talbott. 2010. Fast forward: Ethics and politics in the age of global warming. Brookings Institution Press, Washington. 144pp.

4. Apps, J. 2015. Wisconsin agriculture: A history. Wisconsin Historical Society Press, Madison. 336pp.

5. Apps, J. 2019. The Civilian Conservation Corp in Wisconsin: Nature's army at work. Wisconsin Historical Society Press, Madison. 224pp.

6. Arms, M. 2004. Servants of the fish: A portrait of Newfoundland after the great cod collapse. Upper Access, Hinesburg, Vermont. 255pp.

6x. Audubon, J.J. 1838 (reprinted 2021). The birds of America. Prestel, New York. 448pp.

7. *Backes, D. 1999. A wilderness within: The life of Sigurd F. Olson. University of Minnesota Press, Minneapolis. 408pp.

7x. Baier, L.E. 2023. The codex of the Endangered Species Act: The first fifty years. Rowan & Littlefield, Lanham, MD. 864pp.

7y. Baier, L.E., J.F. Organ, and C.E. Segal, editors. 2023. The codex of the Endangered Species Act: The next fifty years. Rowan & Littlefield, Lanham, MD. 368pp.

8. Baldassarre, G.A. 1978. Ecological factors affecting waterfowl production on three man-made flowages in central Wisconsin. MS thesis. University of Wisconsin, Stevens Point. 124pp.

9. Baldassarre, G. 2014. Ducks, geese, and swans of North America. 3rd edition. Johns Hopkins University Press, Baltimore. 2 volumes: 1027pp.

10. Baldassarre, G.A., and E.G. Bolen. 2006. Waterfowl ecology and management. 2nd edition. Krieger, Malabar, Florida. 580pp.

10x. Barbier, E., and T. Swanson, editors. 1992. Economics for the wilds: Wildlife, wildlands, diversity and development. Routledge, New York. 240pp.

11. Beck, T.H., J.N. Darling, and A. Leopold. 1934. Report of the President's Committee on Wild Life Restoration. U.S. Department of Agriculture, Washington. 28pp.

12. *Becker, G.C. 1983. Fishes of Wisconsin. University of Wisconsin Press, Madison. 1052pp.

12x. Belanger, D.O., and A. Kinnane. 2002. Managing American wildlife: A history of the International Association of Fish and Wildlife Agencies. Montrose Press, Rockville, MD. 334pp.

13. Bellrose, F.C. 1976. Ducks, geese, & swans of North America. 2nd edition. Stackpole. Harrisburg, Pennsylvania. 544pp.

14. Bent, A.C. 1919-1968. Life histories of North American birds. Smithsonian, Washington, DC. 21 volumes.

15. *Berry, B. 2014. Banning DDT: How citizen activists in Wisconsin led the way. Wisconsin Historical Society Press, Madison. 274pp.

16. Berry, D. 1961. A majority of scoundrels: An informal history of the Rocky Mountain Fur Company. Harper, New York. 432pp.

17. *Bersing, O. 1966. A century of Wisconsin deer. 2nd edition. Wisconsin Conservation Department, Madison. 184pp.

18. Bieder, R.E. 1995. Native American communities in Wisconsin 1600-1960. University of Wisconsin Press, Madison. 288pp.

19. *Black, M.R., and E.J. Judziewicz. 2009. Wildflowers of Wisconsin and the Great Lakes region. 2nd edition. University of Wisconsin Press, Madison. 275pp.

20. *Blomberg, K.M. 2017. Up the creek. Orange Hat Publishing, Waukesha, Wisconsin. 176pp.

21. *Blomberg, K.M. 2018. Wisconsin bird hunting tales. The History Press, Charleston, South Carolina. 178pp.

21x. Booth, E.S. 1948. Birds of the west. Stanford University Press, Stanford, California. 397pp.

22. Bortz, D. 2019. Four state men fined $65,000 in illegal bobcat, lion hunts. Wisconsin Outdoor News 26(8):5.

23. *Boyce, M.S., and A. Haney, editors. 1997. Ecosystem management: Applications for sustainable forest and wildlife resources. Yale University Press, New Haven, Connecticut. 361pp.

24. Braband, L., P.D. Curtis, M.S. Fishman, T.L. Hiller, and S.M. Vantassel. 2020. Where do they fit?: Often overlooked, private sector wildlifers play a growing role in conservation. Wildlife Professional 14(1):44-47.

25. Bradley, N.L., C.A. Leopold, J. Ross, and W. Huffaker. 1999. Phenological changes reflect climate change in Wisconsin. Proceedings of the National Academy of Sciences 96:9701-9704.

26. Brinkley, D. 2010. The wilderness warrior: Theodore Roosevelt and the crusade for America. HarperCollins, New York. 940pp.

27. Brinkley, D. 2016. Rightful heritage: Franklin D. Roosevelt and the land of America. HarperCollins, New York. 744pp.

28. *Brockman, K.M., and R.A. Dow, Jr., editors. 1982. Wildlife in early Wisconsin: Collection of works by A.W. Schorger. Student Chapter of The Wildlife Society, University of Wisconsin, Stevens Point. 581pp.

29. Brown, R.D., and L.H. Wurman. 2009. A brief history of wildlife conservation and research in North America. Boone and Crockett Club, Missoula, Montana. 31pp.

30. Bump, G., R.W. Darrow, F.C. Edminster, W.F. Crissey. 1947. The ruffed grouse: Life history, propagation, management. New York State Conservation Department, Albany. 915pp.

31. *Callicott, J.B., editor. 1987. Companion to A Sand County Almanac: Interpretive and critical essays. University of Wisconsin Press, Madison. 320pp.

32. Carson, R. 1962. Silent spring. Houghton Mifflin, Boston. 368pp.

33. *Chizek, L. 1992. Game warden centurion 1879-1979. Flambeau River Publishing, Lodi, Wisconsin. 201pp.

34. *Chizek, J.T. 1999. Protectors of the outdoors: True stories from the frontline of conservation enforcement. Flambeau River Publishing, Lodi, Wisconsin. 232pp.

35. *Christofferson, B. 2004. The man from Clear Lake: Earth Day founder Senator Gaylord Nelson. University of Wisconsin Press, Madison. 416pp.

36. *Corneli, H. 2002. Mice in the freezer, owls on the porch: The lives of naturalists Frederick and Frances Hamerstrom. University of Wisconsin Press, Madison. 336pp.

37. *Court, F.E. 2012. Pioneers of ecological restoration: The people and legacy of the University of Wisconsin Arboretum. University of Wisconsin Press, Madison. 314pp.

38. *Crowley, K. 2003. Gordon MacQuarrie: The story of an old duck hunter. Wisconsin Historical Society Press, Madison. 208pp.

39. *Curtis, J.T. 1959. The vegetation of Wisconsin: An ordination of plant communities. University of Wisconsin Press, Madison. 657pp.

40. *Cutright, N.J., B.R Harriman, and R.W. Howe. 2006. Atlas of the breeding birds of Wisconsin. Wisconsin Society for Ornithology, Milwaukee. 602pp.

41. *Dahlberg, B.L., and R.C. Guettinger. 1956. The white-tailed deer in Wisconsin. Technical Wildlife Bulletin 14. Wisconsin Conservation Department, Madison. 281pp.

42. Danou, C.H. 1997. Habitat use and movement patterns of the eastern massasauga rattlesnake in Wisconsin. MS thesis. University of Wisconsin, Stevens Point. 31pp.

43. Darwin, C. 1859. On the origin of species. Penguin Classics, London. 156pp.

44. *Davis, J.W., R.C. Anderson, L. Karstad, and D.O. Trainer, editors. 1971. Infectious and parasitic diseases of wild birds. Iowa State University Press, Ames. 344pp.

44x. Decker, D.J., and G.R. Goff, editors. 1987. Valuing wildlife: Economic and social perspectives. Westview Press, Boulder, CO. 424pp.

44y. DeFede, J. 2002. The day the world came to town: 9/11 in Gander, Newfoundland. ReganBooks (HarperCollins), New York. 244pp.

45. *Derleth, A. 1985. The Wisconsin: River of a thousand isles. University of Wisconsin Press, Madison. 366pp.

45x. Diamond, J. 2005. Collapse: How societies choose to fail or succeed. Penguin Books, New York. 576pp.

46. Dickens, C. 1861. Great expectations. Chapman & Hall, London. 544pp.

47. Dolin, E.J., and B. Dumaine. 2000. The Duck Stamp story: Art, conservation, history. Krause, Stevens Point, Wisconsin. 206pp.

48. *Dott, R.H., Jr., and J.W. Attig. 2004. Roadside geology of Wisconsin. Mountain Press, Missoula, Montana. 346pp.

49. *Durbin, R.D. 1997. The Wisconsin River: An odyssey through time and space. Spring Freshet Press, Cross Plains, Wisconsin. 237pp.

50. Eisele, T. 2020. Solving the 1971 Neil LaFave murder 1. Wisconsin Outdoor News 27(19):22, 44.

51. Elmer-Dewitt, P., editor. 1999. TIME 100 special issue: Scientists and thinkers of the 20th century. TIME 153(12):64-206.

52. Elton, C. 1927. Animal ecology. Macmillan, New York. 254pp.

52x. Eltringham, S.K. 1984. Wildlife resources and economic development. Wiley, New York. 325pp.

53. *Emlen, J.T., Jr. 1996. Adventure is where you find it: Recollections of a twentieth century naturalist. Self-published, Madison, Wisconsin. 397pp.

54. Engel, T.C. 1980. Effects of urban development on vertebrate wildlife populations in Schmeeckle Reserve, University of Wisconsin-Stevens Point. MS thesis. University of Wisconsin, Stevens Point. 143pp.

55. Engel, T.C., M.L. Lemke, and N.F. Payne. 1992. Live capture methods of sympatric species of flying squirrel. Transactions of the Wisconsin Academy of Sciences, Arts and Letters 80:149-152.

56. *Fassett, N.C. 1931. Spring flora of Wisconsin. University of Wisconsin Press, Madison. 424pp.

57. *Fassett, N.C. 1940. A manual of aquatic plants. McGraw-Hill, New York. 396pp.

57x. Figueres, C. 2023. We hold the pen of history. TIME 201(3-4):50.

58. Flader, S. 1994. Thinking like a mountain: Aldo Leopold and the evolution of an ecological attitude toward deer, wolves, and

forests. 2nd edition. University of Wisconsin Press, Madison. 320pp.

59. *Flader, S.L., and J.B. Callicott, editors. 1991. The river of the mother of God and other essays by Aldo Leopold. University of Wisconsin Press, Madison. 400pp.

60. *Friend, M. 2006. Disease emergence and resurgence: The wildlife-human connection. Circular 1285. U.S. Geological Survey, Reston, Virginia. 388pp.

61. Gabrielson, I.N. 1941. Wildlife conservation. Macmillan, New York. 250pp.

62. Gabrielson, I.N. 1943. Wildlife refuges. Macmillan, New York. 257pp.

63. Gabrielson, I.N. 1951. Wildlife management. Macmillan, New York. 274pp.

64. Gara, L. 1962. A short history of Wisconsin. State Historical Society of Wisconsin, Madison. 287pp.

64x. Gard, W. 1959. The great buffalo hunt. Knopf, New York. 324pp

65. Gaumnitz, L. 2019. Preventive measures. Wisconsin Natural Resources 43(4):22-26.

66. Giles, R.H., editor. 1969. Wildlife management techniques. 3rd edition. The Wildlife Society, Washington, DC. 623pp.

67. *Gjestson, D.L. 2013. The gamekeepers: Wisconsin wildlife conservation from WCD to CWD. Wisconsin Department of Natural Resources, Madison. 473pp.

68. Goc, M.J. 2013. Stewards of the Wisconsin: Wisconsin Valley Improvement Company. New Past Press, Friendship, Wisconsin. 172pp.

69. Gore, A. 1992. Earth in the balance: Ecology and the human spirit. Houghton Mifflin, Boston. 416pp.

70. Graham, E.H. 1947. The land and wildlife. Oxford University Press, New York. 232pp.

71. *Grange, W.B. 1949. The way to game abundance. Charles Scribner's Sons, New York. 365pp.

72. *Grange, W.B. 1953. Those of the forest. Flambeau Publishing, Babcock, Wisconsin. 314pp.

73. *Grange, W.B., J.L. Breitenstein, and R. P. Thiel. 2020. As the twig is bent: A memoir. University of Wisconsin Press, Madison. 324pp.

74. Great Lakes Indian Fish & Wildlife Commission. 2011. A guide to understanding Ojibwe treaty rights. Great Lakes Fish & Wildlife Commission, Odanah, Wisconsin. 52pp.

75. Greenberg, J. 2014. A feathered river across the sky: The passenger pigeon's flight to extinction. Bloomsbury USA, New York. 290pp.

76. *Gromme, O.J. 1998. Birds of Wisconsin. 2nd edition. University of Wisconsin Press, Madison. 240pp.

77. *Hagner, C., and B.E. Small. 2019. Field guide to birds of Wisconsin. Scott & Nix, New York. 368pp.

78. *Hamerstrom, F. 1970. An eagle to the sky. Iowa State University Press, Ames. 142pp.

79. *Hamerstrom, F. 1980. Strictly for the chickens. Iowa State University Press, Ames. 174pp.

80. *Hamerstrom, F. 1984. Birding with a purpose: Of raptors, gabboons, and other creatures. Iowa State University Press, Ames. 130pp.

81. *Hamerstrom, F. 1986. Harrier, hawk of the marshes: The hawk that is ruled by a mouse. Smithsonian, Washington. 171pp.

82. *Hamerstrom, F. 1988. Wild food cookbook. Iowa State University Press, Ames. 126pp.

83. *Hamerstrom, F. 1989. Is she coming too?: Memoirs of a lady hunter. Iowa State University Press, Ames. 156pp.

84. *Hamerstrom, F. 1994. My double life: Memoirs of a naturalist. University of Wisconsin Press, Madison. 316pp.

85. *Haney, A. 2014. Jewels of nature: Delightful birds I have known. Schneider Publishers, Stevens Point, Wisconsin. 256pp.

86. Hardin, G. 1968. The tragedy of the commons. Science 162:1243-1248.

87. *Hawkins, A., and K.M. Blomberg. 2019. Letters from Art: Art Hawkins standing tall in the shadow of Aldo Leopold. Orange Hat Publishing, Waukesha, Wisconsin. 133pp.

87x. Hawley, A.W.L., editor. 1993. Commercialization and wildlife management: Dancing with the devil. Krieger, Malabar, FL. 124pp.

88. *Heberlein, T.A. 2012. Navigating environmental attitudes. Oxford University Press, New York. 240pp.

89. Henke, S.E., and P.R. Krausman, editors. 2017a. Becoming a wildlife professional. Johns Hopkins University Press, Baltimore, Maryland. 232pp.

90. Henke, S.E., and P.R. Krausman. 2017b. Preface. Pages xv-xvi in S.E. Henke and P.R. Krausman, editors. Becoming a wildlife professional. Johns Hopkins University Press, Baltimore, Maryland.

91. Hewitt, C.G. 1921. The conservation of the wild life of Canada. Scribner, New York. 438pp.

92. *Hickey, J.J. 1944. A guide to bird watching. Oxford University Press, New York. 264pp.

93. *Hickey, J.J., editor. 1969. Peregrine falcon populations: Their biology and decline. University of Wisconsin Press, Madison. 596pp.

94. *Hoffman, R. 2002. Wisconsin's natural communities: How to recognize them, where to find them. University of Wisconsin Press, Madison. 400pp.

95. *Hoffman, R. 2019. When things happen: A guide to natural events in Wisconsin. Self-published, Amazon.com. 282pp.

96. Hohensee, P., M.D. Samuel, and D. Drake. 2017. For what it's worth: Appreciating the economic value of wildlife. The Wildlife Professional 11(1):40-43.

97. Hoover, R.L. 1976. Incorporating fish and wildlife values in land use planning. Transactions of the North American Wildlife and Natural Resources Conference 41:279-289.

97x. Hornaday, W.T. 1889 (2021 again). The extermination of the American bison. Smithsonian, Washington. 386pp.

98. Hornaday, W.T. 1913. Our vanishing wild life. New York Zoological Society, New York. 432pp.

99. Hornaday, W.T. 1914. Wild life conservation in theory and practice. Yale University Press, New Haven, Connecticut. 276pp.

100. *Howell, E.A., J.A. Harrington, and S.B. Glass. 2011. Introduction to restoration ecology. 2nd edition. Island Press. Washington. 436pp.

101. Hungerford, H.R., W.I. Bluhm, T.L. Volk, and J.M. Ramsey, editors. 2005. Essential readings in environmental education. 3rd edition. Stipes, Champaign, Illinois. 443pp.

102. Huntington, E. 1931. The Matamek Conference on biological cycles, 1931. Science 74(1914):229-235.

102x. Huq, S. 2022. Bangladesh's media lesson. TIME 200(17-18):56.

103. *Hygnstrom, S., R.T.M. Timm, and G.A. Larson. 1996. Prevention and control of wildlife damage: A handbook for people who deal with wildlife damage problems. Diane Publishing. Darby, Pennsylvania. 503pp.

104. *Jackson, H.H.T. 1961. Mammals of Wisconsin. University of Wisconsin Press, Madison. 504pp.

105. Johnston, O., and F. Thomas. 1990. Walt Disney's Bambi: The story and the film. Stewart, Tabori & Chang, New York. 208pp.

106. *Judd, M.K. 1995. Wisconsin wildlife viewing guide. Falcon Press, Helena, Montana. 95pp.

107. Kahler, K.A., and A. Zani. 2018. From the archives of a 'superagency.' Special Section. Wisconsin Natural Resources 42(2):I-VIII.

108. *Keith, L.B. 1962. Wildlife's ten-year cycle. University of Wisconsin Press, Madison, Wisconsin. 201pp.

108x. Kellert, S.R. 1996. The value of life: Biological diversity and human society. Island Press. Covelo, California. 282pp.

108y. *King, F.H. 1882. (2010). Economic relations of Wisconsin birds. Kessinger Publications. Whitefish, Montana. 174pp.

109. King, R.T. 1947. The future of wildlife in forest land use. Transactions of the North American Wildlife Conference 12:454-467.

110. Knight, R.L., and S. Riedel, editors. 2002. Aldo Leopold and the ecological conscience. Oxford University Press, New York. 216pp.

111. Knudson, G.J. 1963. History of beaver in Wisconsin. Research Report 7. Wisconsin Conservation Department, Madison. 15pp.

111x. Kobilinsky, D. 2021. Diversity in the field. Wildlife Professional 15(3):18-26.

112. Kohn, B.E., N.F. Payne, J.E. Ashbrenner, and W.A. Creed. 1993. The fisher in Wisconsin. Technical Bulletin 183. Wisconsin Department of Natural Resources, Madison. 25pp.

113. Kohn, B.W. 1982. Status and management of black bears in Wisconsin. Technical Bulletin 129. Wisconsin Department of Natural Resources, Madison. 32pp.

114. Koprowski, J.L., and P.R. Krausman, editors. 2019. International wildlife management: Conservation challenges in a changing world. Johns Hopkins University Press, Baltimore, Maryland. 248pp.

115. Kortright, F.H. 1942. The ducks, geese, and swans of North America. Stackpole, Harrisburg, Pennsylvania. 476pp.

116. *Kubisiak, J.F., K.R. McCaffery, W.A. Creed, T.A. Heberlein, R.C. Bishop, and R.E. Rolley. 2001. Sandhill whitetails: Providing new perspectives for deer management. Wisconsin Department of Natural Resources, Madison. 282pp.

117. *Kumlien, L., and N. Hollister. 1903. The birds of Wisconsin. Bulletin of the Wisconsin Natural History Society, Milwaukee. 143pp.

118. Kurtén, B., and E Anderson. 1980. Pleistocene mammals of North America. Columbia University Press, New York. 442pp.

119. Lack, D. 1943. The life of the robin. H.F. & G. Witherby, London. 224pp.

120. Lack, D. 1947. Darwin's finches. Cambridge University Press, Cambridge. 208pp.

121. Lack, D. 1954. The natural regulation of animal numbers. Oxford University Press, New York. 343pp.

122. *Lapham, I.A. 1844. A geographical and topographical description of Wisconsin; with brief sketches of its history, geology, mineralogy, natural history, population, soil, productions, government, antiquities, &c. P.C. Hale, Milwaukee. 264pp.

123. Lapham, I.A., J.G. Knapp, and H. Crocker. 1867. Report on the disastrous effects of the destruction of forest trees now going on so rapidly in the state of Wisconsin. Atwood & Rublee, Madison. 104pp.

124. Lehr, K.M., J. Reneau, and J.E. Spring, editors. 2017. Records of North American big game. 14th edition. Boone and Crockett Club, Missoula, Montana. 974pp.

125. Lendt, D. 1984. Ding, the life of Jay Norwood Darling. Iowa State University Press, Ames. 204pp.

126. Leopold, A. 1915. Game and fish handbook. U.S. Forest Service, Albuquerque, New Mexico.

127. Leopold, A. 1919. Wild lifers vs. game farmers: a plea for democracy in sport. Bulletin of the American Game Protective Association 8(2)6-7.

128. Leopold, A. 1921. The wilderness and its place in forest recreation policy. Journal of Forestry 19:718-721.

129. Leopold, A. 1925a. Recent developments in game management. U.S. Forest Service Bulletin 9(9):1-2.

130. Leopold, A. 1925b. Ten new developments in game management. American Game 14(3):7-8, 20.

131. *Leopold, A. 1931. Report on a game survey of the north central states. The Democrat Press for the Sporting Arms and Ammunition Manufacturers' Institute, Madison, Wisconsin. 302pp.

132. Leopold, A. 1932. Game and wild life conservation. Condor 34:103-106.

133. *Leopold, A. 1933a. Game management. Charles Scribner's Sons, New York. 481pp.

134. Leopold, A. 1933b. The conservation ethic. Journal of Forestry 31:634-643.

135. Leopold, A. 1935a. Wildlife research rapidly growing. American Game 24(1):5, 13.

136. Leopold, A. 1935b. Wild life research in Wisconsin. Transactions of the Wisconsin Academy of Sciences, Arts & Letters 29:203-208.

137. Leopold, A. 1936. Franklin J. W. Schmidt. Wilson Bulletin 48:181-186.

138. Leopold, A. 1939. Academic and professional training in wildlife work. Journal of Wildlife Management 3:156-161.

139. Leopold, A. 1942. Introduction. Page vii in F.H. Kortright. The ducks, geese, and swans of North America. Stackpole, Harrisburg, Pennsylvania.

140. *Leopold, A. 1949. A sand county almanac: And sketches here and there. Oxford University Press, New York. 226pp.

141. *Leopold, A. 1953. Round River: From the journals of Aldo Leopold. Oxford University Press, New York. 173pp.

142. *Leopold, A. 1966. A sand county almanac: With essays on conservation from Round River. Oxford University Press, New York. 209pp.

143. Leopold, A., L.J. Cole, N.C. Fassett, C.A. Herrick, C. Juday, and G. Wagner. 1937. The university and conservation of Wisconsin wildlife. Bulletin of the University of Wisconsin, Serial No. 2211, General Series No. 1995, Madison. 39pp.

144. Leopold, A., et al. 1939. Report of the Committee on Professional Standards [of The Wildlife Society]. Journal of Wildlife Management 3(2):153-155.

145. Leopold, A., and S.E. Jones. 1947. A phenological record for Sauk and Dane counties, Wisconsin, 1935-1945. Ecological Monographs 17:81-122.

146. Leopold, A.S. 1959. Wildlife of Mexico: The game birds and mammals. University of California Press, Berkeley. 581pp.

147. Leopold, E.B. 2016. Stories from the Leopold Shack: Sand County revisited. Oxford University Press, New York. 325pp.

148. Les, B.L. 1979. The vanishing wild: Wisconsin's endangered wildlife and its habitat. Wisconsin Department of Natural Resources, Madison. 35pp.

149. Loew, P. 2001. Indian nations of Wisconsin: Histories of endurance and renewal. Wisconsin Historical Society Press, Madison. 148pp.

150. *Long, C.A. 2008. The wild mammals of Wisconsin. Pensoft Publishing, Sofia, Bulgaria. 544pp.

151. *Long, C.A., and C.A. Killingley. 1983. The badgers of the world. Charles C. Thomas Publications, Springfield, Illinois. 404pp.

152. *Lorbiecki, M. 1996. Aldo Leopold: A fierce green fire. Falcon Press, Helena Montana. 224pp.

153. *Lorbiecki, M. 2016. A fierce green fire: Aldo Leopold's life and legacy. Oxford University Press, New York. 337pp.

154. Lorenz, K. 1949. King Solomon's ring. Methuen, London. 202pp.

155. Lund, T.A. 1980. American wildlife law. University of California Press, Berkeley. 188pp.

155x. McNeely, J.A. 1988. Economics and biological diversity: Developing and using economic incentives to conserve biological resources. International Union for Conservation of Nature and Natural Resources, Gland, Switzerland. 256pp.

156. *MacQuarrie, G. 1995a. Stories of the old duck hunters and other drivel. Willow Creek Press, Minocqua, Wisconsin. 223pp.

157. *MacQuarrie, G. 1995b. More stories of the old duck hunters. Willow Creek Press, Minocqua, Wisconsin. 198pp.

158. *MacQuarrie, G. 1995c. The last stories of the old duck hunters. Willow Creek Press, Minocqua, Wisconsin. 151pp.

159. Madison, M., editor. 2020. Conservation history: Women in conservation. U.S. Fish & Wildlife Service, Washington. 75pp.

159x. Mahoney, S.P., and V. Geist, editors. 2019. The North American Model of Wildlife Conservation. Johns Hopkins University Press, Baltimore. 176pp.

160. *Main, A.K. 1925. Bird companions. R.G. Badger, Boston. 287pp.

161. Mann, C. C. 2006. 1491: New revelations of the Americas before Columbus. Vantage Books, New York. 541pp.

162. Manuwal, D.A., and S. Miller. 2016. Richard D. Taber. Wildlife Professional 10(2):47.

162x. Maraniss, D. 2003. They marched into sunlight: War and peace Vietnam and America October 1967. Simon & Schuster. New York. 573pp.

163. Marsh, G.P. 1864. Man and nature: Or physical geography as modified by human action. Scribner, New York. 312pp.

164. Martin, L. 1965. The physical geography of Wisconsin. University of Wisconsin Press, Madison. 608pp.

165. Martin, P.S., and R.G. Klein, editors. 1984. Quaternary extinctions: A prehistoric revolution. University of Arizona Press, Tucson. 882pp.

165x. Martin, A.C., H.S. Zim, and N.L. Nelson. 1951. American wildlife and plants: A guide to wildlife food habits. Dover Publications, Garden City, New York. 500pp.

166. *Matteson, S. 2020. Afield: Portraits of Wisconsin naturalists, empowering Leopold's legacy. Little Creek Press, Mineral Point, Wisconsin. 728pp.

167. *McCabe, R.A. 1987. Aldo Leopold: The Professor. Rusty Rock Press, Madison, Wisconsin. 172pp.

168. *McCabe, R.A. 1991. Willow flycatcher: The little green bird. Palmer Publications, Amherst, Wisconsin. 171pp.

169. *McCabe, R.E., editor. 1988. Aldo Leopold: Mentor, by his graduate students. Department of Wildlife Ecology, University of Wisconsin, Madison. 125pp.

170. *McCrary, B. 2016. The history of Wisconsin bowhunting: 1930-2016. Bill McCrary, DeForest, Wisconsin. 323pp.

171. McDonald, J. 2012. The Pittman-Robertson Act celebrates 75 years. Wildlife Professional 6(3):74-78.

172. Meine, C.D. 1998. Moving mountains: Aldo Leopold and A Sand County Almanac. Wildlife Society Bulletin 26:697-706.

173. *Meine, C. 2004. Correction lines: Essays on land, Leopold, and conservation. Island Press, Washington. 245pp.

174. *Meine, C. 2010. Aldo Leopold: His life and work. 2nd edition. University of Wisconsin Press, Madison. 638pp.

175. *Meine, C. 2013. Aldo Leopold: A sand county almanac & other writings on conservation and ecology. Library of America, New York. 832pp.

176. *Meine, C. D., and G.W. Archibald, editors. 1996. The cranes: Status survey and conservation action plan. IUCN, Gland, Switzerland, and Cambridge, England. 294pp.

177. *Meine, C., and R.L. Knight, editors. 2006. The essential Aldo Leopold: Quotations and commentaries. University of Wisconsin Press, Madison. 362pp.

178. *Mentzer, M. 1991. The world of Owen Gromme. 2nd edition. Northwood Press, Nevis, MN. 240pp.

179. *Meunier, J., and C. Meine, editors. 2018. Aldo Leopold on forestry and conservation: Toward a durable scale of values. Society of American Foresters, Bethesda, Maryland. 293pp.

180. Montevecchi, W.A., and L.M. Tuck. 1987. Newfoundland birds: Exploitation, study, conservation. Nuttall Ornithological Club, Cambridge, Massachusetts. 273pp.

180x. Moorman, C.E., S.M. Grodsky, and S.P. Rupp, editors. 2019. Renewable energy and wildlife conservation. Johns Hopkins University Press, Baltimore. 280pp.

180y. Morgan, L.H. 1868. The American beaver and his works. J.B. Lippincott & Co., Philadelphia. 330pp.

181. Mosby, H.S., chairman. 1958. Manual of wildlife techniques. Wildlife Society, Virginia Cooperative Wildlife Research Unit, Blacksburg. Unpublished. Various pages.

182. Mosby, H.S., editor. 1960. Manual of game investigational techniques. The Wildlife Society, Virginia Cooperative Wildlife Research Unit, Blacksburg. Various pages.

183. Mosby, H.S., editor. 1963. Wildlife investigational techniques. 2nd edition. The Wildlife Society, Virginia Cooperative Wildlife Research Unit, Blacksburg. 419pp.

184. Mosby, H.S., and C.O. Handley. 1943. The wild turkey in Virginia: Its status, life history and management. Virginia Commission of Game and Inland Fisheries, Richmond. 281pp.

185. Mowat, F. 1984. Sea of slaughter. McClelland and Stewart-Bantam, Toronto. 439pp.

186. Muir, J. 1912. The story of my boyhood and youth. Houghton Mifflin, New York. 294pp.

186x. Murphy, B., and J. White. 2001. Michael W. Gratson, 1952-2000. Wildlife Society Bulletin 29:393-394.

187. Nelson, E.W. 1923. The economic importance of wild life. Scientific Monthly 16(4):367-373.

188. *Nelson, G., S. Campbell, and P.R. Wozniak. 2002. Beyond Earth Day: Fulfilling the promise. University of Wisconsin Press, Madison. 224pp.

189. Nesbit, R.C., and W.F. Thompson. 1989. Wisconsin: A history. University of Wisconsin Press, Madison. 599pp.

189x. Nichols, J.S. 2017. The evolution of the wildlife profession. Wildlife Professional 11(5):55-58.

189y. Norton, N.C. 1981. Food habits, growth, and cover types used by northern Wisconsin black bears. MS thesis. University of Wisconsin, Stevens Point. 48pp.

189z. Ogden, A. 1941. The California sea otter trade: 1784-1848. University of California Press, Berkeley. 251pp.

190. Organ, J.F. 2012. The evolution of a professional society. Wildlife Professional 6(3):24-31.

190x. Orr, D.W. 2002. The events of 9-11: A view from the margin. Conservation Biology 16:288-290.

191. Ostergren, R.C., and T.R. Vale. 1997. Wisconsin land and life. University of Wisconsin Press, Madison. 567pp.

192. Paloski, R.A., T.L.E. Bergeson, A.F. Badje, M. Mossman, and R. Hay, editors. 2014. Wisconsin frog and toad survey phenology manual. PUB-NH-743. Bureau of Natural Heritage Conservation, Wisconsin Department of Natural Resources, Madison. 21pp.

193. Paulson, E.H. 2013. Hamerstrom stories: Recollections of the life of Hammy and Fran Hamerstrom. R. Schneider Publishers, Stevens Point, WI. 336pp.

194. Payne, N.F. 1964. The influence of hunting on rabbit populations in southeastern Virginia. MS thesis. Virginia Polytechnic Institute, Blacksburg. 76pp.

194x. Payne, N.F. 1967. The week of Christmas was pure hell. Third Place. December 21, 1967, Christmas Edition. Evening Telegram. St. John's, NL.

194y. Payne, N.F. 1969. Newfoundland and Labrador fur guide. Newfoundland Wildlife Service, Department of Mines, Agriculture, and Resources, St. John's. 75pp.

195. Payne, N.F. 1975. Trapline management and population biology of Newfoundland beaver. PhD dissertation. Utah State University, Logan. 192pp.

195x. Payne, N.F. 1975. Range extension of the marsh rabbit in Virginia. Chesapeake Science 16(1):77-78.

195y. Payne, N.F. 1975. Aggressive and gregarious behavior of horses. Horse Lovers National Magazine 40(5):42-43, 64.

195z. Payne, N.F. 1978. Hunting and management of the New-foundland black bear. Wildlife Society Bulletin 6(4):206-211.

195zz. Payne, N.F. 1975. Profiles: Newfoundland pine marten. Defenders 50(5):444-446.

195zzz. Payne, N.F. 1980. Trapline management of Newfound-land beaver. Wildlife Society Bulletin 8(2):110-117.

196. Payne, N.F. 1981. Accuracy of aerial censusing for beaver colonies in Newfoundland. Journal of Wildlife Management 45:1014-1016.

196x. Payne, N.F. 1990. Christmas in a Vietnam bunker. December 24, 1990. Stevens Point Journal. Stevens Point, WI.

197. *Payne, N.F. 1992. Techniques for wildlife habitat management of wetlands. McGraw-Hill, New York. 550pp.

198. *Payne, N.F. 2002. More wildlife on your land: A guide for private landowners. Barberie, Plover, Wisconsin. (Self-published.) 158pp.

199. Payne, N.F. 2006. Return to the Falls: Memories of a round trip. Unpublished hard-bound memoir. 199pp.+ pictures.

200. *Payne, N.F. 2011. Wildlife delights and dilemmas: Newfoundland and Labrador. DRC, St. John's, NL. 277pp.

201. Payne, N.F. 2015. The Newfoundland mystique. DRC, St. John's, NL. 245pp.

202. Payne, N.F. 2016. Last surviving Leopold graduate student dies in Montana. Wisconsin Outdoor News 4 March:14.

202x. Payne, N.F., B.S. McGinnes, and H.S. Mosby. 1987. Capture rates of cottontails, opossums, and other wildlife in unbaited wooden box traps. Virginia Journal of Science 38(1):23-26.

203. *Payne, N.F., and F.C. Bryant. 1994. Techniques for wildlife habitat management of uplands. McGraw-Hill, New York. 841pp.

204. *Payne, N.F., and F. Copes. 1986. Wildlife and fisheries habitat improvement handbook. 2nd printing 1988, 3rd printing 1990. U.S. Forest Service, Washington, DC. 402pp.

205. Payne, N.F., and J.C. Harms. 1994. Land use plan for Treehaven. College of Natural Resources, University of Wisconsin, Stevens Point. 203pp.

205x. Payne, N.F., B.E. Kohn, N.C. Norton, and G.G. Bertagnoli. 1998. Black bear food items in northern Wisconsin. Transactions of the Wisconsin Academy of Sciences, Arts and Letters 86: 263-280.

206. Payne, N.F., and R.D. Taber. 1974. Status of 10 uncommon birds and mammals in Snoqualmie National Forest and vicinity. Prepared for U.S. Forest Service. College of Forest Resources, University of Washington, Seattle. 73pp + maps.

207. Payne, N.F., B.P. Munger, J.W. Matthews, and R.D. Taber. 1976. Inventory of vegetation and wildlife in riparian and other habitats along the upper Columbia River. U.S. Army Corps of Engineers and College of Forest Resources, University of Washington, Seattle. 2 volumes, 602pp.

207x. Payne, N.F. 1976. Red squirrel introductions to Newfoundland. Canadian Field-Naturalist 90(1):60-64.

208. Pearson, T.G., editor. 1917. Birds of America. Garden City Books, Garden City, New York. 982pp.

209. Peterson, R.P., and N.F. Payne. 1986. Productivity, size, age, and sex structure of nuisance beaver colonies in Wisconsin. Journal of Wildlife Management 50:265-268.

209x. Peterson, R.T. 1947. A field guide to the birds. Houghton Mifflin, Boston. 290pp.

210. Pinkerton, K. 1947. Bright with silver. William Sloane, New York. 347pp.

211. Pope and Young Club. 2017. Bowhunting big game records of North America. 8th edition. Pope and Young Club, Chatfield, Minnesota. 1028pp.

211w. Raynor, J.L., C.A. Grainger, and D.P. Parker. 2021. Wolves make roadways safer, generating large economic returns to predator conservation. Proceedings of the National Academy of Sciences 118(22):1-10.

211x. Reed, C.A. 1909. Bird guide: Land birds east of the Rockies. Doubleday, Page and Co., Garden City, New York. 228pp.

211y. Reed, C.A., H.F. Harvey, and R.I. Brasher. 1913. Western bird guide: Birds of the Rockies and west to the Pacific. Doubleday, Page & Co., Garden City, New York. 266pp.

211z. Reed, C.A. 1914. The Canadian bird book. Musson Book Company, Toronto. 486pp.

212. Risjord, N.K. 1995. Wisconsin: The story of the Badger State. Wisconsin Trails, Madison. 226pp.

212x. *Robbins, S.D. 1991. Wisconsin birdlife: Population and distribution past and present. University of Wisconsin Press, Madison. 720pp.

212y. Roe, F.G. 1951. The North American buffalo. University of Toronto Press, Toronto. 1006pp.

213. *Ross, J., and B. Ross. 1998. Prairie time: The Leopold Reserve revisited. University of Wisconsin Press, Madison. 256pp.

214. Ryder, T.J., editor. 2018. State wildlife management and conservation. Johns Hopkins University Press, Baltimore, Maryland. 256pp.

214x. Sanders, B. 2023. It's OK to be angry about capitalism. Crown Publishing, New York. 320pp.

214y. Sankoff, I., D. Hein, and L. Maslon. 2019. Come from away: Welcome to the Rock; an inside look at the hit musical. Hachette Books, New York. 224pp.

214z. Sasse, D.B. 2003. Job-related mortality of wildlife workers in the United States, 1937-2000. Wildlife Society Bulletin 31:1000-1003.

215. Saylan, C., and D.T. Blumstein. 2011. The failure of environmental education (and how we can fix it). University of California Press, Berkeley. 241pp.

216. Schemnitz, S.D., editor. 1980. Wildlife management techniques manual. 4th edition. The Wildlife Society, Washington, D.C. 686pp.

217. Schorger, A.W. 1937. The range of bison in Wisconsin. Transactions of the Wisconsin Academy of Sciences, Arts & Letters 30:117-130.

218. Schorger, A.W. 1942. Extinct and endangered mammals and birds of the upper Great Lakes region. Transactions of the Wisconsin Academy of Sciences, Arts & Letters 34:23-44.

219. Schorger, A.W. 1953. The white-tailed deer in early Wisconsin. Transactions of the Wisconsin Acedemy of Sciences, Arts and Letters 42:197-247.

220. *Schorger, A.W. 1955. The passenger pigeon: Its natural history and extinction. University of Oklahoma Press, Norman. 446pp.

221. *Schorger, A.W. 1966. The wild turkey: Its history and domestication. University of Oklahoma Press, Norman. 652pp.

222. Scott, W.E. 1967. Conservation's first century in Wisconsin: Landmark dates and people. Pages 14-42 in N.C. Camp, editor. Conservation centennial symposium: The quest for quality in Wisconsin. Conservation Education Programs, University of Wisconsin, Madison.

223. Seton, E.T. 1909-1928 (reissued in 1953). Lives of game animals. Charles T. Branford, Boston. 4 volumes.

224. Silvy, N.J., editor. 2020. The wildlife techniques manual. 8th edition. Johns Hopkins University Press, Baltimore. 2 volumes.

224x. Sinclair, P. R. 2001. Sustainable development in fisheries-dependent regions? Reflections on the unsustainable Newfoundland cod fisheries. Pages 166-182 in D. McGrath, ed. From red ochre to black gold. Flanker, St. John's, Newfoundland and Labrador.

225. Smith, J.H., and N.F. Payne. 1997. Relationship of birds to various age aspen stands. Passenger Pigeon 59:267-274.

225x. Snow, D.P., W.R. Skinner, and N.F. Payne. 1999. Prescribed burning to improve tundra for willow ptarmigan in Newfoundland. Transactions of the Northeast Wildlife Conference 56:77-83.

225y. Soper, L.R., and N.F. Payne. 1997. Relationship of introduced mink, an island race of muskrat, and marginal habitat. Annales Zoologici Fennici 34:251-258.

226. Stoddard, H. L. 1931. The bobwhite quail: Its habits, preservation, and increase. Scribner's, New York. 559pp.

227. Swift, E. 1946. A history of Wisconsin deer. Publication 323. Wisconsin Conservation Department, Madison. 98pp.

228. *Swift, E.F. 1967. A conservation saga. National Wildlife Federation, Washington. 264pp.

228x. Swanson, T.M., and E.B. Barbier, editors. 1992. Economics in the wilds: Wildlife, diversity, and development. Island Press, Covelo, CA. 237pp.

229. Sykes, B. 2001. The seven daughters of Eve. W.W. Norton & Co., New York. 307pp.

230. Taber, R.D. 1946. The winter birds of Adak, Alaska. Condor 48:271-277.

231. Taber, R.D. 1949. Observations on the breeding biology of the ring-necked pheasant. Condor 51:153-175.

232. Taber, R.D. ca2012. Lucky Dick: The development of wildlife biology. Self-published memoir. 184pp.

233. Taber, R.D., and R.F. Dasmann. 1958. The black-tailed deer of the chaparral: Its life history and management in the North Coast Range of California. Game Bulletin No. 8. California Department of Fish and Game, Sacramento. 163pp.

234. Taber, R.D., R.A. Cooley, and W. F. Royce. 1970. The conservation of fish and wildlife. Pages 143-151 in H. D. Johnson, editor. No deposit—no return: Man and his environment—a view toward survival. Addison-Wesley, Reading, Massachusetts.

235. *Taber, R.D., and N.F. Payne. 2003. Wildlife, conservation, and human welfare: A United States and Canadian perspective. Krieger, Malabar, Florida. 218pp.

236. Taber, D., and P. Taber. 1999. Parties without pain: Your guide to healthy humor. Dog-Eared Publications, Middleton, WI. 136pp.

237. *Tekiela, S. 2000. Wildflowers of Wisconsin. Adventure, Cambridge, Minnesota. 425pp.

238. *Tekiela, S. 2002. Trees of Wisconsin field guide. Adventure, Cambridge, Minnesota. 228pp.

239. *Tekiela, S. 2005. Mammals of Wisconsin field guide. Adventure, Cambridge, Minnesota. 332pp.

240. *Tekiela, S. 2020. Birds of Wisconsin field guide. 3rd edition. Adventure, Cambridge, Minnesota. 324pp.

241. *Temple, S.A., editor. 1978. Endangered birds: Management techniques for preserving threatened species. University of Wisconsin Press, Madison. 466pp.

242. *Temple, S.A., editor. 1983. Bird conservation 1. University of Wisconsin Press, Madison. 156pp.

243. *Temple, S.A., editor. 1986. Bird conservation 2. University of Wisconsin Press, Madison. 188pp.

244. *Temple, S.A., J.R. Cary, and R. Rolley. 1998. Wisconsin birds: A seasonal and geographical guide. 2nd edition. University of Wisconsin Press, Madison. 336pp.

245. *Tessen, D.D. 2009. Wisconsin's favorite bird haunts. Wisconsin Society for Ornithology, Milwaukee. 540pp.

246. *Thiel, R.P. 1993. The timber wolf in Wisconsin: The death and life of a majestic predator. University of Wisconsin Press, Madison. 253pp.

247. *Thiel, R.P. 2018. Keepers of the wolves. 2nd edition. University of Wisconsin Press, Madison. 264pp.

248. *Thiel, R.P., A.C. Thiel, and M. Strozewski, editors. 2013. Wild wolves we have known: Stories of wolf biologists' favorite wolves. International Wolf Center, Ely, Minnesota. 246pp.

249. Thoreau, H.D. 1854. Walden. Ticknor and Fields, Boston. 266pp.

250. *Trainer, D.O., editor. 1970. Infectious diseases of wild mammals. Iowa State University Press, Ames. 417pp.

251. Trippensee, R.E. 1948. Wildlife management: Upland game and general principles. McGraw-Hill, New York. 479pp.

252. Trippensee, R.E. 1953. Wildlife management: Fur bearers, waterfowl, and fish. McGraw-Hill, New York. 572pp.

253. *Tupper, S. 2016. Fran and Frederick Hamerstrom: Wildlife conservation pioneers. Wisconsin Historical Society Press, Madison. 136pp.

254. Udall, S.L. 1963. The quiet crisis. Avon Books, New York. 224pp.

255. U.S. Fish and Wildlife Service. 2018. 2016 national survey of hunting, fishing, and wildlife-associated recreation. U.S. Department of the Interior, U.S. Department of Commerce, and U.S. Census Bureau, Washington. 133pp.

255x. U.S. Fish and Wildlife Service. 2023. 2022 national survey of hunting, fishing, and wildlife-associated recreation.

U.S. Department of the Interior U.S. Fish and Wildlife Service, Washington. 87pp.

256. Valdez, R. 2013. Exploring our ancient roots. Wildlife Professional 7(2):50-53.

257. *Van Hise, C.R. 1910. The conservation of natural resources of the United States. Macmillan, New York. 468pp.

258. Vaugh, G.F. 2002. Pioneer in wildlife conservation: Reuben Edwin Trippensee, 1894-1997. Environmental Institute, University of Massachusetts, Amherst. 30pp.

259. von Humboldt, A. 1845-47, 1850-58. Cosmos: A sketch of the physical description of the universe. Forgotten Books, London. 4 volumes.

260. *Waller, D.M., and T.P. Rooney, editors. 2008. The vanishing present: Wisconsin's changing lands, waters, and wildlife. University of Chicago Press, Chicago. 507pp.

260x. Wexler, M. 2023. Many songs lifting spirits. National Wildlife 61(1): 12-13.

261. Wight, H.M. 1939. Field and laboratory technic in wildlife management. University of Michigan Press, Ann Arbor. 107pp.

261x. *Wilke, R.J., editor. 1993. Environmental education teacher resource handbook: A practical guide for K-12 environmental education. Kraus International Publications, Millwood, New York. 448pp.

262. *Willging, R.C. 2008. On the hunt: The history of deer hunting in Wisconsin. Wisconsin Historical Society Press, Madison. 292pp.

263. *Willging, R.C. 2011. History afield: Stories from the golden age of Wisconsin sporting life. Wisconsin Historical Society Press, Madison. 191pp.

263x. Wilson, A. 1808-1814. American ornithology; or the natural history of the birds of the United States. Bradford and Inskeep, Philadelphia. 9 volumes.

263y. *Wilson, J. 2022. Wrong tree: Adventures in wildlife biology. Cornerstone Press, University of Wisconsin-Stevens Point. Stevens Point, Wisconsin. 276pp.

264. Wing, L.W. 1951. Practice of wildlife conservation. John Wiley, New York. 412pp.

265. Wisconsin Department of Natural Resources. 1998. Wisconsin's deer management program: The issues involved in decision-making. 2nd edition. Wisconsin Department of Natural Resources, Madison. 41pp.

266. Wisconsin Department of Natural Resources. 2005. Wisconsin strategy for wildlife species of greatest conservation need. Wisconsin Department of Natural Resources, Madison. 30pp.

267. *Wisconsin Department of Natural Resources. 2015a. The ecological landscapes of Wisconsin: An assessment of ecological resources and a guide to planning sustainable management. Wisconsin Department of Naturel Resources PUB SS-1131 2015. 2731pp.

268. Wisconsin Department of Natural Resources. 2015b. Wisconsin endangered and threatened species laws & list. Wisconsin Department of Natural Resources PUBL-ER-001-2004. 5pp.

269. Wisconsin Department of Natural Resources. 2016. Revenue options for Wisconsin fish, wildlife, and habitat management. Wisconsin Department of Natural Resources, Madison. 46pp.

270. Wisconsin Department of Natural Resources Bureau of Wildlife Management. 2023. Wisconsin wolf management plan 2023: A plan for stewardship, conservation and management of the gray wolf in Wisconsin. PUB WM-687-23. Wisconsin Department of Natural Resources Bureau of Wildlife Management, Madison. 199pp.

270x. Wisconsin Department of Public Instruction. 1949. Guide to conservation education in Wisconsin schools. Wisconsin Department of Public Instruction. Madison. 94pp.

270y. Wisconsin's Green Fire. 2022. Imbalance of power: How Wisconsin is failing citizens in conserving natural resources and protecting our environment. Wisconsin's Green Fire, Rhinelander, Wisconsin. 32pp.

271. Wright, S.D., and N.L. Bradley. 2008. Thinking like a flower: Phenological and climate change at the Leopold Shack. Pages 41-53 in D.M. Waller and T.R. Rooney, editors. The vanishing present: Wisconsin's changing lands, waters, and wildlife. University of Chicago Press, Chicago.

271x. Writers Program of New York City. 1940. American wild life illustrated. W. H. Wise & Co., New York. 749pp.

272. Wydeven, A.P., and C.M. Pils. 2008. Changes in mammalian carnivore populations. Pages 257-272 in D.M. Waller and T.P. Rooney, editors. The vanishing present: Wisconsin's changing lands, waters, and wildlife. University of Chicago Press, Chicago.

273. Yansa, C.H., and K.M. Adams. 2012. Mastodons and mammoths in the Great Lakes region, USA and Canada: New insights into their diets as they neared extinction. Geography Compass 2012:1-4, 10.

274. Zakaria, F. 2020. Ten lessons for a post-pandemic world. W.W. Norton, New York. 320pp.

275. Zeckmeister, M.T. 1985. Population characteristics of unexploited beaver and muskrat populations. MS thesis. University of Wisconsin, Stevens Point. 45pp.

276. Zeckmeister, M.T., and N.F. Payne. 1998. Effects of trapping on colony density, structure, and reproduction of a beaver population unexploited for 19 years. Transactions of the Wisconsin Academy of Sciences, Arts and Letters 86:281-291.

277. Zeug, D. 2016. Warden Einar Johnson killed. Wisconsin Outdoor News 23(10):31, 36.

*Wisconsin author of a wildlife book or wildlife-related book.

ACKNOWLEDGMENTS

Estella Leopold, Aldo Leopold's daughter and an accomplished and recognized scientist, was gracious enough at age 94 to provide brief remarks about this project via email, for which I am deeply grateful. I thank Adam N. Payne, former Secretary of the Wisconsin Department of Natural Resources, for writing the Foreword to this book.

With my former wife Eileen in full support, for which I am deeply grateful, we moved eight times to six states and one province in 11 years to accommodate my work, which developed perspective for this book.

For reviewing parts of the manuscript, I thank Tom Hauge, former director of the Wisconsin Department of Natural Resources (WDNR) Wildlife Bureau; Chuck Pils, former director of the WDNR Bureau of Endangered Resources; Dave Gjestson, author and former wildlife biologist with the WDNR Wildlife Bureau and policy and planning analyst for the Bureau of Property Management; Dr. Scott Craven, professor emeritus of wildlife ecology and wildlife extension biologist, and Dr. Stanley Temple, professor emeritus of wildlife ecology and Beers-Bascom Professor Emeritus in Conservation, University of Wisconsin–Madison Department of Forest and Wildlife Ecology; Dr. Christine Thomas, Dean Emeritus, and Dr. Scott Hygnstrom, professor of wildlife ecology and director of the Wisconsin Center for Wildlife, University of Wisconsin–Stevens Point College of Natural Resources; and my wife Dr. Jan Payne, professor of nursing, University of Wisconsin–Eau Claire, who proofread the whole thing.

I thank Dr. Robert McCabe's daughter Colleen McCabe; the Aldo Leopold Foundation and University of Wisconsin–Madison Archives; Ruth Hine and Fred and Fran Hamerstrom's daughter Elva Hamerstrom Paulson and the Hamerstrom Family Collection; and editor of *Wisconsin Outdoor News* Dean Bortz, for permission to use their materials as figures in this book. Thanks to Al Cornell for his wildlife photos.

My publisher, Dr. Ross Tangedal, and his team of editors headed by Brett Hill, of Cornerstone Press at the University of Wisconsin–Stevens Point, made many helpful suggestions and professionally and kindly guided me through the process.

Without Jan's love, patience, tolerance, support, cheerfulness, and attendance to household matters that allowed me time to do this thing, I couldn't have done this thing.

INDEX

NEIL F. PAYNE is a Certified Wildlife Biologist and Professor Emeritus of Wildlife Ecology at the University of Wisconsin–Stevens Point, where he was a full-time teacher for thousands of students, a researcher, and a writer. He grew up in Sheboygan Falls, Wisconsin. He received a BA in zoology (1961) from the University of Wisconsin–Madison (captain of UW fencing team), an MS in wildlife and forestry (1964) from Virginia Tech, and a PhD in wildlife science (1975) from Utah State University. He was in combat in the Vietnam War and captain with the U.S. Marine Corps (1964–67). He worked as a wildlife biologist for the Newfoundland and Labrador Wildlife Service (1967–71) and as a wildlife professor for the University of Washington in Seattle (1973–75) and the University of Wisconsin–Stevens Point (1975–98). He wrote technical articles and books on wildlife, including one with Aldo Leopold's former graduate student Richard D. Taber, and three comprehensive techniques books on wildlife habitat improvement. He is a 2026 inductee into the Wisconsin Conservation Hall of Fame.

He is married, with three children and three stepchildren. He lives part-time in Florida, in Newfoundland and Labrador, and in Wisconsin on the shore of the Wisconsin River.

www.ingramcontent.com/pod-product-compliance
Lightning Source LLC
Chambersburg PA
CBHW021705120626
46545CB00004B/1408